*THE WORD OF GOD
AND
THE WORLD OF THE BIBLE*

*In honour of my Mother
and in memory of my Father—
my first and best teachers*

THE WORD OF GOD
AND
THE WORLD OF THE BIBLE

An Introduction to the Cultural Backgrounds of the New Testament

Peter J Miano

DEAR NANETTE,

THANKS FOR BEING PART OF
THIS PILGRIMAGE & FOR
YOUR INTEREST & INSIGHTS —
GRACE & PEACE)

11 MAY 03

MELISENDE

© Peter J Miano 2001

The Word of God and the World of the Bible

First published 2001 by
Melisende
39 Chelmsford Road
London E18 2PW
Tel. +44 (0)20 8498 9768
Fax +44 (0)20 8504 2558
E mail: melisende@cwcom.net
www.melisende.cwc.net

ISBN 1 901764 15 X

Editor: Leonard Harrow
Printed at the St Edmundsbury Press, England

CONTENTS

ACKNOWLEDGEMENTS

Mark Twain once said, 'Good whiskey requires long fermentation.' This book is the product of a long process of fermentation stretching back to my parish ministry days when I was also studying at Harvard. I hope the benefit to the reader justifies the length of that process.

My intent from the outset was to produce a book that would make accessible the best of biblical scholarship to a reader who was intelligent and well educated, but not necessarily initiated into the arcane stuff of biblical studies. In a sense, I wrote for and geared this book to the people in the parish of Calvary United Methodist Church in Arlington, Massachusetts. When I was a parish minister, I was always looking for solid and substantive biblical studies material that did not require a PhD to read. Few parishioners have the appetite for the minutiae to which most PhD students are subjected, not to mention the time required to digest it. I was frustrated also with the syrupy spirituality of much study material available at that time. This book is the first instalment in my quest for satisfying biblical scholarship that is accessible to the broad Church.

My own personal study led me to immerse myself in the region of the Middle East, especially Israel, Palestine, Egypt and Jordan. My research there, my work as a missionary and as a teacher of the Bible there over the past twelve years contributed to this book. There is no teacher quite like the soil and atmosphere of the biblical worlds. During this time, I have been privileged to meet thousands of people who, like the people of Calvary Church, thirsted for a guidebook to substantive, credible biblical scholarship, but did not have the discretionary time to digest PhD dissertations. I am very grateful for the stimulation provided by the students I have had the privilege of meeting and working with in the Holy Land over the past decade. I hope the book will be a help to many more in the future. It is written for them, too.

The many people who gave me encouragement, support and guidance in the research and production of this book deserve to be mentioned, but space does not allow me to mention them all. Their names will be written in the Book of Life. However, I am especially grateful to a number of people in particular. First of all, I am indebted to my professors at Union Theological Seminary (New York City), Harvard Divinity School and Boston University. I am lucky to have had the opportunity to sit at the feet of first-rate scholars, who prodded me, spurred me, chastised me and inspired me.

I am grateful to my colleagues and friends in Israel and Palestine. Their struggles with life and death issues day in and day out over the course of my time living and working in Palestine constantly reminded me of the urgency of biblical study and that the study of the Bible is not merely an armchair exercise, but a vital vocation and an integral component of mission.

In addition, Dr Michael Prior, St Mary's College, University of Surrey, provided much guidance and encouragement before and during the final drafting of the manuscript. I often took peculiar comfort at strange hours of the night and early morning, when writing seemed to proceed at a grinding pace, with his insight, 'Writing is crucifixion.'

My colleagues on the faculty of The Society for Biblical Studies were a great source of information and encouragement. The last stages of this work were handicapped by the untimely passing of my friend and colleague, Daniel W Casey, Jr, who was one of the primary readers of earlier drafts. In the final stages of this project, I am fortunate to have had the assistance and support of Alan Ball and Leonard Harrow of Melisende. Their patient, careful and professional attention to the details of finalizing the manuscript and production is much appreciated. It is gratifying to have my meagre work included among their many fine publications. I would also like to express my appreciation to Harvard University Press for their permission to reprint excerpts from various editions from their Loeb Classical Library series.

Finally and most importantly, I wish to acknowledge my grateful appreciation to my wife, Dana, and our children, Sam and Kate. They tolerated long absences during the research stages and strange hours and work habits during the writing stages. They endured hours of conversation about such fascinating topics as papyri, manuscripts, ostraca, magi, and Josephus. They put up with frequent and peculiar episodes of blank expressions when I suddenly became gripped by an idea. They say I am prone to such episodes. Evidently, those spells can last a long time and can be very disconcerting, not to mention annoying, to people who are trying to have a conversation or are more interested in the outcome of *Horton Hears a Who* than they are in issues like the double taxation of Judea in the time of Jesus. As Hopper, in *A Bug's Life,* says, 'Ideas are dangerous things.' Dana, Sam and Kate also put up with being cajoled, carried and dragged to innumerable archaeological sites, remote deserts, gloomy monasteries, and across tedious border checkpoints to obscure places throughout Palestine, Jordan and Egypt. In particular, Dana agreed to travel with me for months across southern Europe and throughout the Middle East equipped with only the contents of a backpack, while I was exploring the world of the Bible. That she did much of it while pregnant with Sam is all the more meritorious. More than anyone, Dana provided support and encouragement without which this volume would not have been possible.

Peter J Miano
Arlington, Mass.
Easter 2001

Chapter 1
INTRODUCTION

No book is more highly revered, yet more widely misread than the Bible. Generations come and generations go and still the Bible remains an inscrutable mystery to most readers. Many embark on grand resolutions to read the Bible from cover to cover only to get lost in what they perceive as tedious genealogies or mundane and seemingly irrelevant lists of kings. Many are so put off by what seem to be remote, arcane stories, and obscure details of history that they do not even try to read it in the first place. The Apocalypse of John with its vivid imagery and symbolism is particularly intimidating, but even the letters of Paul produce frustration and premature capitulation. The early church read it allegorically. Today, some read it literally, while others read it figuratively and metaphorically. Some take it as history. Others take it as literature or poetry or fairy tale. Not enough, however, take it seriously. This book is about taking it seriously.

Innumerable pages of interpretation and commentary are dedicated to understanding the Bible. Countless hours of research are invested in finding keys to unlock the cryptic secrets locked away in the Bible. Scholars devote their entire lifetimes to the accumulation of data about the Bible intended for the building up of the believer, yet for far too many believers, the Bible is inadequately understood.

Notwithstanding the noteworthy efforts of legions of scholars and the mountains of scholarly material on the Bible, there are several distinct shortcomings in modern biblical scholarship. Sadly, many of the best insights remain the private domain of the Academy, i.e., the almost exclusive domain of professors and graduate students. The academic community is perceived by some as a self-absorbed elite and sometimes it is even accused of being hostile to personal faith. Indeed, the demand for increased specialization among biblical scholars has resulted in the formation of an academic, biblical elite. It is increasingly difficult for this elite to access relevant information from scholars outside their specialities and impossible for them to communicate information to the rank and file of the church.

Second, scholars sometimes succumb to the temptation to think uncritically. Even the best scholars use imprecise and misleading language. The result is that readers are misled and the true meaning of the texts is obscured. The use of the words 'Christian' and 'Jew', for example, while invoked routinely, are often undefined. When we come to defining these terms, their meaning is not as readily clear as one would hope. It is especially misleading to speak of Christians and Jews in the 1st century AD. Uncritical thinking also applies to passing on material and opinions of authorities. Sometimes we are forced to ask ourselves, 'how do we know what we know?' When the answer is, 'because so-and-so leading scholar said it,' then we should give pause.

Third, the scholarly investigation of scripture almost always ignores the moral dimensions of the biblical texts and real life contexts. Bible passages presume values and moral standards. When these go unrecognised, the passages are susceptible to being misappropriated and misapplied sometimes with rather damaging consequences. For this reason, I introduce 'value-critique', the deliberate examination of the value systems presumed by and expressed in the stories of the Bible.[1] Value critique includes description, i.e., the simple activity of listing the value codes that are presumed by or expressed in a particular passage. It also includes the more formal application of a specific value model or system. Together, these processes reveal the contrast between ancient and modern value systems and prevent the misapplication of ancient texts in modern situations.

For all too many, an impenetrable fog obscures the meaning of the Bible. Its secrets are shrouded in the hoary mists of antiquity. Its treasures covered by the musty mildew of time. While this is undoubtedly so, it is also true that the Bible was not written to be mysterious. Its authors did not mean for their messages to be lost on their readers—or hearers, to be more precise.[2] In fact, the words and stories of the Bible which sometimes seem so obscure, bizarre or irrelevant to the modern day reader were clearly understood by their original audiences. It never occurred to any of the writers of the books of the Bible that their words would come to be revered as scripture. They had

---

[1] First introduced by Michael Prior, *The Bible and Colonialism: A Moral Critique*, Sheffield Academic Press, 1997.

[2] It is difficult to estimate how many people were able to read and write at the time of Jesus. Estimates of literacy rates vary from as low as 5-7 percent of the population to as high as 30 percent of the population. I prefer the higher estimate and it is highly probable that many more people could *speak* more than one language than were able to read and write in any language. In any case, the authors of the books of the Bible intended their works to be read aloud and most of their intended audiences *listened to* their works being read rather than reading them for themselves.

no expectations that their legal codes, foundational mythology, hymns, Gospels, letters, apocalypses or romances would be read by anyone other than their original readers. They took it for granted that anyone who read or heard their words would be familiar with the everyday sights and sounds and the cultural values of their 1st-century world.[3] Where the 21st-century reader gropes for meaning in the Book of Revelations, for example, the 1st-century audience immediately understood the meaning, symbolism and wisdom in the apocalyptic narrative. The words that were used to report the episodes contained in the Bible, the writing styles represented in it, the literary allusions to the people and events, and the references to the Hebrew scriptures were well known to audiences of the first and second centuries. What appears to many today to be obscure was crystal clear to the original audiences.

The disadvantage with which modern readers of the Bible are forced to contend is the simple reality that when we approach the Bible, we see it through a thick lens of time. As light is bent when it passes through water, so our vision of the Bible is distorted by history. In order to begin to comprehend the messages contained in the Bible, the modern reader must first become acquainted with its cultural, historical, social, geographical, moral and literary backgrounds. To understand the Word of God, one must first understand the world of the Bible. To take the Bible seriously is to study these contexts.

There is a story told about Rabbi Hillel, the great sage from the time of Jesus. A student approached him and asked, 'Teacher, tell me the meaning of the Bible while standing on one foot.' Instead of giving in to the impatient student, the Rabbi replied, 'Go and study.'

There is a tendency among many to take a shortcut approach to the Bible, to bypass the prerequisites in order to reach the heart of the cabbage. Like the student in the legend about Rabbi Hillel, many want to know the meaning of the Bible while standing on one foot, i.e., in a nutshell. Such an approach, however, is laden with pitfalls.

Many adopt the fallacious assumption that the world has not changed in the past two thousand years and that the meaning of words we think we recognize in the Bible are unchanged from their original context. Thus, when Jesus speaks about divorce (Mark 10: 2-12), many fail to recognize that divorce as it is known in 21st-century America and divorce as Jesus knew it are two entirely different phenomena. Not only is the meaning of the Bible distorted if we impose our modern assumptions and values on it, but hurtful damage can result as well. For women of the 1st century, divorce meant social and economic disaster. It threatened social stability. It was a

---

[3] The same applies no less to the authors of the books of the Hebrew scriptures and their audiences as well.

form of cruelty. By denying the possibility of divorce, Jesus was redressing a social wrong. Further, by extending to women the same rights of divorce as men (Mark 10: 12), Jesus issued a revolutionary social reform. In fact, women in Israelite society[4] had no rights to divorce when Jesus made that statement. If we do not understand this, we will fail to appreciate a key element in Jesus' character, namely his progressive social outlook and free interpretation of scripture, to say nothing of the extent to which Jesus' culture had been Hellenised. While the Gospels suggest that Jesus addressed divorce in his day, scholars debate whether he did so or not.[5] Notwithstanding this debate, it is certain that Jesus made no comment on divorce as it is practised in 21st-century America. To apply Jesus' words about a 1st-century phenomenon to today with wooden literalism risks causing harm.[6]

Another popular fallacy when approaching the Bible is the assumption that the world has changed so much that its lessons cannot possibly impart anything of value to us who live in the 'advanced'[7] world of modernity. Quite the opposite is the case. Indeed, when approaching the study of the world of the Bible, we must familiarize ourselves with 'the principle of continuity'.

Kenneth Bailey was one of the first biblical scholars to recognize and utilize the cultural continuity between ancient and modern Near Eastern cultures in his research.[8] It is a widespread misconception that the region that we call the Middle East today has been a place of constant strife and turmoil throughout its history. Nothing can be further from the truth. In the

---

[4] In stark contrast, an abundance of material shows clearly that in the dominant Hellenistic culture, women did indeed enjoy the same rights to divorce as men.

[5] Any thorough treatment of this subject must address the question, 'Did Jesus actually make these remarks or did the author of the Gospel put them on Jesus' lips?' The historicity of the Gospels falls into the purview of historical Jesus research. I take the position that we cannot with reliable certainty distinguish between Jesus and his words as they are presented in Gospels and Jesus as his contemporaries may have experienced him. The Gospels are our best source for knowing Jesus of Nazareth, but they do not enable us to reconstruct a reliable picture of Jesus as his contemporaries knew him. They record a picture of Jesus as believers in him experienced him at least one generation removed from him. Irrespective of the historicity of the statements attributed to Jesus in the Gospels, understanding the cultural background on the issue informs our understanding of the reading of the passage.

[6] This, of course, is not to say that we cannot apply Jesus' words to contemporary situations, only that to do so requires skill and care.

[7] 'Advanced' is perhaps not the correct word to describe a century that has seen the deaths of 75 million people in warfare.

[8] Bailey, Kenneth, *Poet and Peasant*, William B Eerdmans, Grand Rapids, MI, 1976; Bailey, Kenneth, *Through Peasant Eyes: More Lucan Parables, Their Culture and Style*, William B Eerdmans Publishing, Grand Rapids, MI, 1980.

field of Near East studies, it is widely recognized that in fact, the Near East is characterized by striking stability across the ages. Its social fabric is based on tradition. The past is knitted to the present. By observing modern Near Eastern cultures, we can, if we are careful in our methods and conclusions, gain insight into the past. By the same token, insights from sociological, anthropological and historical studies yield insight into present day social and political dynamics. The present informs the past and vice versa.

A second aspect of the principle of continuity is that in spite of the dramatic changes that have taken place over the past 2,000 years, there is also a fundamental continuity that unites people in every age to each other. Regardless of when and where we are born, people seek to understand their temporal, finite lives in relation to a more enduring story. Human life is more than the material necessities of physical health, shelter and sustenance. Even more, it is intangibles such as meaning, purpose and identity. These are real commodities that are expressed in symbol, conveyed in images and contained in narratives, i.e., stories of where we come from, who we are, what we value and where we believe we are going. People seek to associate themselves in some way with an eternal, transcendent reality in narratives of identity. We want to make sense of our human experience, the fundamentals of which—finitude, loneliness, the quest for fulfilment and meaning in life—do not change. People in all generations and places seek identity, meaning, purpose and belonging in a community. How people do this is the stuff of religion and the raw material of the Bible.

We share a kinship with our forebears throughout the ages. Their story is our story. Their dilemmas are our dilemmas. This is why we still read and find meaning in Euripides, Sophocles and Shakespeare, as well as the Bible. This is why today, as much as ever before, we need a mature, viable understanding of scripture. What were the conflicts and contradictions that obsessed the sage authors of the ancient world? What were their fears, their hopes and their challenges? More importantly, how did the movement that arose from the person of Jesus of Nazareth and grew into the phenomenon we know as Christianity satisfy these concerns? To answer these questions is to learn the secret of Christianity's stunning conquest over paganism. To take the Bible seriously is to study these questions.

An understanding of the contexts of the Bible is so important to our understanding of scripture, that the world of the Bible—not just Israel/Palestine, but the entire Greco-Roman world—has been called the 'fifth Gospel' and the '78th book of the Bible'. Jesus is depicted in the Gospels as an artful communicator who knew and utilized the best and most effective literary devices of his day. Paul was a master of rhetoric, i.e., the art of persuasion. Both used common, everyday sights and metaphors to illustrate key theological points. Jesus referred to the birds of the air, the lilies of the field, indications of weather and the sight of cities perched on mountaintops surrounding the Sea of Galilee. Paul invoked common images, such as that of the body and its parts (Romans 12: 4-5, 1 Corinthians 12: 12), which was a widely used metaphor for the Roman legion and the Empire itself. He employed rhetorical devices that were well known across class lines. The psalmist refers to the deep v-shaped valleys of the Judean wilderness, 'Yeah though I walk through the valley of the shadow of death ...' (Psalm 23) Amos invokes the imagery of the plumb line. If we do not understand the world that produced the scriptures, we cannot begin to understand these object lessons, literary and rhetorical devices or words of scripture itself.

To illustrate the way in which unfamiliarity with the world of the Bible has distorted the meaning of the Bible, one should consider the passages in scripture in which references are made to faith that is so powerful that the faithful one could '... say to this mountain 'Move from here to there' and it will move.' (Matthew 17: 21) Paul writes, '... and if I have all faith, so as to remove mountains, but do not have love, I am nothing.' (1 Corinthians 13: 2). Here Jesus and Paul use the same metaphor and perhaps the same visual object lesson to illustrate a point. Such references can be and have been used to equate faith with supernatural power. However, when one comes to know the world in which Jesus and Paul both lived, worked and walked, one comes to know the startling realization that mountains of substantial size were, in fact, moved from one place to the another, entirely without the aid of magic.

From the slopes of the Mount of Olives in Jerusalem, a locale with which both Jesus and Paul were well familiar, one can look south and clearly see a conical shaped mountain about seven miles distant. This mountain is called the Herodian and was one of Herod the Great's palace fortresses. Herod's workers, who levelled a neighbouring mountain—also plainly visible—and piled the rubble on the top of the Herodian, constructed the fortress. The Herodian is the product of mountain moving activity of an entirely natural kind.

From the same position on the Mount of Olives, one could in Jesus' day and still can today look West and see the human made platform known in Arabic as the Haram al-Sharif—Noble Sanctuary—and what many call the Temple Mount. Constructed on the top of Mount Moriah, a place of religious significance even before the arrival of the Israelites, it was built when Herod had his workers expand the platform on which Solomon had built the first Israelite temple. This platform is about thirty-five acres in area. It is entirely human made and was built by moving rubble from distant mountains and using retaining walls, building up the platform. It is the largest artificial platform in the world.

Herod did not rely on magic, wishful thinking or supernatural power to accomplish these mountain-moving feats of construction. Instead, he utilized a legion of workers—probably not slaves—who were skilfully organized to perform coordinated work. When the Bible refers to faith that is able to move mountains, it is almost certainly a reference to the vision, determination, perseverance and skill of Herod, his architects, engineers and workers.

In the case of Paul, perhaps he was referring to the well-known building accomplishments of Herod the Great. Or, perhaps he was referring to the failed attempts to move mountains of earth from the isthmus separating the Saronic Gulf from the Gulf of Corinth. The Peloponnesian Peninsula is an area about half the size of the Greek mainland, almost isolated from the mainland except for a short, narrow isthmus. Corinth benefited economically from its location at the entrance to the isthmus. Its two ports gave it access to both gulfs and control of maritime trade. In Paul's day, the isthmus was a barrier to sea traffic and ships were dragged overland on wheels at the place where today we see the Corinthian Canal. For centuries, rulers had dreamed of enhancing economic prosperity by opening a passageway across the isthmus, but had been thwarted by the massive earth-moving feat it required—not to mention their superstition that sea level on either side of the isthmus was different! What better way to dramatize for the Corinthians the imperative of love than by comparing it to human power which such massive ambition would have required. Learning about the world of the Bible can unlock the secrets of the Bible.

Clearly, the sights and sounds of everyday life in Galilee had a deeply profound impact on Jesus' thought. According to the Gospel writers, he drew object lessons for his listeners from the imagery of the region. Indeed, the Gospels indicate that Jesus was a genius when it came to using everyday sights to illustrate his points. His parables relied heavily on agricultural and rural imagery, such as that of the sower and the seed, the mustard seed, the farmer and the wheat and tares, the shepherd and his sheep. He alluded to vineyards, fig trees, the birds of the air, the lilies of the field. Similarly, Jesus invoked images from domestic scenes such as a woman sweeping her house, and the baking of bread. He also drew illustrations from the realm of commerce and industry. Fishing was a major occupation along the shores of the Sea of Galilee and Jesus frequently made reference to that occupation. He likened the kingdom of heaven to a fisherman casting his drag net and gathering fish of all kinds. Discipleship itself was likened to being fishers of people.

One of the most poignant of Jesus' object lessons was drawn from the conspicuous location of cities perched on the tops of the mountains that surround the Sea of Galilee. Referring to these cities overlooking the region and visible far and wide, Jesus observed, 'A city set on a hill cannot be hid.' (Matthew 5: 14) Carrying the illustration further, Jesus remarked, 'No one after lighting a lamp puts it under a bushel, but on a lampstand ... Let your light shine before people ...' (Matthew 5: 15-16) The reference here is not simply to household lighting, but to the system of warning fires that would be lit from each of the hilltop cities in the event of approaching danger. Learning about the world of the Bible can unlock the secrets of the Bible.

Biblical authors had no other language with which to tell the biblical story except the common language of faith in their day. When they spoke of Jesus as 'Son of God', 'Son of Man', 'Saviour', or 'Messiah', they were not coining new phrases or inventing new categories of expression. The phrase 'Son of God,' for example, had had a long history of usage prior to its application by Gospel writers to Jesus of Nazareth. The Greeks had long assumed that political leaders were endued with a divine spirit. Alexander the Great, the first universal monarch, minted coins that referred to him as 'son of god'. Even before Alexander, however, the concept of divine sonship was well known in the ancient world. The Gilgamesh Epic, a Mesopotamian poem the original version of which probably dates to about 3,500 BC, depicts Gilgamesh, the mythological king, as having divine origins. The ancient Egyptians appear to have developed this concept by 2,000 BC. Browse through the lists of Pharaohs and one marvels at the profusion of names which use the root *mses*, which means 'child'. The name Ramses, which was the name of at least twelve Pharaohs, is a compound of the word 'Ra', the Egyptian sun god and *mses*. It thus means 'child of the god Ra'. 'Thutmoses' means 'child of Thuth', i.e., the moon god. 'Kamoses' means 'child of Ka'. It is not a coincidence that the legendary leader of the Exodus, Moses, was given an Egyptian name. These are early and poignant examples of the phenomenon of 'syncretism,' or cultural blending.[9] The ancient near eastern world was a cultural melting pot, each civilization giving and receiving ideas, insights and wisdom.

Similarly, broad theological concepts contained in the Bible, such as immortality, resurrection, monotheism[10] and the habit of depicting gods in

---

[9] Syncretism is a complicated phenomenon. For a thorough discussion see Koester, Helmut. *History, Culture, and Religion of the Hellenistic Age*, Fortress, Philadelphia, 1982.

[10] Although the term 'monotheism' is anachronistic, appearing in literature only in the 17th century, it is widely used to describe the religion of ancient Israel and other ancient near eastern peoples. In fact, ancient Israel understood that there were many, many gods. Israel's claim was not that there was only one god, but that *its* God was supreme among many. The religious reforms of Akhenaten, the 15th-century BC Pharaoh, are closer to 'monotheism' than Israel's was.

groups of three were not original with Christianity, but were taken by early writers of the Bible from previous religious settings to express their new faith. The concept of the immortality of the soul is at least as old as the oldest monumental architecture of ancient Egypt. Immortality was not a well-developed concept among the Greeks or even the ancient Israelites. The building of the pyramids and other tombs by the Egyptians is a testament to their belief that the pharaoh's life, and at least the lives of the nobility, if not the general populace, would not end with the death of the body. They were sure that the pharaoh, his—and occasionally her—family and select others would need to make provisions for the life of the soul after death.

This book seeks to fill a void in study material for conscientious, thoughtful people who take the scriptures of the New Testament seriously. It is meant to introduce a general audience to contemporary biblical scholarship. I mentioned above several shortcomings in scholarship. As a corrective to increased specialization, I advocate generalization. To the temptation to uncritically accept opinions and terms advanced by the academic community, I will offer alternatives. I will attempt to show where loose language is better discarded in favour of precision. In place of simplistic traditions passed down from one generation of popular theologians to the next, I will present a number of seemingly unconventional opinions. Where the tendency is to retreat from the world to the texts, I will return to the world to illuminate the text.

This study also carries some risks and liabilities. The main one to take care against is the temptation to think that complex subjects can be distilled into easily accessed paragraphs of information. There is a good reason why scholarship has tended toward specialization, even if this tendency has become problematic. The reason is that the subject matter is massive. The prodigious efforts of generations of scholars cannot be treated lightly. For this study, however, in the effort to make scholarship accessible, I have made decisions about which information to pass on. Entire lifetimes have been dedicated to subjects given less than a chapter here. Further, no book can be a substitute for contextual study. No amount of armchair activity can replace the necessity of study in the field where the soil and atmosphere is the classroom. Experience is the ultimate teacher. Biblical study is best undertaken experientially where one's heart, head, soul and body—all five sense along with intuition, imagination and perception—is engaged. When people first heard the words of Jesus and Paul, they were immersed in specific settings to which those words spoke. Immersion in the world is a prerequisite for Bible study that no book can replace. This study is an introduction and not a conclusion.

Christianity and its scripture did not spring forth from a theological, spiritual vacuum. The soil of the ancient Near East had been prepared by millennia of cultural cross-fertilization. Christianity is the heir of a long and rich Near Eastern tradition of religious reflection. It is the apex of an accumulation of religious insights, ideas and developing concepts. While early Christianity certainly went beyond the developing traditions from which it grew, its debt to its theological antecedents should not be underestimated or ignored. To fully appreciate the meaning and significance of Christianity and its scripture for the world and for each individual believer, it is imperative to understand the Bible in its historical, cultural, social, moral, literary and geographical contexts. To study these is also to learn how Christian scripture stood out from these same contexts. This is what it means to take the Bible seriously.

The Bible is an extraordinarily rich anthology. It is the product of not one, but many hands over a period of many centuries. It has undergone many stages of transmission, from word of mouth to a variety of written forms. It represents a broad range of theological outlooks and it bears witness to an evolutionary theological process from the religion of wandering nomads who lived five thousand years ago to the sophisticated cosmopolitan religion of the city dwellers of Paul's churches. It reflects the collective spiritual insights of the ancient Near East. No other document in the history of human civilization represents such diversity. In terms of literary beauty, theological sophistication, religious wisdom, inspiration and enduring meaning, no other book comes close to the Bible. But to understand the Word of God, one must first understand the world of the Bible.

Chapter 2
THE TEXT OF THE NEW TESTAMENT

The best approach to the world of the New Testament is the text of the New Testament itself. The New Testament is the first and best window to look through to see the world that produced it. There are those who question the reliability of reading the New Testament texts for historical information.[1] In addition to meaning and inspiration, the texts are full of confusing puzzles and mysteries. Yet, they are highly reliable historical sources, once they are properly understood and properly read. There are, of course, other texts such as those of the Israelite historian Josephus and non-canonical Christian writings that yield helpful historical insight about the 1st century world. None, however, surpass the New Testament in historical reliability and insight. We cull historical information from other written sources in order to understand the New Testament, but the latter can also be read to glean information about the world that produced it.

While the New Testament is particularly important to people of faith, we are fortunate that there are other collections of writings to examine for the purpose of gaining insight into it. We are the beneficiaries of a priceless bequest. The secrets of the ancient world are open to us through a vast treasury of literature that has survived through the ages.[2] First, the classics of the ancient world are preserved. We have sources such as the writings of

---

[1] Some New Testament scholars discredit the historical reliability of the texts of the New Testament, suggesting that the interests of the authors or the early churches obscure historical information and compromise historical reliability. These scholars favour non-canonical writings and hypothetical documents, such as Q, as sources for historical information. While these texts are enormously valuable in reconstructing the world of the first centuries, they themselves also include biases that are no less obvious than those of the canonical texts.

[2] Archaeological artefacts are another source of information. Indeed, archaeological research sometimes yields literary finds, as in the case of the Qumran and Nag Hammadi texts. The role of archaeology in reconstructing history will be discussed later.

the philosophers Plato and Aristotle, and later thinkers such as Zeno, Epictetus, and Lucretius. We have the works of historians such as the Greeks Thucydides and Herodotus and the Romans Tacitus, Pliny the Elder, and Seutonius. We can read the speeches, letters and memoirs of statesman such as Cicero. We have treasuries of official documents such as the letters of Pliny the Younger to his boss, the Emperor Trajan. There are letters and other writings from the emperors themselves, such as the memoirs of Marcus Aurelius. There are rhetorical handbooks, the works of playwrights, books on grammar, politics, natural phenomena, as well as examples of light reading akin to our dime novels. Virgil, Horace, Dio Cassius, Plutarch, Philodemus, Livy—these are but a few of the many authors who have bequeathed literary treasures to us. In addition to these, we have a vast reservoir of papyrus notes, letters, contracts and piles of ostraca that pertain to everyday matters. There are marriage and divorce contracts, love letters, petitions to the gods, and, among other things, bids to receive contracts or procure employment. Last but not least, there are inscriptions on coins, pottery, civic monuments and tombs that give us yet another angle from which to view the ancient world.

In addition to literature from secular Roman and Greek sources, there are significant Israelite works. These include books of the Old Testament Apocrypha, the Dead Sea Scrolls and the works of Israelites[3] such as Philo of Alexandria and Josephus. Philo and Josephus require further mention.

Philo was known as Philo the Judean. He lived at the same time as Jesus and wrote a number of works that survive in complete form. Among these works are Philo's efforts to interpret to his Roman audience the history of the people of Israel and their religion. His works are particularly important because they are the only sources from his time (ca. 20 BC to AD 40) written by Judeans outside Palestine. Although it is difficult to determine how representative his views are, they provide an important angle from which to learn about at least one Judean view.

Joseph ben Mathias is better known by the name he took later in life, Flavius Josephus. Josephus states that he was born into a priestly family and was also descended from the Hasmoneans, who ruled Judea during the late Hellenistic period (*ca.* 160-63 BC).[4] He is clearly a member of

---

[3] Scholars and laypersons alike often misuse and misapply the terms such as 'Judean', 'Jew', 'Israel', 'Israelite'. Important corrections and clarifications are warranted and I offer a more thorough discussion of these in chapter 6. The glossary also discusses these terms.

[4] 'Hellenism' is thoroughly discussed in chapter 4. There is a concise definition of it in the glossary.

the privileged classes. He also identifies himself with the Pharisees, which he says are one of three or four 'sects' of the Judeans, along with Sadducees, Essenes and rebels. When the revolt against Rome broke out in AD 66, he reluctantly joined it and took command of the rebel forces in Galilee. He defected during the revolt and, when he was brought before Vespasian, the Roman general, he predicted that Vespasian would eventually ascend to the throne. When his prediction came true, he became a confident of the new emperor. He lived the rest of his life in Rome under the patronage of two emperors and the wife of another. His patrons supplied him with an apartment, money and protection from false accusations, among other benefits. In Rome, he wrote the treatises that have become the most important sources of information for events in Palestine in the 1st century.[5] Often, he is our only source. He authored a number of works that survive in full. These include his autobiography, the *Antiquities of the Judeans*, and *The Wars of the Judeans*. In each of these works, Josephus addresses a Roman audience with the purpose of interpreting to them the history of Israel. He is writing in the aftermath of the first Judean revolt especially keen to persuade the Roman public that Judeans are loyal subjects. Notwithstanding his inestimable value in historical reconstruction, like all other authors his biases must be understood. He was obliged by the rules of society to honour his patrons, who were Roman aristocrats. He himself came from an aristocratic family. Thus he represents the views and values of the aristocracy.[6]

Finally, Christian authors supply invaluable information about the early Jesus movement, the growth of the church and about the Roman Period history in general. I will refer to their writings as 'non-canonical' Christian writings.[7] These are diverse texts about Jesus and the Apostles that were eliminated from the Christian canon.[8] They include additional gospels, 'acts' of various Apostles and disciples, letters and apocalypses. The texts of the

---

[5] It is easily arguable that Josephus' value as a source for general Palestinian history in the 1st century exceeds that of the Gospels, because he treats a wider window of time and has a broader interest.

[6] All literary testimony from the ancient world bears a similar bias. Those who could write were members of the upper classes.

[7] The use of the term 'Christian' is not entirely appropriate, because at that time there was no Christianity. The term was applied early to a diverse group of people who were related in some way to their central figure, Jesus who some was called Christ. The beliefs about Jesus, however, were so varied that it would be incorrect to think of a cohesive movement that shared similar outlooks, perceptions or rituals.

[8] 'Canon' means measure or standard. The process of canonization was long, complicated, and the criteria used in distinguishing canonical from non-canonical are not entirely known today. The canon is those books recognized historically as authoritative.

New Testament are a select subset of all Christian writings we know of. Indeed, there are far more Christian writings that are outside the canon than there are inside the canon. All of it, however, is valuable to the task of reconstructing a picture of the early movement that came to be called Christianity.

Thus, our literary sources are drawn from several centuries, from the 2nd century BC to the 2nd century AD. This window of time, the later Hellenistic and Early Roman periods, can be thought of as the time of the New Testament. Also, our sources are drawn from places and people across the Mediterranean basin. Together, all these literary sources contribute to enabling us to reconstruct the world in which the seed of Christianity was sown, in which it germinated and in which it sprung forth.

What, however, is the New Testament? Is it simply a source of history? Is it merely literature or is it revealed Truth? The answers to these questions, of course, will vary from one reader to the next. One need not be a Christian to appreciate the historical and literary values of the New Testament. For some Christians, the New Testament is little more than a collection of fanciful stories devoid of historical value and with little literary value either. For others, however, the New Testament is a collection of writings with historical, literary *and* sacred value and meaning. Readers search its pages for spiritual insight and wisdom, for existential meaning, to discern a sense of purpose in life, for moral guidance and to discover God revealed in Jesus Christ. In either event, a historical and literary approach to the New Testament is indispensable. Historical investigation informs revelation. It prevents revelation from being trivialized and parochialized. The claim of Christian preaching across the ages is that God is revealed in Jesus Christ *in history*, i.e., in a particular time and place. The historical context of revelation is neither irrelevant nor ancillary to that which is revealed. For the understanding of revealed Truth, history is essential. The appeal to revelation can be and is abused. Historical investigation, properly undertaken, prevents the specious appeal to revelation in support of personal preferences. It is our interest in revealed Truth, i.e., God's presence in history in the person of Jesus Christ, on the other hand, that elevates the pages of the New Testament from the level of simple history or mere literature to the level of sacred scripture.

The historical approach to the Bible begins with distinct questions. Who were the authors of the New Testament? When and for what purpose did they write? How did they write? A general understanding of the answers to these questions, even when they cannot be answered completely, helps us position the New Testament in its religious, social, political, moral and historical contexts.

The first point to make is that modern readers of the New Testament do not read it with the same spiritual, social, literary lenses. For many of us today, especially those who take faith personally and seriously, the New Testament is *scriptural*, i.e., sacred writing. This cannot be said for any readers in the 1st century. In fact, those who wrote the texts that eventually became the New Testament had no idea they were writing scripture. Neither did their original audiences realize that they were reading or listening to writings that would eventually be understood as scripture.[9] For many early writers, such as the apostle Paul, the only scripture they knew anything about was the Hebrew Bible. Thus, their writings had value for the original audiences of these texts aside from the value we attach to them today. Yet, just as the original readers could read and listen to the texts of the New Testament on levels other than scripture, so can we. In fact, learning to see and read the texts as they were originally seen and read is one of our primary challenges.

I have already implied that the New Testament is not one text, but many. It is an anthology of a variety of different types of writings. Not all of the texts represent the same type of literature and there are many different authors. The Gospels and Acts had four different authors. Their true identities are not known. The names of the authors cannot be determined from the titles of the Gospels , because in the ancient world, it was customary to name books in honour of someone. This custom is called 'pseudonymous authorship'. The names in the titles of the Gospels might be the figures that inspired the works, a writer's mentor or the names of the leaders of a particular community that produced the works. They might be the names of the one who taught the meaning, significance or purpose of Jesus. 'Paul's letters' are not necessarily written by Paul. Of the letters that bear Paul's name, scholars consider only seven to have been written by Paul. In general, scholars accept that the writings that contain the name 'John' in their titles were written by different authors who may have had some connection to one another. While we do not know the true identities of the authors of the Gospels, we do know, that the author of Luke is also the author of the Book of Acts.[10]

Nor do we know exactly the geographical locations of the writers of

---

[9] It is probably more correct to refer to the first *listeners* to the books of the New Testament, rather than *readers*. Although reading and writing were skills that many possessed, most people in the 1st century AD were illiterate. Even the literate, however, probably *heard* these texts for the first time. When Luke 4: 16 says that Jesus stood up to *read* in the synagogue, he obviously had an audience, i.e., listeners. *Listening* to texts was much more common than *reading* them and an audience would most likely have included the literate as well as non-readers.
[10] Cf. Luke 1: 1-4, Acts 1: 1.

the Gospels. The consensus is that the Gospels were written outside Palestine, most likely in Asia Minor, perhaps, in the case of Matthew's Gospel, in Antioch. We know that the Gospels were written after the destruction of the Temple in Jerusalem (AD 70). While the biographical details of the authors of the Gospels remains a mystery, we have direct access to their thought and experiences. That the authors produced writings at all shows that they were relatively well positioned in society. The authors did not come from the lower classes.

When contrasted with Paul's letters, the Gospels are very different in style, substance and purpose. They are largely narratives and include large sections in which Jesus teaches his audiences. These are called 'discourse sections'. The Gospels agree with one another most thoroughly in the passion material. These are the sections that relate the events of Jesus' final hours with his disciples, arrest, and crucifixion. Each Gospel presents unique perspectives on Jesus and accent different aspects of his ministry. Mark contains no information about Jesus' birth and childhood, but accents the events of Jesus' passion. Matthew and Luke include infancy material and expand Mark's information about Jesus' earthly ministry. John does not mention anything about Jesus' birth, but includes a prologue that identifies Jesus as the 'logos', and ties Jesus' ministry to God's work in the act of creation. John also includes an extensive discourse section that makes up half of the Gospel.

In contrast to the Gospels, Paul's letters are clearly a different sort of writing. There is no narrative material. Paul shows almost no interest in Jesus' earthly ministry or in his birth. He accentuates the fact of Jesus' crucifixion and resurrection. He is clearly motivated by concern for specific issues in specific situations. Paul's writing shows that he was well educated and positioned high on the social ladder. He is well acquainted with his society's rules of social engagement, i.e., he accepts patronage, honours his patrons and expects reciprocal treatment. He is skilled in the arts of persuasion. Indeed, he is a master of rhetoric.

In addition to the Gospels, Acts and letters of Paul, the New Testament contains letters from authors other than Paul as well as the Apocalypse or Book of Revelation. This last book in the canon of the New Testament is of a sort of writing that is distinct from that represented in letter or gospel writing. The Book of Revelation, which appears to be in the form of a letter, but is not a letter, is an example of a distinct genre of writing. It is called 'apocalyptic'. Apocalyptic was a common form of writing in the centuries leading up to the New Testament period. It also occurs in the Gospels, the Book of Daniel and the Qumran texts. Apocalyptic is characterized by striking imagery and symbolism. The symbols tend to be animal and numerical figures. Spectacular celestial events are featured in apocalyptic. It sees the world as a battleground between the forces of good and evil. It expects the ultimate and imminent victory of good over evil and God's vindication. While many find the Book of Revelation to be confusing, intimidating, or even bizarre, its original audience would have recognized its style and would have been able to understand its meaning.

Within the various texts, different types of writing occur. The Gospels and Acts, for example, contain genealogies, narratives, speeches, parables and proverbs, among a great many other types of writing. Paul's letters contain exhortation, rebuke, instruction, and personal greetings, all of which are expressed in terms that would have been easily and readily recognized and understood by his original audience. The writings of the New Testament display all of the features common in Hellenistic writing.

One important truism should never be forgotten, but often is. All scripture was written to be understood. No author of a book of the New Testament deliberately wrote to be obscure or to be misunderstood. Modern readers sometimes find the books of the New Testament inscrutable, because they do not know the types of writings they are reading, the world that produced them and consequently, the techniques for reading them. Learning the various writing styles and the rules of writing that pertain to them is one of the first steps in understanding the words and the world.

The art of writing was highly prized by the upper classes of ancient society, but it was not restricted to the elite, which represented three to seven percent of the population. Men were more likely to read and write than women, but there are many examples of documents written by women. Some estimates put the general literacy rate as low as five percent. This estimate is probably too low. Writing as a fine art or in formal, official functions was, indeed, an elite occupation, but writing was important not just for the production of fine literature, but for such mundane needs as writing receipts, making dates, issuing warnings, announcing a condemned person's offence and identifying tombs. Such uses of writing suggest that people other than the elite enjoyed some level of literacy. The introduction to Claudius' letter to the Alexandrians discovered in Oxyrhyncus states that the purpose of posting the emperor's letter was to enable 'the populace' to read it. Such a posting would be unnecessary, unless the general public was able to read. A sign in Pompeii warns, 'Beware of the dog.' There was a sign on the Temple Mount warning non-Israelites not to enter the sacred precincts. Are these kinds of signs intended only for a select few? Such signs were effective only if they could be read. The sign placed on Jesus' cross read 'King of the Jews'. Pilate was asked to change it to read, 'This man *said* he was King of the Jews,' which would have been more appropriate to what we know of the custom of crucifixion. The condemned person's offence was announced on a sign. Was that sign only meant for the elite? Any sign intended for the general public would be an absurdity unless a wide constituency enjoyed some level reading skills.

The tools for writing were ink, pens and papyrus. It was important to use the best quality writing implement and opinions on quality abound in ancient literature. Pens were made of reeds, sharpened with a knife to a fine point. Ink was made of chimney soot mixed in a solution and contained in ceramic or metal jars. The English word 'paper' is derived from the Greek word 'papyrus'. Papyrus is a reed-like plant that grows in Egypt. It can grow ten feet tall.[11] The stalks were cut, laid in sheets, pressed on top of each other, dried and then refined. After the sheets of paper were made they were joined by glue at the ends and rolled into scrolls.

Another material for scrolls was parchment. This was processed animal skin that was also cut and glued together. This process was developed in the Asia Minor city of Pergamum, from which the word parchment derives. The king of that city wanted to build a huge library. This ambition was irritating to the Egyptian king, so he put an embargo on the sale of papyrus to Pergamum, thus necessitating the development of another material for writing.

Papyrus or parchment could be used for scrolls. The length of a scroll was determined by convenience in handling. They were about 30 feet long and required two hands to manage. Our word 'volume' derives from the Latin name for a scroll, *volumen,* which means 'something rolled up'. The two longest books of the New Testament, Luke and Acts, would fill one scroll each. Scrolls were the standard for written works until codices or books replaced the use of scrolls, especially among Christians, in the Late Roman Period.

A codex is a book type of text, made by folding one or more sheets of papyrus or parchment in the middle and sewing them together to make pages. It is easier to manage than a scroll, easier to find one's place in a text, both sides of a sheet of parchment or papyrus could be used and longer manuscripts could be produced. All four Gospels, for instance, could be contained in one manuscript.

Even when a person was skilled at writing, the dictating of letters, documents, records, etc. was normal practice. The author of the document was not the writer of the document. Rather, he or she was the one who dictated the text to the scribe. There are several instances when Paul is

---

[11] Pliny the Elder gives a lengthy account of the process of making paper, which was a major industry. See appendix, Ancient Texts.

clearly using a scribe. Occasionally the scribe announces his presence (Rom 16: 22) or Paul differentiates the scribe's writing from his own hand (1 Cor. 16: 21, Gal. 6: 11, Phil 19). Typically, when multiple copies of a text were required, as in the case of copying sacred texts, the author would dictate to a room full of scribes who would each write what was heard. The scriptorium, or room in which this process occurred, was discovered at Qumran replete with a desk and writing tools.

Anyone who went to school learned reading, writing and the skills that went along with them. Writing was taught by the use of dictation. Dictation was a very important part of the process of transmission of texts and shorthand was widely used by professional scribes. When it came time to send a letter or other document, there were several options. One could entrust an important document to someone reliable with a special commission to deliver the document. Paul probably used this method to send his letters. It is clear that he receives letters from his churches in this manner (1 Cor. 7: 1). Alternately, one could take a chance and send a less important document with someone who happened to be headed in a particular direction. Augustus Caesar instituted a delivery system for sending official documents. It involved relaying correspondence from one carrier to the next. The carriers were positioned at stations or *positus* along the way, hence the origin of our word 'post'. The system was modified eventually so that instead of changing carriers, a carrier simply changed horses, in the manner of the pony express. Thus, one person from its sender to its recipient would carry a letter. The one who delivered the document could also convey verbal information from the sender and be questioned as well. Paul clearly has the advantage of questioning Chloe's people who come to him from Corinth with a letter from the Corinthians (1 Cor. 1: 11).

Even though the author of a document did not necessarily do the physical writing of the document, he or she was responsible for the composition of the document. Sometimes authorship was done alone, but there are many examples of joint authorship as well (2 Cor. 1: 1, Phil. 1: 1). Sometimes the composition was the sole product of the author's thought process. Sometimes the author would incorporate pieces of earlier documents into a new composition. Composition required skill with very complex rhetorical rules and devices. In fact, in the ancient world, the most important subject taught by tutors or in schools was rhetoric, the art of persuasion. The purpose of the document determined its form and the rhetorical strategies. Just as today there are specific forms for a business letter, a will, various kinds of contracts, so in the ancient world there were specific forms associated with specific literary functions. A scribe might be commissioned to simply copy the dictated material or he could be entrusted to correct style and form as well. He was a professional writer who knew the rules of writing and the forms of various documents. Once the document was complete and delivered, it might be subject to further revision or adaptation.

Modern biblical scholarship recognized distinct genres, forms and sources in biblical writing very early. By the turn of the twentieth century, the so-called 'historical-critical method' had developed. Even today, this method is still predominant in seminaries, although it has been refined and developed. This method is an approach to the Bible that seeks information about the development of the texts by examination of different aspects of the texts.

Form criticism recognizes differences between letters and narratives and different types of narratives. For example, Paul's letters have a distinct 'form' that distinguishes them from other types of writing. It includes formal greetings, the sender and recipient are identified, thanksgivings, the body of the letter, and a conclusion, which could include blessings, a benediction, informal greetings, an expression of peace and a postscript. The Book of Revelation is a narrative document, but includes part of a letter from John to the seven churches, so its form is sometimes misunderstood. Different documents require different forms. Deciding which form to use is an important part of the process of composition. The genealogies of Jesus conform to a specific form, as do the beatitudes.

Literary forms help us to determine the origin of a passage. Sometimes the occurrence of a distinct form suggests that a story circulated in oral form before being committed to writing. For example, angelic annunciation stories follow a distinct form: 1) the angel greets the recipient, 2) the recipient registers fear, 3) the angel reassures the recipient, 4) the message follows, 5) the recipient expresses surprise or disbelief, 6) the angel provides a sign, 7) the recipient carries out the command given in the message (cf. Luke 1: 26-38). A modern analogy is the form of the 'knock-knock' joke. These are transmitted orally across generations and around the world without losing any details, because they conform to a tight, distinct form. The form aids memory and is thus, an extremely important device in a culture in which information is processed orally, such as the ancient world.

Source criticism recognizes that in the composition of a document, earlier documents may have been recycled. It is particularly important when reading the Gospels, but pertains to all New Testament writings. The author of Revelation used a letter of John to the seven churches as one of his sources. 2 Corinthians is a composite of more than one letter from Paul. Source theory has helped determine the chronology of the Gospels. Scholars recognize that the Gospel of Mark is contained, almost in its entirety in the Gospels of Matthew and Luke. But which came first? Did Mark condense

Matthew and Luke or did Matthew and Luke rely upon and expand upon Mark? What about those parts that are common to both Matthew and Luke, but do not occur in Mark? This material is mostly sayings of Jesus. And what about material that is unique to Matthew and Luke respectively? Today, the overwhelming consensus among scholars is that Mark is the earliest of the four Gospels and was written sometime in the decade of the seventies. Scholars believe that Matthew and Luke did not know of each other's writing and both relied upon Mark. Their Gospels were produced sometime in the eighties. Further, both had a written source that circulated prior to their writing. Finally, both contributed their own information based on their own understandings. Neither Mark, nor Matthew, nor Luke was aware that their works would be included one day as scripture in the New Testament. They used writing conventions that were common in their day. They did not have any compunction about sorting through available sources and including only the material that they felt was the most important to convey.

Another component of the historical-critical method is *text theory*. This is an ancient technique that has been applied to ancient and modern literature, including the works of Homer and Shakespeare. It developed when discoveries of ancient manuscripts showed that different versions of the same books circulated widely. The form of the Bible we have today is not the original form. Although many modern readers hold the Bible in a type of reverence that prompts them to resist the idea that the text of the Bible has been, can or should be modified in any way, all modern English versions are modified versions. They have been translated into a different language, chapter and verse designations have been added, many versions include section headings and many others include notes of various kinds in margins and footings. These are examples of intentional modification and similar modifications have been made throughout history.

When an ancient text reached the stage that it was copied for wide circulation, it was susceptible to a variety of unintentional modifications. When copying from a manuscript, a scribe might misread one word for another that was very close in spelling. He might misread two similarly written letters or even miss a line, if his eye wandered. When taking dictation, a scribe might mishear a particular word. Occasionally, a scribe would reverse the order of letters in a word, thus changing a word without realizing it. Different words that are very near to each other in spelling are easy to confuse. More significant textual variations occur as well.

A well-known example of the importance of text theory is the case of the long ending of Mark. Most modern English translations, such as the Revised Standard Version, end with 16: 20. However, they include a note at the end of Mark's Gospel stating that the most ancient manuscripts end with 16: 8. They also indicate that other ancient manuscripts end with a ninth verse, still others add an alternate verse nine, and yet others add more verses after verse fourteen. Text theory tries to figure out which reading was the original.

Finally, *redaction criticism* examines passages where there is evidence of the work of an editor. The ending of the Gospel of John appears to be one such instance. John 21: 24 is written in the first person plural ('*we* know that *his* testimony is true') and refers to another who 'has written these things.' Then in verse 25, another voice appears and speaks in the first person singular (I suppose).

More importantly, redaction criticism enables us to discern the thinking of the authors of the Gospels. An author's selection of a particular source reveals his thinking. Both Matthew and Luke, for instance, use the Gospel of Mark and the source called 'Q' as sources in compiling their gospels, but they use these sources selectively. For example, Luke is careful only to relate resurrection stories that occur in or near Jerusalem in order to emphasize his understanding of the particular importance of that city. We get our clearest view of the authors of Matthew and Luke, however, in their respective preambles. The infancy material in both Matthew and Luke do not derive from earlier sources. As far as we know, written narratives about Jesus' birth and childhood originates with Matthew and Luke. Thus, when we read these sections of their Gospels, we can almost feel the authors' outlook. Matthew is interested in stressing the continuity of Jesus' birth with Israelite tradition. Luke displays a keen interest in the relationship between Jesus and John the Baptist. Both authors display unique techniques to depict the birth stories as portents for events in Jesus' adult ministry.

The historical-critical method is unavoidable. It has produced enormous insights into the Bible. It has advanced our understanding of scripture immeasurably. Yet it is deeply flawed. With the historical-critical method, the scholar approaches the Bible the way a scientist approaches a specimen under a microscope, i.e., with measured objectivity. As if the Bible were composed of atoms and molecules, he/she stands outside it and looks in. He/she breaks it down into its component parts. Indeed, biblical scholars have adopted some of the fundamental presuppositions of science. This is not surprising since the scientific method and its assumptions pervade modern life. Neither is it unproductive. Modern scholarship has produced startling and inspiring insights into the Bible. It is not, however, the ultimate, final, sole or most productive approach to scripture, because the Bible is not only about texts, but also about *contexts,* i.e., life situations, the human experience.

Modern biblical scholarship demands specialization. The level of specialization is now so great that biblical scholarship has become the domain of an academic elite. Further, specialization leads away from contexts and toward concentrated areas of textual expertise. It draws the scholar deeper into the text, but further from real life contexts. It leads toward isolation rather than engagement with the world. The assumption that knowledge is derived by breaking down an object into its component parts is at the root of the ever increasing demand for specialization, but it does not respect the complexity of the Bible. While this assumption itself is by no means self-evident, scholarship accepts it uncritically. The demand for greater control over smaller component parts prevents us from integrating the Bible into life, understanding the human experience or giving ultimate meaning to temporal existence. It has lead to increased isolation of biblical disciplines from one another. Rarely do scholars have the ability to access information from other areas of study. The best that it can produce is detailed information about isolated parts. Compartmentalization of information, however, cannot produce a cohesive, coherent outlook on either the Bible or on human life. Instead, a contextual approach requires experience with a real life situation to which the Bible can be applied and continually requires us to engage the world. Contexts produced the texts. Understanding these contexts takes us back out of the pages of the book to the world. The best biblical study leads us into the world. The Bible is not an object to be examined objectively from the outside looking in. Cool, disinterested, detachment does not necessarily lead us to the Bible's wisdom. The Bible is concerned to reveal wisdom, impart insight, instil value, meaning, purpose, and identity. These things are not revealed by the scientific method. Thus, *examination* of the Bible is less productive than *experiencing* the Bible. Instead of standing outside the Bible and looking at it from a distance, it is necessary to immerse oneself *in* the Bible and look out toward the world.

Chapter 3
THE GEOGRAPHY OF
THE BIBLICAL WORLD

There are three principles that pertain to understanding the relationship between geography and biblical literature: location, location, location. The literature of the Bible must be understood in its geographical context. As the noted Near Eastern scholar, Georges Roux puts it, 'Nowhere, perhaps, is the influence of geography upon history as clearly demonstrated as in the group of countries which extend from the Mediterranean Sea to the Iranian plateau and form what we call the Near East.'[1] While Roux seems to overlook the reality that geography informs history in every context, it is important to stress this point here, because modern New Testament scholarship almost entirely ignores biblical geography.

When it comes to reading the Bible with comprehension and insight, an acquaintance with the lands of the Bible is an absolute necessity. There are two main areas in which geography plays pivotal roles in the development of the biblical texts and the biblical faith. The first, which I alluded to in the introduction, is that the land itself is a reservoir of object lessons, images and metaphors at the disposal of the biblical actors and authors. The second is that geography dictates where and how societies develop.

Geography is the point of departure for the discipline of Near East studies, because the nature and characteristics of the land determine the forms taken by various societies. For instance, desert terrain encourages the development of nomadic society, while better agricultural land leads to the establishment of more permanent, sedentary societies. Without an operating familiarity with the Biblical landscape, the insights and inspirations of scripture all to often remain cryptic, remote and obscure. It is a sad commentary on contemporary New Testament studies that biblical geography is not taken seriously.

To know the land of the Bible is to read the words of the Bible in an altogether new light. It is to read colourful scripture rather than black and white newsprint. It is to see beyond the flat pages of a bland manuscript into a multi-dimensional world of sensory stimulation, spiritual inspiration, intellectual satisfaction, and moral reorientation. The biblical authors presume acquaintance with this multi-dimensional world. The striking imagery of the

---

[1] Georges Roux, *Ancient Iraq,* London: Penguin Books, Ltd., 1964, 1.

Psalms takes on a deeper meaning when we are familiar with the changing landscapes and seasons of Palestine. Until we have experienced the harsh desert environment of the Negev or Sinai, we cannot fully identify with authors who described their relationship with God in terms of the desert experience. 'As a hart pants for water, so my soul longs for you, O Lord.' (Psalm 42: 1) 'Like unto the shadow of a great rock in a barren wilderness ... ' (Isaiah 32: 2) Only after familiarizing ourselves with the barren terrain of the Judean wilderness with its deep, v-shaped ravines and precipitous cliffs do we understand the psalmist's words of grateful assurance, 'Yea, though I walk through the valley of the shadow of death, I will fear no evil.' (Psalm 23: 4) The story of the Good Samaritan, set in the heart of the Judean desert, becomes less of an abstract tale and more of a real life paradox when we understand that the story is set in a region which was a haven for outlaws where ambushes were common. Until we have seen a Galilean hillside carpeted with flowers blossoming in a rainbow of colours, we cannot fully identify with Jesus' poetic description, 'Behold the lilies of the field, how they grow; they neither toil nor spin, yet even Solomon in all his glory was not clothed as one of these.' (Matthew 6: 28) Likening the prolific bloom of the Galilean countryside to the legendary splendour and opulence of King Solomon, Jesus, in his first century way, anticipated the modern adage, 'There is no springtime like winter in Galilee.'

Or consider the picturesque, tactile imagery of the Song of Solomon. It seems so bizarre to us when we have never seen or eaten a pomegranate (4: 13, 6: 7). Until we have seen a gazelle bounding over the hills (2: 8), until we have seen a flock of goats moving over a hillside (6: 5), we cannot fully appreciate the author's descriptions. How can one understand the sensuous beauty described in the Song of Solomon never having seen the vineyards of Ein Gedi, or not knowing the rhythm of the seasons or the lifestyle of the nomadic shepherds who make the stark desert landscape their hospitable kingdom?

The stories of the Bible often sound puzzling or like far-fetched fairy tales and their details can seem inconsequential until one learns the geographical context in which the story is placed. For instance, in the episode reported at the beginning of Matthew 13 (cf. Mark 4: 1), the author mentions that Jesus drew such a large crowd that he is forced to preach from a boat just offshore. To one who is unfamiliar with the shoreline of the Sea of Galilee, this may seem like a meaningless detail. In fact, it helps us identify the probable location of this particular episode and one of the places Jesus frequented.

We know from the gospel testimony that Jesus' Galilean ministry was cantered in Capernaum. We know also that the shore of the Sea of Galilee in the vicinity of Capernaum is often very hilly. Indeed, within an easy walk from the ruins of Capernaum, one will come to a place where the water has carved out small semicircular bays. The hills slope gently to the water. The combination of the curve of the shoreline and the slope of the hills coming down to the sea at a 45 degree slope forms perfect natural amphitheatres, i.e. natural acoustical shells are formed that are strikingly similar to the shape of the Roman theatres found throughout the ancient world. The reference in Matthew to Jesus' preaching from a boat to a crowd on the shore informs us that Jesus used these natural acoustical shells along the shore to broadcast his message to the gathered crowd. Thus, such a detail helps us locate the setting of this passage.

The meaning of the Bible expands and our appreciation for scripture multiplies when we learn the dimensions of the Holy Land and the proximity of one place to another. To one unacquainted with the landscape of Palestine, perhaps the story of the visitation of the magi (Matthew 2) seems magical or mystical. Who were these magi? Where in the East did they come from? And when Herod sent them on to Bethlehem from Jerusalem how far did they have to travel and why didn't he go with them? If we picture this distance to be great, we will have missed an important point of the story. In fact, Bethlehem is only a few short miles from Jerusalem. Herod did not need to send the magi there to gain the information he sought. He could have gone there himself or sent a delegation on his behalf. Rather, he sent the magi in his place as if he was prevented by some divine power regulating the events of this episode, as if he was playing a part in some drama even he did not comprehend. As a result, the story functions to tell the story of salvation. Specifically, Herod became a foil in the plot to help the author of Matthew interpret this birth narrative in light of important Old Testament antecedents.[2]

By the same token, our appreciation for the drama as well as the meaning of the biblical word is enhanced when we understand the geographical relationships between places. In John's telling of the events following the last supper and Jesus' arrest (John 18), many are left in the dark due to their lack of familiarity of the Jerusalem landscape. When Jesus finished his words to the disciples, he left the place where they were gathered, crossed the Kidron valley and waited in a place where there was a garden, namely Gethsemane. The location of this garden has been known throughout the

---

[2] The story of Balaam and King Balak (Numbers 22, 23) is the likely literary allusion in Matthew's mind. In that story, a non-Israelite noted as a seer, i.e., an occult visionary (Numbers 23: 23) of some sort who comes from the East accompanied by two servants, is called upon to curse Israel. Baalam spoiled the wicked designs of a treacherous King Balak by delivering a oracle of future Israelite greatness and the greatness of its king. Likewise, Herod sought to use the foreign magi in his plan to seek out and destroy Jesus. Like Baalam, however, the magi end up honouring Jesus.

ages. The name means 'oil press' and it is located on the shoulder of the Mount of Olives. It was a walk of perhaps one mile for Jesus on the night he was betrayed from the place of the Last Supper to the garden where he was arrested. It could be accomplished in about twenty minutes. If we imagine it as a trek of major proportions, we miss the point that Jesus was intentionally making himself accessible to the Roman soldiers and the detachment from the chief priests and the Pharisees. An acquaintance with the land informs us that Jesus was not hiding or trying to escape. This is reinforced by the observation that he could have escaped easily by simply walking another twenty minutes to the top of the Mount of Olives and beyond to the safety of the Judean wilderness just on the other side.

Geography determines where and how culture develops. The Book of Exodus records a historic promise made by God to Moses (Ex. 3: 8). 'I have come down to deliver them (Israel) from the Egyptians and to bring them up out of that land to a good and broad land, a land flowing with milk and honey ...' That it was such a good land, one formed by the coming and going of many cultures, is underscored by the important observation that it was a land already peopled by a variety of ethnic groups from the earliest times of recorded history. Even at the time of God's covenant with Abraham (Gen. 17: 8), the land was already populated and Abraham was required to negotiate with the indigenous population to purchase property for a burial place for his wife, Sarah (Gen. 23). The narratives relating the covenant between God and Abraham give Abraham no unconditional prerogatives over other peoples' lands. However, the weight of the land traditions of the Old Testament display remarkable disregard for the rights of the people resident in the land when, according to the narratives, the Israelites arrived.[3]

Deuteronomy lists its specific resources. In contrast to the popular perception that the land of the Middle East is barren desert, Deuteronomy tells us that it was '... a land with flowing streams, with springs and underground waters welling up in valleys and hills, a land of wheat and barley and vines and fig trees, and pomegranates; a land of olive oil, and honey; a land where you can eat bread without scarcity, where you will lack nothing, a land whose stones are iron and from whose hills you can mine copper. (Deuteronomy 8: 7-9)

The expression of the 'land flowing with milk and honey' was a proverbial one signifying that the land was productive. It referred specifically to two different types of productivity. A land of milk refers to a region suitable

---

[3] In his 1997 book *The Bible and Colonialism: A Moral Critique*. Sheffield Academic Press, Sheffield, England, Michael Prior focuses on ferocity and consistency with which the land traditions of the Old Testament not only legitimate the ethnic cleansing of Canaan, but insist that such is the requirement of God.

for shepherding. A land of honey signifies a zone that was good land for settled farming communities. This latter region yielded dates from which a form of honey is derived. The biblical phrase 'a land flowing with milk and honey' denotes a place with two different types of agricultural productivity and two different types of society to which they correspond. These two geographical zones define the region of the Middle East. The societies that developed in these distinct zones were ideally suited to their environments. We see the tension between them reflected in the Bible (Cain and Abel) and in other ancient near eastern literature. The Epic of Gilgamesh records the history of the creative tension between the hero of the story, Gilgamesh, a town dweller and Enkidu, who comes from the desert. The two need each other, but collide with one another.

Another example of the way in which geography determines how and where history unfolds is in Jesus' choice of villages to be his primary locus of ministry. Jesus' choice of Capernaum as a centre of his Galilean ministry was probably more strategic than coincidental. Capernaum was located at the intersection of the Via Maris and spur of the second of the two great trade routes, i.e. the King's Highway.

Capernaum was not a backwater. Even though it did not have the status of a city, which would have given it special privileges, it was a thoroughly Hellenised town with a relatively diverse economy. We know that it was Hellenised from both archaeological and literary testimony. Excavation of the site shows that even though the town was small, with a population of approximately 1,500 people who lived modestly but were not destitute. They made their living as fishermen, artisans (the production of millstones was an important industry there) or in commerce. Certainly there were farmers, as well as those who had amassed some modest wealth. Its streets, which date to the time of Jesus, are clearly laid out on a grid, showing the Hellenistic influence. The Gospel testimony is that people from a wide variety of ethnic groups and social strata frequented it. There, Jesus could come in contact with travellers from all corners of the world, due to its proximity to the Via Maris and the King's Highway.

Some say that Jesus chose Capernaum because it would afford him a refuge from Herod Antipas. However, a good sized town with a tax collection booth and a detachment of royal soldiers that was only about 5 miles from the provincial capital of Galilee (Tiberius) would not give Jesus much refuge from a king. Others say that Jesus chose Capernaum, because its population was more open to his teaching in contrast to that of his native village Nazareth. Yet, Jesus condemned the village along with Bethsaida and Chorazin precisely because his message was *not* received.

A third hypothesis is that he chose the site of Capernaum for the access to people and ideas it afforded. His was no parochial world of narrow, remote interest, but a world which was cosmopolitan in the truest sense, a world which was hungering for a new philosophical framework. Jesus lived in a dramatically changing world that was clamouring for a global self consciousness. Not only did Jesus absorb the spirit of this changing new world from his upbringing in Galilee and position in Capernaum, but from there his ideas were transmitted far and wide by those who heard him hold forth. Thus, when the apostles set forth from Jerusalem after Jesus death to carry the Gospel into the world, they came across enclaves of people who had already heard of Jesus.

There is a widespread fiction about Galilee that it was strictly separated into 'Jewish' and 'gentile' areas. This is a fiction that is perpetuated largely by people who have an interest in legitimating separation of peoples and by tour guides for whom the saying, 'Never let the facts get in the way of a good story' has the force of a sacred creed. The only problem is that such a view is supported neither by archaeological evidence nor by literary support. It is almost impossible to tell ethnic identity from foundations of buildings.

In fact, the Galilee was populated from earliest times with a variety of ethnic groups and so it earned the epithet 'Galilee of the nations' (Isaiah 9: 1). Indeed, its Judean population was a distinct minority. Nor is there any evidence that Judeans and non-Judeans separated themselves from each other. From the perspective of religious Judeans living in Jerusalem, the Galilee was a backwater of sorts and Capernaum would have seemed like a frontier town to a Jerusalemite, but class and ethnic chauvinism cannot be the basis of historical reconstruction.

Recent New Testament studies reflect a trend toward considering the distinctiveness of regional cultures.[4] Regional variations are better appreciated now than they were a generation ago. The Pharisees considered Galileans boorish and uncultivated. People from there were distinguishable by there dress and accent (Matt. 26: 73). They were considered unimportant and noteworthy for very little (John 2: 46). Galilean Judeans observed different customs from those in Jerusalem. For instance, a newly married couple was allowed to be alone on their wedding night. There were differences in the rights of a widow and no work was done on the day before Passover.

Without question, however, the Galilee is best known from the events

---

[4] Freyne, Sean, *Galilee from Alexander the Great to Hadrian, 323 BCE-135 CE: A Study of Second Temple Judaism*, Michael Glazier, Wilmington, Del., 1980; Horsley, Richard A, *Galilee: History, Politics, People*, Trinity Press International, Valley Forge, PA, 1995.

of the life of its best known citizen, Jesus of Nazareth. Almost all of Jesus' ministry occurred within the borders of Galilee, which by the middle of the first century had become a Roman province with a fixed area.[5] Although he travelled from time to time, the gospel record suggests that Galilee was the centre of his attention. The vast majority of stories are connected not only with the Galilee, but more specifically with the Sea of Galilee. Moreover, Jesus seems to have been a product of his environment in a number of ways. As indicated above, Galilean Judeans observed slightly different customs than those in Jerusalem, which was the centre of ritual worship. Traditionally, Galileans displayed a spirit of independence from the Jerusalem cult. They were known to be hard to subjugate. Clearly, that many of them chafed under Roman rule when it did arrive after AD 44 is reflected in the fact that resistance to Rome during the first revolt was stiff there. Perhaps because of their isolation from Jerusalem, they were less inclined to strict observance of Temple ritual, which would have required frequent travels to Jerusalem 120 miles away. Contrary to popular misconceptions, there is no evidence that Jesus regularly attended festivals in Jerusalem, although the Gospels suggest that he occasionally went there for such events. Perhaps as a corollary of his free spirited approach to ritual worship, Jesus was known for his unorthodox interpretation and application of the Law. For instance, in one exchange with the Sadducees (Mark 11: 18-27), Jesus invokes an argument which must have seemed rather unorthodox to his interlocutors in order to explain his belief in life after death. Again, in justifying the behaviour of his disciples before a dubious group of Pharisees (Mark 2: 23-28), Jesus resorts to free interpretation of scripture and eschews strict application of the Law. Jesus' Galilean nature was licence enough for him to speculate freely and develop theological positions that must have seemed independent if not idiosyncratic to Israelite authorities in Jerusalem. While he did not share the revolutionary spirit of some of his contemporaries and seems to be neutral regarding Roman domination, in the end, it was his defiance of the Temple establishment in Jerusalem that prompted his execution.

Jesus' upbringing in Galilee not only imparted to him a spirit of free interpretation of Judean Law, it also exposed him to influential international social currents and philosophical winds. Not only was he exposed to broad cultural diversity due to the large number of ethnic groups represented in the Galilean population, but also, the trade routes which crossed Galilee carried ideas and social trends as well as commercial goods for consumption.

---

[5] It was not, however, under direct Roman rule at the time of Jesus' adult ministry, so the popular spin on Jesus' ministry that he was issuing a direct challenge to Roman Imperial rule is a bit hasty, if not outright reductionist.

Galilee was productive territory not only because of the fertility of its soil, but also because of the fertility of the intellectual atmosphere. Jesus lived in a place and time which was extraordinary for the fermentation of ideas.

Finally, no one can even begin to comprehend the cross fertilization of ideas that took place in the region of Palestine in particular and the ancient Near East in general unless one appreciates Palestine's geographical position relative to the rest of the world. It was at the intersection of civilizations— Egypt in the south, Mesopotamian kingdoms and Persia to the East, Greece and Rome to the West. Palestine had no mineral resources or economic power. Throughout most of its history, it was a political backwater. Control of the trade routes that ran through it, however, in particular, the Via Maris, were of critical importance to neighbouring empires and empire builders. As a result of its location, its populations along the trade routes were far less isolated than peoples in more remote regions. A person who grew up in lower Galilee could not be kept insulated from the influences of surrounding cultures and peoples. It is not a coincidence that the seed of Jesus' life and ministry germinated in the soil of ancient Palestine. Neither did it happen by mysterious chance that this seed sprang up and grew into the first universal religion in the region of the ancient Near East.

Scholars have known for decades that the culture of the Near East was a particularly fertile field for the development of civilization. Civilization was born there. People learned to farm there, leaving behind the nomad's existence for permanent dwellings grouped in communities. The first irrigation systems and the introduction of a system of the division of labour contributed to this development. In Sumer, situated in the area of modern Iraq, the first written language emerged around 3,500 BC. The clash of empires over the course of thousands of years and the intermarriage of cultures eventually gave birth to a universal culture which ultimately required a universal religion, one which bore the traits of the family of religions in which it was reared.

That there was a fluid exchange of ideas between various ancient civilizations cannot be contested. Evidence for this exchange of ideas is abundant from Genesis to Revelation. The biblical stories of creation and flood, for instance, are mirrored in the literature of other ancient Near Eastern cultures. In their myths, the Sumerians portrayed themselves as being formed by the gods from clay, not unlike the account of the creation of Adam in Genesis 2: 7. Their myths also testify to the ancient antagonism between tillers of the ground, i.e. farmers and keepers of sheep, i.e. herders, a tension that is also described in scripture in the story of Cain and Able. The report of the portent in Revelations 12 describes a scene and events that seem to draw heavily on ancient Egyptian mythology. The only questions are, how did this exchange occur and why Palestine? These cannot be answered without an understanding of the geography of the Holy Land and so, one of the first principles of biblical study is to learn the relationship between the Word of God and the land of the Bible.

The Lands of the Bible

Although modern day Israel is often referred to as 'The Land of the Bible', not one book of the Bible was written there. In the case of the Hebrew scriptures, the consensus among scholars is that the form in which we currently know them took its shape in Mesopotamia, even if the stories are about places in the land of Canaan. In the case of the New Testament, scholars overwhelmingly agree that the nearest to Palestine any of these writings originate is *perhaps* the Gospel of Matthew. Some assert that Matthew was written in Antioch, which is in modern day Turkey on the Syrian border.[6] On this point there is much debate, however. As for the rest of the New Testament, the consensus among scholars is that the books of the New Testament were written in Asia Minor (modern day Turkey), Greece or Italy.

The land of the Bible is, thus, much larger than the area known to most pilgrims as the 'Holy Land', a term used by Christians which usually designates the region within which Jesus was active during his earthly ministry. In addition to Palestine, the lands of the Bible encompass Egypt, Mesopotamia (modern Syria and Iraq, also known as the Fertile Crescent), Arabia, Asia Minor or Anatolia (modern Turkey), Greece and Rome. Together these regions comprised the core of the Hellenistic world. Alexander the Great united this area through conquest and cultivated it through enlightened administration. It was here that Christianity first flourished. The Coptic Church, which derives its name from the Greek word for Egypt, was the first fully constituted Christian Church. Armenia, in eastern Asia Minor was the first nation to officially accept Christianity. Paul's missionary activity started in Damascus and took him through a region he refers to as Arabia (Gal. 1: 17, probably the mountain and plateau regions in the south of Jordan, but possibly further) and the Mediterranean basin as well as to Palestine and Jerusalem. The churches to which he wrote were located in Asia Minor, Greece and Rome, not in Palestine. All seven churches to which the letter known as the Apocalypse of John is written were in western Asia Minor (Turkey). We should properly consider all the countries of the Mediterranean

---

[6] Historically, Antakya (ancient Antioch) had been part of Greater Syria, but it ended up under Turkish rule when the borders of the modern Middle East were drawn by Europeans subsequent to the Ottoman collapse in World War 1.

basin, along with the countries of the Near East among the lands of the Bible.

Biblical testimony to the far-flung frontiers of the ancient world and the proclivity of the ancients to wander throughout the world is abundant. Genesis tells us that Abraham's ancestors made their way from the east, to the southeastern extent of the Fertile Crescent, to the land of Shinar, the Bible's name for ancient Sumer (Gen. 11: 2). Abraham himself was born in Ur, the capital of the Sumerian empire (Gen. 11: 26-27) and from there travelled caravan routes the entire length of the Fertile Crescent to the Land of Canaan (Gen. 12: 5). During his lifetime, Abraham travelled as far as Egypt (Gen. 12: 10). The Queen of Sheba made a 1,200 mile trek from her kingdom at the southern tip of the Arabian peninsula to Jerusalem to visit King Solomon, offering him '... 120 talents of gold, and of spices very great store, and precious stones.' (I Kings 10: 10) Isaiah mentions the ' ... multitude of camels ... from Sheba.' (Isaiah 60: 6) From the another direction, Egyptian armies travelled the Fertile Crescent north through the Levant's coastal plain, subjugating all the land as far as Babylon. Thutmoses III made at least sixteen military expeditions throughout the region. Ramses captured Ashkelon and Acco on the Mediterranean coast of the Levant and subdued the Hittites at Kadesh in Syria. Asian kings appealed to Pharaoh Akhenaten for help against their foes. All left legacies recorded on stone monuments, personal and official correspondence and in scripture. In 724 BC Assyrian armies conquered the northern kingdom of Israel (II Kings 17: 5-6, 18). Later, under the command of King Sennacherib, Assyrian forces advanced on the southern kingdom of Judah, conquering Lachish (II Chronicles 32: 9), but left Jerusalem after exacting tribute from King Hezekiah (II Kings 19: 36). Tiglath-pilesar conquered Hazor in Galilee and under King Ashurbanipal, Assyrian power reached deep into Egypt. The Bible records that the Babylonian King Nebuchadnezzar conquered Jerusalem in 597 BC and ten years later commenced the mass deportation of Judeans to Babylon. There they were immersed in the ways of a foreign culture. The Bible relates their struggle to avoid foreign abominations even as they absorbed foreign culture (Isaiah 44: 9-20).

All this is to say that we vastly underestimate the extent of the territory of the biblical world in general and the New Testament in particular when we reduce it strictly to the so-called Holy Land. Even more so, to presume that the Bible reflects the culture of some isolated backwater is a gross error. The geography of the Bible includes all the territory of the Graeco-Roman world in the first century AD. For millennia prior to the birth of Jesus, the world had become well accustomed to the ebb and flow of empires. It had been formed by the slow fermentation of a variety of cultural ingredients. A melting pot in the truest sense, it had developed an appetite for foreign cultures and the cultural benefits they offered. The cultures of all this territory contributed to the formation of the Bible, which bears the fingerprints of a wide variety of influences. Yet, the mixing bowl for the ingredients from these cultures was a more specific region. The crossroads of the civilizations of the ancient Near East was a compact area. To distinguish it from its component parts, including Palestine and Greater Syria, it is useful to avail ourselves of the name given it by European explorers, merchants and military men, i.e. the 'Levant' which means 'the rising', so named because of its location on the eastern Mediterranean where the sun rises.[7] In Arabic, it is referred to as *al-fajr*, i.e., the dawn. Its hospitable countryside with abundant water and good farming is able to sustain sophisticated society. It was easy to traverse it by roads. Two major 'superhighways' facilitated traffic through it. Its strategic location destined the region to play an integral role in a broader world drama.

The Levant: A Land Bridge

By the 18th century, the region on the eastern shore of the Mediterranean Sea had been dubbed 'the Levant'. One of the most important observations to be made about the Levant is that it constitutes a bridge of land connecting the continents of Africa, Asia and Europe. The strategic importance of this observation cannot be understated. Located on the eastern shore of the Mediterranean Sea, the Levant is bounded by the sea on the west and the Greater Syrian Desert in the east. The distance from sea to desert is about 55 miles. It is about 400 miles long, from Aleppo in the north (ancient Khaleb) to Gaza in the south. Any travel between empires in the south (Egypt), the east (Assyria, Babylon, Persia) or the west (Greece and Rome) took place on this thin strip of hospitable terrain called the Levant. This feature alone is enough to give the region geopolitical significance disproportionate to its size.

The Levant is coextensive with the western half of the Fertile Crescent, a semi-circular region of highly fertile land with enough water to support large-scale agriculture and sustain large populations. The eastern half of the Fertile Crescent lies between the Tigris and Euphrates rivers, includes modern day Iraq and extends as far east as the western mountains of modern day Iran and the Persian Gulf. It is a region of fertile agricultural land and reliable supplies of water, the ingredients necessary for it to have developed in such a way that it is appropriately called the birthplace of civilization.

---

[7] There are no politically or culturally neutral labels for this region. Any choice of terms represents value judgements.

The geography of the biblical world

The Levant is divided into smaller regions by natural geographical divisions, including plains, mountains, rivers and desert areas. There are six distinct geographical zones: the coastal plain, the ridge of the central highlands, the rift valley, the mountains of Transjordan, also known as the eastern heights, the Negev and the Jezreel Valley. In general, these divisions run longitudinally, i.e. in a north-south direction. The exceptions are the Negev and the Jezreel Valley, which run in generally east-west directions.

On the Mediterranean coast is a narrow region, known as the coastal plain, which runs the entire length of the Levant. It is up to 10-12 miles wide in some places and as narrow as a few miles in others. In the north, it was known as Phoenicia. In the south, it was called the Philistine plain. Important sea ports, including Ashkelon, Dor, Caesarea Maritima, Acco, Tyre, Sidon and Byblos developed here that facilitated trade with Mediterranean civilizations. That Jesus was familiar with this region is known from his references to its cities, including Tyre and Sidon (Matthew 11: 21,22), and from the assertion in Matthew that Jesus travelled to those cities which, today, are in Lebanon. (Matthew 15: 21 cf.: Mk 7: 24, 31)

The apostle Paul embarked on his missionary voyages from ports on the coastal plain, including Caeserea Maritima where he was imprisoned and Tyre (Acts 18: 22; 21: 7) Evidently, this region was dependent on the Judean kingdom of Herod Archelaus for its commercial vitality (Acts 12: 20). This is not surprising, since commercial interdependence is well attested in the first century. Moreover, goods from regions far off in the east made their way across overland routes to the coastal ports and were shipped throughout the Mediterranean world. By the same token, manufactured goods from North Africa, southern Europe and Greece reached the Levant by sea and then were shipped overland to a variety of destinations in the east. Archaeological research, specifically the discovery of coins from kingdoms far and wide as well as potsherds distinctively decorated from far off regions, testify to the vitality of trade among far flung regions of the world.

Alongside the coastal plain to the east is a long narrow region of mountains, which runs from the Negev in the south to the mountains of Lebanon and anti-Lebanon in the north. The heights of these mountains range in elevation from 3,000 feet in the south at Hebron to over 7,500 feet in Lebanon. Obviously, the presence of mountains posed an impediment to travel and trade which influenced the development of civilization in significant ways. These mountains can be considered the hinterlands of the civilization of the ancient world. Their ruggedness discouraged travel and trade and therefore isolated these regions from the mainstream of traffic. The mountains also discouraged the development of a single, unified kingdom. Consequently, smaller kingdoms developed there off the beaten track as it were. Indeed,

45

most of Old Testament history took place in the isolated hill country of the southern Levant, which was inhabited by Canaanite tribes before it was conquered by the Israelites. Largely due to its isolation, Israelite culture was able to flourish during brief periods of time when it was unmolested by neighbouring superpowers, such as Egypt.

East of the mountains lies the Afro-Syrian rift valley. This rift valley is over 4,000 miles long and runs from Ethiopia to Syria. It includes the Gulf of Aqaba, the Araba (from a Hebrew word for desert), the Dead Sea, the Jordan River Valley, the Sea of Galilee, the Huleh Valley and Lebanon's Beqaa' Valley and Latani River. The rift valley is a deep, wide fissure with high, mountainous slopes on either side. Its average width is ten miles. Its depth varies from north to south. At its lowest point, at the Dead Sea, it is 1,300 feet below sea level, the lowest point on earth. In Lebanon, the Litani River in the Beqaa' valley collects water shed from the mountain slopes on either side of the river and is one of the most important sources of water in the Near East. The Jordan River valley, further to the south was known from the earliest times as a region of great productivity. 'And Lot lifted up his eyes and saw that the Jordan Valley was well watered everywhere, like the garden of the Lord, like the land of Egypt.'[8] (Genesis 13: 10) The climate along the entire length of the rift valley is dramatically different from that even a few miles on either side of it.

East of the Afro-Syrian rift valley, the mountains of Transjordan rise to heights up to 5,500 feet and the eastern plateau. Along the ridge of these mountains ran a major trade route called the 'King's Highway.' Moses appealed to the kings of Edom and the Ammorites to allow the children of Israel to pass along this road, but was rebuffed. (Numbers 20, 21) In the north, these give way to the high plateau called the Golan Heights. This plateau is very fertile and receives abundant rainfall in the winter, so it has been an important region for agriculture. Moses was given a view of the promised land from the top of Mt. Nebo, opposite Jericho, but was allowed only to see it from afar (Deuteronomy 34: 4). Moses and Aaron are said to be buried in these mountains, at Mt. Nebo and Mt. Hor which are in modern day Jordan. John the Baptist was imprisoned in one of Herod's fortresses there.

Beyond the eastern plateau and the mountains of Transjordan, the Greater Syrian desert forms the eastern frontier of the Levant. This is not a clear boundary as the transition from hospitable plateau to harsh desert is nebulous and gradual. Moreover, from time to time, various kingdoms were better able than others to tame the desert by introducing water collection

---

[8] This verse represents hyperbole, but still accurately describes the northern reaches of the Jordan Valley, where it meets the Jezreel Plain.

techniques and thus, extend control further out into the desert. On the other hand, during times of decline, nomadic tribes harassed frontier settlements, sometimes forcing the frontier to recede.

Throughout most of history, the Levant was considered a complete geographical unit. Egyptian sources refer to the land of the 'sand dwellers,' a reference to the population centres along the coastal plain. From the point of view of empires from Mesopotamia and beyond, the Levant was considered the place 'beyond the river,' i.e. on the other side of the Euphrates from a Persian point of view. While foreign empires always considered it one region, no indigenous government ever emerged that was able to control all the Levant and protect it from subjugation from empires. I have indicated above the biblical evidence for military traffic from Egypt in the south and Mesopotamian kingdoms in the north and east. Invading armies, such as those of the Hittites also entered the region from the north and of course, Greece and Rome appeared on the scene from the west.

Even though it afforded quality land for the cultivation of complex society, its strategic position between empires determined that the Levant would be most important as a staging area, a land to be controlled for the purpose of getting somewhere else or attaining something else. It can be said that the importance of the region stems from its being in the way.

From time to time, when foreign empires were in periods of decline, regional kingdoms were able to exert control and gain a measure of sovereignty. One such period took place at the time of the United Monarchy in Israel and another was the Hasmonean kingdom. At these times, the people called Israel were able to exert a modicum of local hegemony.[9] Normally, the kingdoms that came and went in the Levant depended on foreign protection and pledged loyalty to some foreign empire. Such was the case when the Herodian dynasty ruled Judea on behalf of their Roman benefactors, as it was during the Hasmonean dynasty before it.

Strategically, the Levant was crucial to empire builders far and wide.

---

[9] Until recently the idea that there was a independent 'Israelite State' during the time referred to as 'The United Monarchy,' was the unchallenged consensus among scholars. Now, however, significant dissent from this notion is gaining ascendancy. Keith Whitelam, in his book *The Invention of Ancient Israel: the Silencing of Palestinian History,* Routledge, London and New York, 1996, shows that the idea of ancient Israel rests on biased historiography and partial evidence. Certainly, when it is envisaged as anything even remotely similar to a 'state', as we understand that term today, there can be no question that such historiography is anachronistic at best. Clearly, the Hasmonean kingdom, notwithstanding its guerilla warfare successes against the battlefield armies of the Seleucids, was never more than a semi-independent vassal kingdom. Even at the height of its success, its rulers still depended upon their Seleucid patrons for support in their claim to the office of the High Priest in Jerusalem.

Its long coastline, backed by productive agricultural land afforded ports for shipping and trade and access to Mediterranean countries. It was located centrally between empires and, most importantly, its hospitable geography rendered it highly suitable for building roads for international trade and travel. The unique conjunction of factors which are determined by its geography— the presence of water, easily passable plains and valleys for the construction of roads and its location at the crossroads of empires— made the Levant the strategic intersection of ancient world history. If Egypt wanted to expand into Asia Minor or Mesopotamia, it had to cross the Levant. If Assyria or Persia wanted to expand west to gain access to the Mediterranean, it had to pass over the Levant. Subsequent to the death of Alexander the Great in 323 BC, the generals who succeeded him each endeavoured to expand his realm by exerting control over the resources and roads of the Levant. Control of the great trade routes which converged in the Levant assured prosperity and therefore increased military power, because these trade routes provided access to foreign markets for the sale of manufactured goods and the purchase of raw materials or other desirable commodities.

The Promised Land, the Holy Land

The term, 'the Holy Land,' denotes an area that roughly corresponds to the Promised Land or the Land of Canaan. Ironically, in spite of the emotional and spiritual attraction which the Holy Land holds for many, none of the Gospels were written there and it is doubtful than any book of the New Testament had its origin there. This is not to say that the Holy Land, including the people who lived there at the time of Jesus, their customs, religion and social-political circumstances was irrelevant to the writing of the New Testament scriptures. On the contrary, the geo-political situation of the Holy Land, which has been known as Palestine throughout most of history, is the very stuff of the Gospels. What's more, several non-canonical books which give us invaluable information about the early church, the compilation of the canon and the New Testament world, were, indeed, written in the Holy Land. Examples of these are the Dead Sea Scrolls.

The Holy Land is about 150 miles long and forty miles wide. Its approximate boundaries are defined by the biblical phrase 'from Dan to Beersheva,' (2 Sam. 24: 2; 1 Kings 4: 25). This phrase is the biblical equivalent of the expression 'From Maine to California'. The Holy Land would fit comfortably within the boundaries of Massachusetts, Vermont or New Jersey. Today, the Holy Land consists in Israel, the occupied Palestinian territories and small parts of Jordan, Syria and Lebanon where Jesus probably travelled. Its strategic position always offset its physical size.

Relatively speaking, Jesus was a home sticker of sorts.[10] Although allusions are made to his journeys in the Gospels (see below), it appears that the scope of his itinerant ministry was not greater than 120 miles in length. His public ministry was centred in Galilee, but he made occasional trips to regions bordering Galilee. He travelled through the Decapolis, in Batanea, to the regions of Tyre and Sidon, and beyond the Jordan, as well as to Jerusalem. Still, it seems that Jesus relied less on personal travel to carry his message than he did on others to carry his message for him. Moreover, the evangelists indicate that people would travel great distances themselves to hear Jesus preach and to have him treat the sick (Mark 8: 3).

Geography is the point of departure for the discipline of Near East studies, because the nature and characteristics of the land determine the forms taken by various societies. For instance, desert terrain encourages the development of nomadic society, while better agricultural land leads to the establishment of more permanent, sedentary societies. Without an operating familiarity with the Biblical landscape, the insights and inspirations of scripture all to often remain cryptic, remote and obscure. It is a sad commentary on contemporary New Testament studies that geography is not taken seriously.

---

[10] Paul, on the other hand, is known to have made several lengthy missionary journeys and tradition holds that the Apostle John journeyed to Asia minor, Thomas made his way as far as India.

Chapter 4
FROM ALEXANDER TO JESUS

When we ponder the names of people who shaped history in the first century AD, several names immediately stand out. Ask yourself the question, 'who was the most important person in the time of Jesus?' No doubt the names Jesus, Paul, Herod, Josephus and Augustus Caesar will come to mind. Certainly all of these people influenced the course of history. No one was more powerful than Augustus Caesar in his day. Over the course of time, no one has exerted more influence in history than Jesus has. But the most important person in the first century is not included in the foregoing list. In fact, he died over three hundred years before Jesus was born. The most important person in the first century AD was Alexander III of Macedon, who was called 'Alexander the Great'. He lived in the fourth century BC, but his contribution to history continued to be felt during the time of Jesus. Were it not for Alexander, we would not know Jesus the way we do.

Alexander was born in 356 BC. He was the son of Philip II of Macedon. He received his education under the supervision of the great philosopher, Aristotle, who was Alexander's private tutor. At the age of 20, he ascended to the throne of his father, whose assassination was arranged—in a touching gesture—by his mother. She wanted to be sure of her son's succession.

In a series of decisive battles, Alexander defeated the Persians, the traditional enemies of the Greeks. He pushed south to the Levant and on to Egypt. Then he looked and moved toward Mesopotamia. Indeed, Alexander would have been happy to subdue the entire world had it not been for his generals and armies who forced him to stop at the Indus River. They were already homesick as it was without going even further. Between the years 335 BC and 323 BC when Alexander succumbed to malaria (probably) and died an untimely death, his armies succeeded in taking control of all of Greece and bringing under Alexander's rule all of what had been the Persian empire. Upon Alexander's death, the empire was divided among his generals who tried to continue his legacy. Economics, politics, science, and technology, as well as literature, philosophy and religion would never again be the same. Daniel 11: 3-4 appears to refer to Alexander. There is explicit reference to him in 1 Maccabees 6: 2. In 1 Maccabees 1: 1-8 there is a summary of Alexander's rule:

After Alexander, son of Philip, the Macedonian, who came from the land of Kittim, had defeated Darius, the king of the Persians and the Medes, he succeeded him as king (he had previously become king of Greece.) He fought many battles, conquered many strongholds, and put to death the kings of the earth. He advanced to the ends of the earth, and plundered many nations. When the earth became quiet before him, he was exalted, and his heart was lifted up. He gathered a very strong army and ruled over countries, nations, and princes, and they became tributary to him. After this he fell sick and perceived that he was dying. So he summoned his most honoured officers, who had been brought up with him from youth, and divided his kingdom among them while he was still alive. And after Alexander had reigned twelve years, he died.

The consequences of Alexander's achievement spread like ripples across the world, touching remote peoples and places. For the first time in history, there was a 'universal' monarch of a 'universal' empire.[1] The concept of 'kingship' had a whole new meaning. Prior to his conquest, Greece had been a collection of independent city-states in loose confederations or competing with each other for trade markets and the economic and political power they afforded. Persia, the world's superpower with its capitals in what is today Western Iran, had been unable to develop a uniform society throughout its empire. The conquest of Persia, which had threatened Greece for years, reinforced the Greek notion of the supremacy of Greek social institutions and political philosophy. This gave impetus to the conscious spread of Greek culture throughout the new empire. Even though Alexander's untimely death led to bitter fighting among his generals to determine who would succeed him and ultimately the fragmentation of his short-lived empire, the legacy of universal empire persisted. Henceforth, the old political concept of individual city-states in loose confederation with each other or in direct competition with one another gave way to an ideal of one realm with interdependent regional parts. People no longer saw themselves as citizens of isolated cities or kingdoms, but rather as members of one universal realm.

Long after Alexander's empire broke apart into separate kingdoms, attempts were made to reunite the empire by force. Eventually, it was Rome that succeeded in doing so, but even when earlier attempts failed, the kingdoms of the former empire continued to see themselves as the heirs of

---

[1] The term 'universal' is, of course, a relative term. There had been empires and there had been monarchs, but no one before Alexander had managed to assert rule over the such a large extent of the world of the Mediterranean and Near East.

the one universal culture with special responsibility to protect and cultivate that culture. Thus began the period in history called Hellenism (from 'Hellene,' the Greek word for 'Greece',[2]) The conscious spread of Greek culture throughout Alexander's former empire and the absorption of foreign cultures characterize Hellenism. By the time Jesus was born, Palestine had been under 300 years of Hellenistic influence. Israelite culture was so thoroughly Hellenized that its major institutions had taken Greek names, such as the *Sanhedrin*, from the Greek word meaning council, the *synagogue*, from the Greek meaning gathering. Some of the most well known titles for Jesus are taken from the prevailing Hellenistic culture, such as 'saviour' and 'son of god'. The nascent Jesus movement adopted Greek designations. The word 'church' is from the Greek word *ekklesia*. Before it acquired its Christian meaning, it was the word used to denote those who were eligible to vote in the Greek *demos* or voting district. Their scriptures were written in Greek. They drew the term 'gospel' from the Greek word *euangelion*, which meant 'good tidings' and designated the announcement of the birth of a political ruler (cf. Luke 2: 10).

That the civilizations of the ancient world drew from each other's cultural reservoirs and freely exchanged ideas with one another is beyond question. Just as they traded agricultural goods and manufactured products, so they participated in a common market of ideas. That this give and take between ancient cultures far and wide took place for centuries is born out by the similarities in their literature and art. For example, stories of floods and the metaphysical battle between the forces of good and evil are common to all ancient Near Eastern cultures. Stories of ancestral wanderings over great lengths of time are common ancient themes. Odysseus, no less than Abraham and Moses, went through an extended period of wandering before finally reaching his destination. Likewise, the concept of human beings as the offspring of gods is common to a number of ancient cultures. Jesus was hailed as the Son of God. So were Alexander, Apollo, Asclepius, and Augustus Caesar, among others. Such a distinction was not unusual. Yet, the process of the mutual absorbing of cultural assets dramatically accelerated with the conquest by Alexander the Great of all the territory of the eastern Mediterranean basin, Asia Minor and the Near East all the way to India. Hellenism is characterized by the phenomenon of cultural blending. The technical word for this is 'syncretism'.[3]

Alexander articulated for the first time an ideal of universal brotherhood the appeal of which resonated harmoniously with Greeks and

---

[2]   The English words 'Greece' and 'Greek' derive from the Latin word *Graece*.

[3]   Helmut Koester, *Introduction to the New Testament*, vol. 1, 164-167.

foreigners alike. The occasion for this defining moment in world history was a banquet at which Alexander prayed for a union of hearts among all peoples and a joint commonwealth of Greeks and Persians. The Stoics were the first to take up and transmit this new vision. Zeno, the founder of the Stoic school of philosophy was not a Greek, but a Phoenician from Cyprus. He envisioned a world city in which individual members were bound to each other by Love. Thus, the word 'cosmopolitan', derived from the Greek word *cosmos* meaning 'world' and *polis* meaning 'city', came into vogue and became part of the philosophical atmosphere of the Hellenistic Age. The city-state became obsolete, not only in economic and political terms, but conceptually as well.

There seems little doubt that the early Christians absorbed these ideals. Jesus understood that Love was a principle that was far more authoritative and compelling on individuals than the force of human made laws. The Apostle Paul, echoing Alexander's prayer that there be neither Greeks nor Persians in his new empire, explicitly stated that distinctions of race, class, gender and nation were artificial and that all people were united in universal brotherhood in Christ Jesus. To the Romans, he wrote, 'For there is no distinction between Jew and Greek; the same Lord is Lord of all ...' (Romans 10: 12) To the Galatians, he was even more explicit and more expansive. 'There is no longer Jew nor Greek, there is no longer slave nor free, there is no longer male nor female; for all of you are one in Christ Jesus.' (Galatians 3: 28). This transcendence of class, ethnic origin and gender is predicated on the new reality that the law has been superseded by faith in Jesus Christ. 'Therefore the law was our disciplinarian until Christ came ... But now that faith has come, we are no longer subject to a disciplinarian for in Christ Jesus you are all children of God through faith.' (Galatians 3: 24-26) As Zeno had before him, Paul believed that humanity was bound by a deeper power than human laws. Moreover, Paul could see himself not only as a Judean, but also as a Roman citizen as well, i.e., a member of the world-city.

These themes of universal brotherhood were part of the spiritual atmosphere of the Hellenistic age. They did not originate in the first century with either Jesus or Paul. Rather, Jesus and Paul were spokespersons for themes that had been circulating for generations. Their words had strong appeal because the hearts and minds of their listeners were already attuned to such moving ideas.

With Alexander's conquests a period of reinterpretation began. The old territorial gods and the cults that had grown around them, provincial and parochial as they were, were no longer able to satisfy the fundamental needs of their constituents. People sought to understand themselves in a new light to go along with the New World order that had taken root. The old gods were given new names and associated with gods from other regions with whom there seemed to be a natural affinity. Zeus, for instance, was identified with the Egyptian god Ammon-Ra. Sometimes, entirely new gods were consciously invented bearing features of a variety of gods from across the Hellenistic world. This was the case with the establishment of the cult of the god Sarapis who became popular in Egypt in the third century BC. Greek education was established throughout the world. Greek political and social values were transmitted far and wide. The Greek language became the *lingua franca*, i.e., the universal tongue which was spoken by almost everyone and was the language of business, literature, religion and politics, just as English is today.

Tangible evidence of the far-reaching success of Hellenism is the adoption of Greek styled cities and city life throughout the eastern Mediterranean and the Orient. In fact, the planting of Hellenistic cities across the Hellenistic world was one of the primary mechanisms for advancing Hellenistic ideals. Not only were new cities built on a Greek model, old cities were rebuilt in Greek styles and renamed, often with Greek names. Alexandria, founded by Alexander, Ptolemais (Acco), Scythopolis (Beit Shean) and Philadelphia (Amman) are examples. At first, new cities were established as military colonies and peopled with former soldiers. Frequently, people from the Greek homeland would be recruited to take over the administration of these cities.[4] Additionally, important cities along key trade routes would be reconstituted or newly established according to Greek ideals. All this served to facilitate the spread of Greek culture. Even after the rise of Rome and the extension of its authority through most of the territory of the Hellenistic kingdoms, the process of promoting and advancing Greek culture continued. The Romans were fascinated and awed by Greek culture. They saw themselves as the heirs and stewards of the Hellenistic legacy, just as the Hellenistic kingdoms themselves did. As modern day Greeks like to say, 'Rome conquered Greece with its armies. Greece conquered Rome with its culture.' Eventually, Herod the Great rebuilt even Jerusalem in Greek style. The Roman Emperor Hadrian did the same and renamed it Aelia Capitolina. Consequently, today, the ruins of these cities can be seen from North Africa and the Italian peninsula in the West to Iraq in the East and throughout the countries of the Mediterranean basin. Greek styled cities, remarkably uniform in architectural style and institutional features, can be found wherever Alexander himself travelled and wherever the Romans expanded his territories.

---

[4] Alexander employed novel tactics to maintain order and build loyalty. In addition to recruiting administrators from the ranks of the indigenous peoples, he kept existing political structures intact. This combination of tactics yielded great benefits in terms of stability and loyalty.

An acquaintance with the architectural style of Hellenistic cities is important if one is to visualize the world of Jesus, because by the first century AD, the world had become thoroughly Hellenised. Moreover, the layout of these cities provides clues about the values that had taken root in the Hellenistic world in which Christianity grew and flourished. City plans were fairly uniform. They were laid out in grids with a main street, called the *cardo maximus*, running the length of the city in a north-south direction. East-west running streets called *decumani* intersected the *cardo*.[5] This pattern, still in style today, is called the *Hippodamian* plan, after the fifth century BC urban planner who developed it. So widespread was this urban plan that by the time of Jesus, even small villages were laid out this way.[6] Columns lined the stone paved streets supporting aqueducts and roofs that covered sidewalks. Shops fronted the streets and monumental architecture, such as majestic gates, fountains and statues of important citizens punctuated major intersections. Modern day visitors to the ruins of these cities can still marvel at the feats of architecture, engineering and construction that these cities required. Heating systems for the baths, underground sewers replete with manhole covers and indoor plumbing were standard features of the infrastructure.

The ubiquitous presence of theatres bears witness to the cultural sophistication of the Hellenistic world and the priority of the dramatic and rhetorical arts. Each city in the ancient world had a theatre that satisfied a need not only for entertainment, but functioned as a forum in which ideas were cultivated and expressed. In the theatre, the population was educated and enriched. Professional actors performed plays by contemporary and classical writers. Poetry was read out loud. Lectures were presented. Concerts of vocal and instrumental music were given. So important was the theatre in the life of the city, that the author of Acts makes note that when a group of artisans in Ephesus stirred up trouble against Paul and his travelling companions, the town theatre was the venue in which the complaints were aired (Acts 19: 29,31). Josephus reported that the death of Herod Agrippa (cf. Acts 12: 21) took place in the theatre in Caesarea where the populace had gathered for festivities in honour of the Roman emperor. Paul himself betrayed his own acquaintance with Greek theatre when he quoted Menander, a Greek playwright who died in 291 BC. 'Bad company ruins good morals' (I Corinthians 15: 33).

---

[5] These Latin terms were adopted in the Roman period.
[6] Attesting to the extent which Galilee had been Hellenized by the time of Jesus, archaeological excavations of Bethsaida and Capernaum revealed the Hippodamian plan. Neither were cities at the time of Jesus but both were oriented around the north-south running cardo.

The Hellenistic theatre was built into a hill, if the city had one, but frequently was expanded by building vaults and arches to support additional seating. Frequently, the theatre could accommodate tens of thousands of spectators. Seating was arranged in a semi-circle around the orchestra section, rising from front to back at a forty-five degree angle. Each seat was numbered to enable the ticket holder to find his or her place and social status was expressed in the location of one's seats. The seats closest to the stage or orchestra were occupied by the elite classes. Average citizens would take seats higher up and further from the stage.

The shape of the theatre was extremely uniform from city to city. This is because the shape was determined by acoustical requirements. In an age when voices could not be amplified electronically, architects utilized natural acoustic dynamics to project the performers' or speakers' voices. This form of vocal projection was so effective that an actor or speaker could stand at the exact centre of the orchestra, speak at a normal level and be clearly heard throughout the theatre to as many as fifty thousand spectators![7]

The role of the theatre and dramatic arts was so important to Hellenistic culture that the language of the theatre eventually found its way into the Bible. In the Gospel of Matthew, Jesus lambastes the scribes and Pharisees repeatedly invoking the term 'hypocrites' (Matthew 23). The Greek word *'hypocrites'* had a long history by the time of Jesus.[8] Originally it designated the actors in a play who held up masks in front of their faces in order to dramatize a particular role. In a play, the actor's job is to present him or herself as something that he or she is not. By the time of Jesus, the word 'hypocrite' had come to denote a faker, i.e. an actor in the worst sense of the word. By invoking this term, Jesus was consciously drawing from the language of his culture with which his listeners were well acquainted. In an unmistakable reference, Jesus was calling the scribes and Pharisees fakers. He was pulling off their masks, so to speak, and revealing them to be

---

[7] Evidently, Jesus himself utilized the same acoustic principles as the architects who designed the theatres when speaking to crowds. Not far from Capernaum which was the center of Jesus' Galilean ministry, along the shores of the sea of Galilee, one will find a place where the bank forms a natural acoustic shell carved out by the waters of the lake. These coves exactly approximate to the curve and angle of the Hellenistic theatres of the first century. The gospel of Mark reports an episode in which the crowd which came to hear Jesus was so large that Jesus was forced to get into a boat and speak to the crowd on the shore from the boat just off shore (Mark 4: 1). Mark's mention of this otherwise irrelevant detail and Jesus' action make sense only if the episode occurred at this location. Jesus knew how to make himself heard as much as the designers of the theatres did. He was not an amateur speaker.

[8] Ulrich Wilkens, 'Hypocrites,' in *Theological Dictionary of the New Testament,* ed. Gerhard Kittel, 559-569.

pretenders. Needless to say, this would not have endeared Jesus to the scribes and the Pharisees, but his listeners certainly would have understood his meaning.[9] In case they missed it, however, Jesus fanned the flames further by calling the Pharisees and the scribes, 'sons of snakes'.

Jesus' verbal broadside on the scribes and the Pharisees may well reflect another development in Hellenistic society at large. During the period preceding Alexander's conquests, Greek civilization had produced remarkable advances in many fields of inquiry. This was the golden age of science, art and philosophy. Plato was a contemporary of Alexander's father. Alexander's teacher, Aristotle, was Plato's student. In the Hellenistic age, however, new advances in learning slowed dramatically. Instead of new discoveries and new learning, the Hellenistic age was an age of popularising trends. Instead of producing new scientific discoveries, Hellenistic scholars produced compilations of earlier ones. Jesus' indictment of the Pharisees highlights the contrast between surface appearance and underlying reality, between the sizzle and the steak, so to speak, between style and substance. It could be that the Pharisees of Jesus' day had become spiritual copiers of a former golden age. Perhaps they had become uninspired and run of the mill, replacing vital spiritually with a rigid formalism such as simple obedience to ritualistic rules. In that case, Jesus' sharp words could be a challenge to them to return to their authentic spiritual roots.

It is important to note also, that the cultural priority given to the theatrical arts is a testament to the egalitarian spirit of the Hellenistic age. The theatre was something that everyone enjoyed. It was not a pastime

---

[9] Jesus' intent when he invokes this term is misunderstood, when it is assumed that he applies it to his enemies. The subject of Jesus' intent is complicated by the reality that we have his words as they are presented to us by a particular author who had his own axe to grind. Matthew 23 seems to use Jesus' words in a polemical way, but it is possible that when they were originally spoken, they had an entirely different meaning. In fact, in Jesus' world, the rules of decorum precluded direct denunciation of one's enemies. Direct discourse was reserved for use among friends and colleagues or between a teacher and his disciples who had an interest in improving one another or responsibility to prevent the friend or the charge from straying from the path of moral rightness. A teacher would rebuke his disciples, for example, if their actions or thinking was unbecoming or dangerous. The use of direct speech or *parrhesia* was a finely cultivated craft that required sensitive application. Paradoxically, its use did not indicate a state of enmity, but one of friendship, even intimacy. Thus, the words of Jesus in Matthew 23 may, in their original context, be an expression of Jesus' care for and closeness to the Pharisees, rather than his disdain for them. His purpose was to correct them and bring them back to proper behaviour, not because they were his enemies, but because they were his friends and colleagues. Indeed, he may have held a position of esteem among them that required him to speak in such a manner, i.e., as a teacher of moral discipline would be required to chastise his students.

reserved for any particular social class. That it was the venue of the spoken, audible word meant also that it was accessible not only to the literate, but to the illiterate as well. Contrast this with our own era in which theatre going is a pastime of the affluent. In Jesus' day and in the Hellenistic period in general, going to the theatre was more akin to us going to a baseball game. Everyone goes, irrespective of his or her social class or educational level. Thus, the theatre and the events it fostered served to engender a sense of community and commonality among the broad constituents of a diverse cosmopolitan society.[10] This community value was transmitted to Christianity, which included a broad range of people from the aristocracy to slaves.

Another way in which the architectural features of the Hellenistic city reflect the spirit of the age is in the preponderance of public buildings and the correlative abundance of public art. The idea that each individual, although unique, was a participant in a culture that transcended its individual members and that culture was a shared commodity was expressed in the inclination on the part of government and individual citizens to foster the public good. Instead of buying a work of art for his personal and private enjoyment, the custom was for people to buy art, which would be seen and enjoyed by everyone. Hence, buildings and streets were lavishly decorated with sculpted statues and monuments of all kinds. Some memorialised historical events like victory on the battlefield, others testified to the significant contributions of individual members of society. Usually the latter were commissioned and paid for by the one who was being honoured. Still, the overwhelming tendency was for these works to be put on public display, rather than coveted for private enjoyment.

Kings were particularly generous in funding the construction of public buildings, such as libraries, fountain complexes, temples and shrines to various gods, and, of course, governmental buildings and public works projects. In contrast to our own day when national pride is expressed in the cultivation of a strong military and individual achievement is expressed in the size of personal homes, in the Hellenistic era, kingdoms expressed themselves in the construction of public buildings such as theatres or stadiums for athletic events. In general, even the homes of the wealthiest citizens were relatively modest. Instead of purchasing art for personal enjoyment or building

---

[10] The constituents of an audience in a theatre cannot be determined from archaeological evidence. Nor does clear literary evidence exist to help us determine who attended theatres. It is not likely that those from the countryside made special dates to attend the theatre, like we would drive to a movie today, but it is clear from the Gospel narratives that large, outdoor gatherings where people would come to hear a speaker or be otherwise entertained were commonplace. In the cities, however, it is likely that the theatres were attended by anyone who lived there.

opulent houses for personal use, the custom was for affluent individuals to pay for public works projects of various kinds. This system was known as *leitourgia*. Thus, in Luke's version of Jesus' healing of the centurion's slave, the Judean elders report that the centurion is worthy and that he paid for the building of the synagogue (Luke 7: 5).[11] The centurion's philanthropy should be understood in light of the system of *leitourgia*.[12] It was the civic duty and honour of an individual who was able to take responsibility for the construction of a bridge or a fountain or other public work and pay for it from his own pocketbook. *Leitourgia* is the root of our word 'liturgy'.

In addition to having a theatre, each Hellenistic town had an *agora*. The *agora*, or marketplace, was usually a rectangular open area surrounded on all sides by *stoa*, or covered colonnade. It was one of the city's centrepieces and a place where all people eventually came, exchanged greetings with one another, heard the latest happenings and took care of business, whatever business they had. In a way, the *agora* functioned in the manner of the general store in American hamlets today. It was also the place where merchants would come to sell their wares, where artisans would perform, and where magicians would ply their craft. The *agora* was where insurrections would be plotted and where the spokespersons of the myriad new religions and cults would hold forth on the benefits to be gained for those who became adherents to their favoured religion or philosophy. In other words, the *agora* was the social clearinghouse to which all citizens, city dwellers and travellers would be drawn whenever they were in town. It was a public, open-air forum with the atmosphere of a bazaar. Textiles, foodstuffs and manufactured goods such as pottery would be traded here. It was also a marketplace of ideas, rumours and lifestyles. The *agora* fulfilled the critical function of bringing different parts of society together, thereby creating a sense of public, common identity. It also served as a sort of public tribunal in which philosophies, cults, and performers alike would be given a hearing and be tested for their authenticity. Those with genuine talents and commodities of high worth who passed the test would receive instant acclamation. Those who were deemed to be charlatans or hucksters would also receive an immediate verdict and would be lucky to get out of town unharmed.

---

[11]/ Contrary to the emerging consensus among scholars that there is no archaeological evidence for synagogue *buildings* in Palestine in the first century, here is documentary evidence. The passage suggests, at least, that Luke considers it natural and normal that the building of a synagogue would occur and that a non-Israelite could pay it for. For the question of the building of synagogues in the first century, see Horsley, 1995, 1996 and Kee, 1999.

[12] R Meyer and H Strathman, 'Leitrougew, Leitourgia,' in *Theological Dictionary of the New Testament, vol. 5,* ed. Gerhard Kittel, pp.215-233.

In the sixteenth chapter of Acts, an episode in Paul's travels is told which helps us understand the Hellenistic world on several different levels. Paul and his companions came upon a slave woman while they were travelling in Macedonia in the vicinity of the city of Philippi. The woman apparently had a 'spirit of fortune telling'. This talent made a profit for her owners. When the woman persisted in announcing loudly that Paul and his companions were 'slaves of the most high God,' Paul became annoyed and ordered the spirit to come out of the woman. Of course, the spirit obeyed, the woman's stock crashed and her owners lost a lot of income. So, they dragged Paul and Silas into the *agora* where they were tried before the magistrates and judged in the tribunal of public opinion. The judgement went against them and they were stripped, beaten and thrown in jail (Acts 16: 16-24). So much for the verdict of public opinion, but the story serves to illustrate the important role the *agora* played in Hellenistic and Roman times.

The New Testament references to the *agora* and its function are numerous. While in Athens, Paul went to the *agora* everyday in order to engage in disputations with the proponents of pagan religions. This was simply the Hellenistic thing to do. There he also came into contact with representatives of two of the leading schools of philosophy in the 1st century, Stoicism and Epicureanism (Acts 17: 18). A marketplace for all kinds of goods (Mark 7: 4), material as well as spiritual and philosophical, the *agora* was the place of gathering for all peoples for all purposes (Acts 17: 16-21). Jesus used the habits of the marketplace to illustrate the importunity of 'this generation'. (Matthew 11: 16-19, Luke 7: 32). Jugglers, magicians and even storytellers would perform there, but like those who see the performers in the *agora*, but pay them no heed, so 'this generation' refuses to heed the calls of the prophets.

Jesus alludes to the *agora* as a place where an employer would seek out daily workers (Matthew 20: 03). In the passage in which Jesus lambastes the Pharisees and scribes, he identifies the *agora* as the public place where the 'hypocrites' come to be seen and admired (Matthew 23: 7, Mark 12: 38, Luke 11: 43, 20: 46). The *agora* is the place where people brought their sick to be healed by Jesus (Mark 6: 56) and it is a place where merchants market their goods (Mark 7: 4).

In I Corinthians 9: 24 onward, Paul alludes to another form of entertainment that was as popular in his day as it is today. 'Do you not know that in a race, the runners all compete, but only one receives the prize?' In the ensuing verses, it is evident that Paul was familiar with the forms of athletic competition of the Hellenistic world and appreciated the value of sports to society. He utilized imagery from sporting events often enough in his letters that it is evident that he was a fan himself. Running, boxing, and wrestling were popular sports in Paul's day and he was familiar enough with these events that he could use sports metaphors easily and without apology. He referred to the 'goal' and 'the prize' the winner would receive when he wrote to the Philippians (Philippians 3: 14). He mentions the 'good fight' and 'the race' (2 Timothy 4: 7). He cites 'the crown' the athlete would receive and the 'rules' of competition (2 Timothy 2: 5). That he mixes his metaphors does not mean that his acquaintance with athletics was sketchy. Preachers do the same today. That he used these metaphors at all indicates that he as well as his readers was familiar enough with sports that sports imagery was an effective medium of communication. After all, Paul meant to get his point across, not to have it lost in obscure references.

It is likely that Paul and his readers in the first century were intimately acquainted with athletics, since the Hellenistic world placed a high premium on physical competition. Sports were a major form of entertainment and were a part of the educational curriculum. In fact, our word 'gymnasium' derives from a Greek word that designated the place where young boys went for training, not only in athletics, but also in reading, writing and arithmetic. Each city had its stadium for foot races and perhaps a hippodrome for chariot racing or an arena for more brutal competition such as gladiator fights. Sometimes a city had all three. The ruins of these ancient sports facilities are quite impressive even by modern standards. They could accommodate tens of thousands of fans. It is said that the Circus Maximus in Rome had a capacity of over 250,000 people. Major game events took place in festivals, such as the Olympiads or the Isthmian games that were held near Corinth or the Caesarean games instituted by Herod the Great. In addition to symbols of victory, the 'perishable wreath' mentioned by Paul (I Corinthians 9: 25), competitors were often well paid and honoured by their adoring fans. Sometimes, statues of athletes would be erected in honour of their achievements and placed in temples. Usually, athletic festivals were held in honour of a deity or the emperor and would begin with religious ceremonies, just as today football teams say a prayer before taking the field. Perhaps, the association between sports and religion was a further incentive for Paul to invoke sports imagery in writing on religious themes. In fact, other cults did utilize sports imagery in this way.

The Hellenistic values of community life and freedom of association found expression in the system of social clubs that spread throughout the world. After the family, which ordered personal life and the civil administration, which ordered public and state interests, the 'associations' were the most important institution of the first century. The clubs gathered members who shared common interests. There were clubs for members of the same trade, for those who enjoyed an interest in a particular sport, and, among many other types, for those who were foreigners living abroad. There were even dinner clubs.

Originally, the associations were religious in nature and the religious character of the clubs was maintained to a degree throughout the Hellenistic period. Most clubs were associated with one or the other deity and had some cultic flavour, such as the requirement of the members to make appropriate sacrifices from time to time. They often met in temples, but could also meet in public buildings or in the homes of members. Membership in the clubs was usually based on recommendation of a club member and required the affirmation of a majority of club members. Today's Masons and Lions' Clubs share similar customs. The purpose of the club was the enjoyment of socializing and the building of community. Each member paid dues, participated in a certain number of regular meetings, subscribed to a code of behaviour regulated by rules and got his wife to produce something for the yearly bake sale. Often, the association took care of funeral arrangements for deceased members. The associations were administered by officers whose term was considered a service to the club or, in Greek a *leitourgia*. The number and variety of associations in the Hellenistic world is truly astounding and more often than not, a club served more than one purpose. Thus, an association of merchants, for instance, could satisfy members' interest in a stimulating social life, as well as facilitate business contacts, promote the economic interests of the merchants, cultivate piety toward a particular deity and, in the end, provide for the burial of the member.

That the clubs were the medium of choice for people to enter into some form of satisfying social life is an important factor in understanding the early organization of the Christians. What's more, that the role of the deity in the life of the club was often nominal and a mere formality helps us understand some of the background of Paul's letters. Religious groups had for some time organized themselves into associations. Judeans gathered in one called the synagogue. When the book of Acts depicts Paul as seeking out the assembly of Judeans in each new town he visits, this is tacit acknowledgment of the role of these associations for Judeans in such cities.

It was only natural that when it came time for those devoted to the new religion preached by Jesus' disciples to organize that they utilized the standard social form to which they were accustomed. So, they gathered themselves into associations to which Paul applied the term *ekklesia*.[13] This term was already in common usage and originally meant 'assembly'. In particular, it was the assembly of eligible voters in the Greek democracy. In the gospels it refers to the Christian community.

[13] Karl Ludwig Schmidt, 'Ekklesia,' in *Theological Dictionary of the New Testament, vol. 3*, ed. Gerhard Kittel, 501-536.

It is evident from Paul's first letter to the Corinthians that some of the members were confused about the nature of that particular assembly. Like many other clubs, that one served more than one purpose, dining included. As accustomed to club life as first century people were, many looked at that new assembly as just another social outlet. Inevitably, however, issues of identity arose and Paul had to struggle to distinguish the assemblies dedicated to God and the Lord Jesus Christ from other clubs. When he learned that some were treating the Lord's Supper as just another meal at another dinner club, Paul applied the appropriate corrective (I Cor. 11: 7-22). He implored the membership to be of one mind and purpose (I Corinthians 1: 10). Gatherings of the church were even disrupted by disputes about who would serve as officers, some supporting Apollos, some Cephas and still others, Paul. Apparently, some of the members were quite nonchalant about the role of the deity in that association, as the deity in other clubs was often a nominal presence. Paul's insistence that 'our Lord Jesus Christ' was the central focus of the church can only be understood in this context.

Like many associations, membership in the Corinthian church crossed class, gender and ethnic lines. Paul responded to a message from 'Chloe's people' (I Cor. 1: 11). Chloe is a woman's name. Indeed, of forty personal names Paul invoked in his letters, sixteen are feminine. Some of these, for instance Phoebe (Romans 16: 1), are identified as 'deacons'. Chloe herself must have been quite influential with Paul. He went on to try to sort out issues that arose because of the pluralism in the church. Specifically the Judeans and the Greeks had different demands. If this were not so, he would have had no reason to make the comments he did (I Corinthians 1: 22-25). Further, the Corinthian congregation was made up of slaves, as well as free people (I Cor. 7: 21). Paul insisted that social status was irrelevant in the church just as it was in the associations.

There is no question that as to social status, one's class mattered little when it came to membership in the Pauline churches. Paul included slaves as well as members of the aristocracy as members of his churches and as travelling partners. One Secundus is mentioned as one such partner. *Secundus,* meaning 'second' in Latin is a slave's name. In his letter to Philemon, Paul made an appeal on behalf of Onesimus to whom he refers as a child (Phil v 10). *Onesimus,* which means 'useful' or 'beneficial', was also a slave's name. On the other hand, Paul sent greetings to the saints of Caesar's household (Phil 4: 22) which surely included some who were born to privilege and lofty position.

Jesus also included members of all layers of society into his company. His compassion touched slaves (Luke 7: 10, 22: 50) as well as members of the local elite. First century society was stratified and privilege was a function of position, but with respect to spiritual values and membership in various religious societies, there was a clear recognition that status was largely irrelevant. It did not matter to Jesus that the centurion in Capernaum (Luke 7: 1-10) was wealthy, powerful, non-Israelite and a slaveholder.[14]

In Luke 7: 1-10, Jesus is prevailed upon to heal a centurion's slave. Popular interpretations of this passage sentimentalise the centurion's interest in having the slave healed. In English translations, the slave is said to be 'dear' to the centurion, but the Greek word *entimos,* is better rendered, 'valuable,' i.e. in a monetary sense.[15]

In this light, Jesus' actions are much more troubling. Not only does he not object to the centurion as a man of power, privilege and position, Jesus registers no objection whatsoever to his holding slaves. He even goes so far as to restore the slave to a useful condition and then, instead of ordering him to be freed, he announces to all that the centurion is a paragon of faithfulness!

Slaves were often the spoils of war and consequently, more often than not, they were well educated and therefore valued for their skills. Sometimes, a person would be sentenced to slavery as punishment for a crime and would serve a fixed term. Others were forced into slavery in order to pay off a debt. In any event, slavery was not necessarily a hopeless condition. It was possible to earn one's freedom as many did. These were known as 'freedmen' and constituted a distinct social class. The act of freeing slaves was also considered a good work, especially among Christians.

The role of slavery in the ancient world is popularly misunderstood by many people today. By the time of Jesus and Paul, slavery was no longer depended upon as it had been in earlier times. In fact, it was coming to be

---

[14] While slavery was an obvious fact in the Hellenistic world, it would be a mistake to associate the ancient institution of slavery with that to which we are familiar. Slavery as it was practiced in colonial and 19th century America was far more brutal than the slavery common in the world of Jesus and Paul. There were three different types of slaves in the first century— household slaves, farm slaves and industrial slaves. Of these, industrial slavery was the most severe. Industrial slaves were sentenced to work in mines, manufacturing and construction and many lived a desperate existence. As a result, they were not expected to live long. Farm slaves performed all the tasks of agricultural production and worked on huge estate plantations. Household slaves were charged with all the domestic chores associated with running a large estates, from cleaning and cooking to grinding flour, baking, producing clothing and even entertaining guests. Frequently household slaves were given the task of raising the children. Often they were responsible for taking care of tasks such as bookkeeping and letter writing. All in all, they were quite well off and were considered an integral part of the family as a whole.

[15] Bauer, 268-9.

seen as an economic liability. It was expensive to hold slaves and rulers recognized that prosperity was better promoted through the uplifting of society rather than by maintaining a class of slaves. Public attitudes about slavery ranged from outright rejection to indifference. The most popular philosophies insisted that slavery was not a disqualification of one's value as a human being. Many religions saw class and status as neutral factors relative to membership in the cult. In this respect, Christianity was typical. The attitudes expressed by Paul were standard for his day, but at the same time, there was no call for the abolition of slavery. On the contrary, the freeing of slaves on mass was seen as a social liability since it would flood the market with unemployed workers and cause significant dislocations in the economy. Consequently, slavery was carefully managed during the Roman Imperial period.

One final aspect of Hellenistic culture which figures enormously in the background of the New Testament and early Christianity is the prominence and function of the ruler cult. Long before the time of Alexander the Great, Greeks had been accustomed to giving special honour to important people after their deaths. By the time of the Hellenistic age, the Greeks had effectively canonized the idea that specially gifted people were worthy of special distinction and privilege. While they believed that the best form of government was the absolute monarchy, a ruler was entitled to power not because of heredity, but because he was considered to possess extraordinary qualities for the office. Thus, legitimate rule was based on public recognition of the ruler's qualifications. That the ruler was not considered to be above the requirement of public authorization is reflected in fact that in the Hellenistic period, the king's quarters were situated in the centre of the city among the populace, instead of in the acropolis, high above and removed from the people.

The Stoics postulated that earthly rule mirrored the divine rule of Zeus. This was the logical outgrowth of the ancient assumption that earthly and heavenly events corresponded to each other. These factors, combined with the influence of eastern political concepts after Alexander's conquests resulted in the development of what has come to be called the ruler cult, i.e. the conscientious cultivation of the idea that the ruler was worthy of special distinction and devotion.

When Alexander the Great visited Egypt, he was received at the temple of Ammon-Ra at Siwa oasis as the son of the god Ra. As pharaoh, he was entitled to such distinction. For thousands of years, all pharaohs had received such honours. This was the first time among Greeks, however, that this occurred while the king was still living. Coins bearing Alexander's profile include the title 'son of god'. Subsequently, his successors claimed and expected similar honours. Ptolemy II and his sister were honoured as 'brother and sister god'. Ptolomy IV claimed to be a descendent of Dionysus. Marc Antony was proclaimed as the new Dionysus and Cleopatra as the new Isis. Julius Caesar was accorded the status of a god after his death and his successor and adopted son, Augustus Caesar, was called *divus filius* or son of god.[16] Royal authority was frequently reinforced by using genealogies to show that a ruler had divine ancestry. It was not uncommon for the genealogies to be adjusted in a manner we would call fudging in order to establish the connection between the ruler and the god.

By New Testament times, the idea that rulers were somehow imbued with divine qualities was so widespread that any notion to the contrary would have been considered a quaint novelty. In an episode in which the people of Tyre and Sidon come to Caeserea Maritima to appeal to Herod Agrippa over a dispute related to food supplies, the king was lauded as one who spoke with a god's words (Acts 12: 20). Moreover, the concept that certain human beings were endowed with divine qualities was extended beyond kings to any person who displayed extraordinary characteristics. In Acts, Paul and Barnabas were acclaimed as gods after Paul healed a cripple. (Acts 14: 11) The language used over and over again in the Bible in which human beings and gods are associated with one another is abundant and should be understood in light of popular Hellenistic concepts. Human distinction was interpreted and expressed in terms of one's being related in an intimate way with the divine.

The application of divine honours to Jesus is not only an acknowledgment of who Jesus was, but also an expression of who Jesus was interpreted to be by those who believed in him. The only language available to the first century believers in Jesus and those who wrote about him for the benefit of others was the customary language used to express adoration and adulation. Jesus had so distinguished himself in the eyes of his believers that they had no choice but to interpret him to others in terms of his being related to God. This interpretation put Jesus in direct competition with the emperor—a distinction which Luke, for example, intended to advance. Augustus was emperor at the time of Jesus' birth and Luke takes pains to contrast the royalty and majesty of Jesus with that of Augustus.

---

[16] Archaeological excavation at Capernaum revealed a Roman marker inscribed with the name of the Emperor Trajan, who is identified as god and the son of the god Nerva. The identification of humanity with divinity is more plausible in a culture in which gods were the highest beings in a hierarchical systems of beings, but were substantially the same as people in their nature.

Chapter 5
RELIGION IN THE ANCIENT WORLD

The people who lived at the time of Jesus and Paul were among the most religious in the history of the world. Religious speculation was an ancient and revered craft by the time of Alexander. The ancient world prized religious practice and personal piety to such an extent that by the time Jesus and Paul were born, a great spectrum of religious cults had developed. One can easily imagine what it was like to visit a city such as Rome or Athens or Jerusalem at a time when a religious event was taking place. Impressive monuments dominated the squares. Streets were lit with torches and filled with people. The air tingled with excitement. For people coming from the city and the country, foreigners and natives alike, participants in the festivities and onlookers, a religious event was a spectacle.

According to Acts, when Paul entered Athens (Acts 17: 16-33) he beheld a city full of idols. His spirit was provoked within him, but he must have been partly taken by the spectacle of it all. The spirit of the age predisposed the public to entertain a variety of religious ideas. In spite of its reputation for persecution, religious pluralism was the norm during the Roman Empire. The people were eager to hear something new. So Paul addressed them, 'Men of Athens, I perceive that you are in every way religious. For as I passed along, and observed the objects of your worship, I found also an altar with this inscription, "To an unknown god".'

Paul could have seen such an altar in any city. One of Rome's most impressive monuments is the 'Pantheon', dedicated, as its name suggests, to all the gods. Built as the largest domed structure in antiquity, it even had a special niche for a god who was not yet known. Honouring such a god was a wide spread practice, since no one wanted to offend any of the gods. A person could choose from among a long menu of cults and belong to more than one. Observance of the cults was considered a civic duty. In fact, devotion to more than one god was the norm—the more the merrier. After all, one had to cover all of one's bets. If one cult god didn't work, the other would. Those who were dedicated to only one god, such as the Judeans and the new group that came to be called 'Christians', were considered with curiosity or suspicion, sometimes with disdain, disgust and hostility.

Religion in any age endeavours to elevate the individual above the plain of temporal existence to the realm of the eternal. Religion lifts individuals out of the physical isolation and transience of human life and associates them with a permanent world of enduring value. All religions claim to satisfy this deep human thirst for transcendence. Not all are successful. Thus, a sort of religious Darwinian principle has operated throughout human history. Religious cults compete with one another for supremacy. This competition between religions was particularly lively during the Hellenistic age and the Early Roman Period.

The contest among religions to win devotees took place against a backdrop of philosophical and spiritual assumptions that most people shared. There was a sort of common market of spiritual values. Illustrative of these commonly held religious values is Plato's allegory of the cave.

In this allegory, someone is chained deep inside a dark cave such that he can only look forward. In front of him is a wall upon which he sees shadows cast by figures behind him. A fire that he is not even aware of causes the shadows. Until he is released from his chains, he thinks that the shadows are all that is real. He is, in effect, a prisoner to these images. When he gains his freedom, he learns that the shadows were illusions produced by the light of the fire and by people parading statues and objects in the likeness of animals between the fire and the place where the man had been confined. The light from the fire is painful to look at, because he is not accustomed to it. Then the former prisoner is dragged reluctantly upward from the recesses of the cave to its opening. Upon reaching the entrance to the cave, he looks out on the world, illuminated by the sun. The light is dazzling, but he is enjoying the wonders of true reality for the first time. Ultimately, he casts his eyes skyward, beholds the sun and realizes that what he had taken to be real were dependent upon the sun. In the end, he arrives at the knowledge that the sun is the source of what is truly real.

Plato taught that the world of ideas was far more real than the physical world. His philosophy had no theory of physics whatsoever. This idea persisted with great force for many centuries. In the allegory, Plato presented his understanding of the unfolding of knowledge, from opinion to truth, from shadows and images, representing error, to opinion, faith and, finally, to the source of Truth, the sun. For Plato, the sun represented the world of ideas. The realm of ideas is that which is changeless, ordered, eternal, incorruptible, true, good and ultimately real. Even the world of ideas itself was ordered and all ideas were subordinate to the idea of the Good.

Plato's allegory of the cave illustrates the prevailing cosmological assumptions of the ancient world. He understood the *cosmos,* the world in its entirety, to be an ordered and orderly place, arranged hierarchically. Each level in the allegory represents a level of knowledge. Knowledge was ordered hierarchically and ranged from the level of error, occupying the lowest levels of the hierarchy to knowledge of the realm of Truth, the level of Ideas which occupies the highest level of the hierarchy. While he is chained in darkness, deep inside the cave, the man is unable to understand his world. When he emerges into the light, after his upward journey from the depths of the cave, the man is able to comprehend the true nature of the world. Plato never doubted that the cosmos could be known through the exercise of the mind. Just as the outside world was ordered hierarchically, human faculties were also ordered hierarchically and the mind was the highest function. Human beings were endowed with Reason for the purpose of understanding the universe and perceiving directly the realm of the Divine.

Aristotle, Plato's student, dramatically modified his teacher's theory of the cosmos. Still, he understood the world to be arranged hierarchically. It was a rational and knowable place. Aristotle introduced further stratification to Plato's theory of the cosmos.[1] Heaven was arranged with one ruling god above lesser gods who were assigned status relative to one another and were relegated to specific levels in their stratified heaven. Beneath these lesser gods were the stars and the planets, which themselves were believed to be deities. Beneath these were the sun and the moon. The physical realm, occupied by human beings and their fellow creatures, was material, imperfect. It was subject to change, deterioration, irrationality and moral corruption. Naturally, Aristotle understood this realm to be ordered hierarchically as well. Reason differentiated people as the highest in the created order, but even people were arranged according to status. Below the earth was the lowest level of Aristotle's cosmos—the underworld, the realm of evil and corruptibility. It had the status of non-being. It was opposed to life, reason, order, and goodness. It too was arranged hierarchically.

The entire classical world assumed that ultimate reality was so defined. From Plato and Aristotle to Augustine, Aquinas and Dante, people in the ancient world shared fundamental presumptions about the order of the universe. These suppositions were nuanced, but basically unchallenged until the Renaissance. The writings of Josephus, Philo, the Qumran community and the Old and New Testaments are saturated with expressions of the commonly held beliefs about the world. The ancients presumed a

---

[1] Subsequent philosophers continued to modify Aristotle's reification of Plato's stratified model of the cosmos. Eventually, heaven became a highly stratified place.

hierarchically ordered universe in which the real was above and the unreal below. The gods, of course, dwelt above in the heavens. Heaven was the realm of light, changelessness, goodness, rationality and perfection. It was non-material, spiritual, and eternal. The heavens were stratified and different levels of beings occupied different levels in the heavens. In the Hebrew Bible, we read, 'But will God dwell indeed with man on earth? Behold, heaven and the highest heaven cannot contain thee ...' (1 Kings 8: 27) Paul writes, 'I know a man who fourteen years ago was caught up to the third heaven—whether in the body or out of the body I do not know ...' (2 Cor. 12: 2)

Between the heavens and the earth, many layers of intermediaries could be found—semi-divine angels, *daimon*, forces and powers. Paul writes, 'For I am sure that neither death nor life, nor angels, nor principalities, nor things present, nor things to come, nor powers, nor height, nor depth, nor anything else in all creation, will be able to separate us from the love of God in Christ Jesus our Lord.' Paul's world is a lot more than matter and energy. The principalities and powers are not political entities, but rather astral forces and the powers of nature. To the Galatians he asserts that freedom from the 'elemental powers of the universe' (Gal. 4: 3) is achieved through the Redeemer, God's son, Jesus. He reminds them, 'Formerly, when you did not know God, you were in bondage to beings that by nature are no gods,' and asks them, '... now that you have come to know God ... how can you turn back again to the weak and beggarly elemental spirits, whose slaves you want to be once more? You observe days and months and seasons and years!' (Gal. 4: 8-9)

The reality of the spiritual world was not only taken for granted, it was a fundamental supposition of the ancient world upon which all religious speculation and devotion depended. That the scope of the world was far greater than what was reported by the senses was a virtually uncontested notion in ancient times. Our modern preoccupation with physical proof and empirical evidence would have seemed excessive to the ancients, if not bizarre. To the ancients, all the proof showed that you had better take the invisible world of the spirit seriously. Theirs was a world thickly settled with unseen spirits, beings, powers and demons. Today's widespread agnosticism of things unseen and the spiritual realm would have seemed peculiar to our cultural ancestors.

The multiplicity of gods and the cults associated with them is one reflection of the widespread trust that the spiritual world was every bit as real as the physical world. The failure to show appropriate reverence was considered a peril. Participation in the cult of at least one god was normative. By the Hellenistic age, the gods of classical Greece had assumed a spiritual back seat. Their temples continued to operate and their cults persisted, but not with the vitality that was typical several centuries earlier. Still, the gods of classical Greece left their mark on the religion of the Hellenistic age. The names of the gods changed and the focus of religious speculation shifted eastward. Eastern cults gained wide acceptance. The conduct and character of the gods, however, stayed the same. They remained a capricious lot, involving themselves in human affairs in ways that could even be malicious. The gods continued to be pictured in human forms and possessed human qualities. In general, they were unaffected by human affairs, but could be provoked easily, so it was prudent to make the appropriate gestures at the right times.

With the advent of the Hellenistic period, eastern religions and eastern spiritual ideas began to exert great influence on the West, but the Greek religious tradition influenced the development of religion in several significant ways. While the Olympian gods faded, one continued to hold sway. She is Fortune. Fortune represented an essential power in individual lives. She was neither blind chance nor rigid determinism. She was an incomprehensible order in the world. She was visible but not fully understandable. Perhaps Paul referred to her as an 'elemental spirit'. If a king ascended to the throne, his rise was due to Fortune. If one was toppled, Fortune was behind it. Each person had their Fortune, i.e. their individual guiding light or personal spirit. Fortune in her personal form was one's *daimon*. Our word 'demon' is derived from *daimon*, but the *daimon* did not have the negative associations that we attach to demons. Fortune could be good as well as bad.

The counterpart to Fortune was Fate, an idea which originated in Babylonia and which came to wield tremendous power in the thinking of the average person. Fate was non-moral. It was impersonal. It was immutable. Thus it was feared. Men and women sought to escape its grip. The fear of Fate became an enormously motivating power. How does one escape it?

The idea had long since developed that earthly events correspond to heavenly phenomena. Ancient observers had noticed that the stars and the planets moved according to fixed laws. Since they believed that heaven is the realm of the gods, they took the motions of the stars and the planets to be regulated by the gods. If the movements of stars were fixed and there was correspondence between heavenly and earthly events, then it followed that earthly events must be fixed, as well. Thus, people were not really free. Their actions were determined.

Determinism has never been a comforting concept, since it precludes the freedom which humanity so highly values. But if human events are determined by a non-moral, indifferent or a malevolent power, instead of a benevolent one, then the oppressiveness of the doctrine of determinism or Fate as it was called looms even more threatening. Such was the case with respect to the eastern concept of Fate.

Observance of the stars and heavenly phenomena grew to become a much valued occupation. If the secrets of the stars could be discovered, humanity could gain knowledge of the divine, gain release from the rule of Fate and bring their lives into conformity with the realm of the divine. This is why the observance of calendar events became so important in religious observance. If human life could be regulated in accordance with the heavenly world, then people could gain a measure of control over their lives. So, the Galatians were persuaded to watch the calendar. The observance of special days and events fixed by the calendar was a way to maintain harmony with the realm of heaven. Those who did not observe these calendar events could easily be blamed for calamities.

The ancients saw the movements of heavenly bodies as portents of earthly events. Those who studied the stars came to be revered as sources that could free men and women from the tyranny of fate. Astrology as we know it makes similar presumptions about the effect of stars on individuals, but it lacks the oppressiveness that accompanies the ancient concept of Fate. The influence of star reverence persists to our own day. Our language is full of mildewed allusions to this anachronistic creed. People are called 'jovial', 'mercurial,' and 'earthy', i.e. their natures are related to specific planets. Some believe in lucky and unlucky numbers and thank their lucky stars. The use of the number seven still has special significance. That our week has seven days stems from the Hellenistic belief that there were seven planets and that each controls a specific day.

The modern vestiges of ancient star reverence are only a pale shadow of their use in the ancient world. The Greek language had seven vowels, corresponding to each of the seven planets—the sun, the moon, Venus, Mercury, Mars, Saturn and Jupiter. The Hellenistic world boasted seven wonders. People spoke of the seventh heaven, as Paul referred to the third heaven. The goddess Isis had seven stoles and Mithras had a seven-stepped ladder. Testifying to the extent of the influence of astrology, even the Book of Revelation incorporates its terminology. John wrote to the seven churches of Asia and speaks of seven lampstands, seven stars, seven spirits of God, seven torches of fire, seven seals, seven horns, seven eyes, seven angels, seven trumpets, seven thunders, seven heads, seven diadems, seven thousand people killed, seven plagues, seven golden bowls, and seven kings. The number seven occurs forty-three times in Revelation.

The widespread ancient assumption that earthly events corresponded to heavenly events is reflected in another ancient tradition. Heavenly events were believed to be portents of earthly ones (Rev. 15: 1). Thus, when a particularly important ruler or public figure was born or died and when significant events took place, corresponding celestial happenings were sought as confirmation or sited as proofs. In Revelation, the earthly battle between the forces of good and evil is foreshadowed in a parallel heavenly battle (Rev. 12: 1-7). Cicero reported that an extraordinary dawn light accompanied the birth of Alexander the Great. Persian magi to boot interpreted this celestial light as a portent. Virgil reported that a star guided Aeneas to the place where Rome was to be founded. Josephus mentioned a star that stood over Jerusalem and a comet that lasted one year at the time of that city's fall. Several kings were said to have been born to the accompaniment of a special star. It would not have come to anyone's surprise in Jesus' day that Christ's birth was accompanied by the appearance of a star. Neither would anyone have wondered much that magi from the East had observed his star and were keenly interested in it.

The birth story of Matthew's gospel, especially its reference to mysterious magi and their star may strike some today as bizarre and miraculous, but it would have struck a first century reader as rather to be expected. Even the threatening actions of Herod the Great (Matthew 2: 16-18) would have seemed unexceptional in the first century, since rulers were known to have taken drastic measures to ward off events foretold by the stars. When Nero saw a comet for several nights in a row, he took it to be a sign that an important person was going to die. To make sure that that person was someone other than himself, Nero ordered several Roman nobles to be killed. It was said that when Augustus' birth was foretold in the heavens, the Roman senate forbade the rearing of any male children for one year. Herod's treachery would not have seemed uncommon in light of such customary happenings.

The mysterious, exotic magi of Matthew's Gospel were not so mysterious after all. Long before Matthew ever beheld the works of the saviour and even longer before he wrote his Gospel, the Greek historian Herodotus had captivated his readers with stories about a priestly caste who lived in Media beyond the Tigris and Euphrates rivers in what is today western Iran. These Median magi were known to have the power to interpret dreams.[2] They diversified their powers into all areas of secret lore and magic, were particularly fond of stargazing and developed a reputation for reading the signs of the heavens.

The Book of Daniel includes numerous references to magi whose celebrated powers had become well known throughout the world by that

---

[2] When the Persians assumed control of Medes, Zoroastrianism ascended to religious dominance and the magi became influential in its hierarchy.

time. Philo of Alexandria, the Judean historian who lived in Jesus' day, knew of magi who were more or less scientific and others who were known to be charlatans and hucksters. Other first century writers testify that magi were well known figures. In Acts, Luke tells the story of Simon, a *magus* in Samaria who amazed everyone with his powers (Acts 8: 9-24) and also of Elymas or Bar Jesus, a Judean magus and false prophet on the island of Cyprus (Acts 13:6-11).

All in all, by the first century, magi were those who were practised in any of a variety of occult arts, including fortunetellers, augurers, sorcerers, magicians, astrologers and astronomers. Not all magi were flaky. Some were credible scientists, at least by first century standards. In any event, Matthew's story of magi from the east who discern a rising star, tips the scales in favour of these magi being visionary astronomers of some sort. The gifts of frankincense and myrrh can also be seen in the context of the Magi's craft. They were substances commonly used in the process of embalming and in conjunction with incantations and other occult practices. This suggests that Matthew's magi may have been practitioners of magic.

Over the centuries, it has been popular to see the magi who came to worship the newborn Jesus as practitioners of occult arts who repented and came to revere the higher power resident in the newborn king of the Judeans. It could very well be that Matthew's purpose was to clarify that the powers of pagan magic were subordinate to the power of Jesus. However, Matthew's narrative contains not even a hint of repentance on the part of the magi. Nor are they depicted as anything but noble and admirable. Thus, it is better to see the magi as representatives of the best of pagan religious perception who discerned in nature authentic revelation of the dawning of a new age.

In any event, the Hellenistic and Roman ages were times when men and women saw themselves as being at the mercy of impersonal, even malevolent cosmic forces. Escape from these forces or gaining control over them became a popular preoccupation. In order to aid people in the endeavour to escape the grip of Fate and other capricious forces from the ethereal world, a wide variety of practices developed, including star telling, magic and sorcery. Additionally, all of the religions promised to render the initiate immune to the power of immutable Fate. Elaborate systems grew up to aid in the warding off of malevolent forces.

Magic was one of the choice methods for enabling individuals to avoid the many supersensory pitfalls and snares set before them in their daily lives. The gods might decide to amuse themselves by capriciously meddling some day. The *daimons*, which were individual spirits, lived unseen upon one's death and were a sort of intermediary between the natural and spiritual realms. These were to be guarded against, since they could bring down calamity unless proper precautions were taken. Consequently, all kinds of charms and incantations were invoked to ward off the *daimons*. These magical charms and formulae could also be invoked to aid in the attainment of some desired object or another. In any case, magic was widely used to help alter one's fate. Judeans in particular were known to be skilled practitioners in the arts of magic.

Of all the charms and incantations invoked to ward off the *daimons* or keep them in their place, none was more effective than to utter the *daimon's* name. Knowledge was considered power and to know the daimon's name was to gain power over it. *Daimons* were not stupid, however, and took care to keep their identities concealed. Consequently, the magician who was worth his salt would utter long strings of names in the hope of hitting the right one. Sometimes the name would be spoken in a variety of languages and dialects, just to make sure. Judean magicians invoked the name Yahweh and Josephus tells us that the Essenes were sworn never to reveal the names of angels— a sure sign that they were keeping the names secret for use in magic.

New Testament references to the practice of magic are abundant. They occur in association with the powers of the spiritual world. In his farewell address to the disciples, Jesus charged his disciples to proclaim the good news, saying that those who believe will be known by certain signs. One of the signs is that they will cast out demons using Jesus' name, i.e. as a charm (Mark 16: 17). Also in Mark, Jesus is reported to have had an encounter with a demon whose name was legion. When Jesus approached, the demon yelled out Jesus' name, certainly in the hope that by so doing, Jesus could be controlled. To the demon's dismay, however, Jesus turned the tables and forced him to reveal his name, demonstrating that Jesus is more powerful than the destructive power of the demon. Jesus forced the demon to enter the herd of swine and they plunged into the lake (Mark 5: 1-13). The lake itself was known to have been the abode of powers and spirits. Archaeologists have discovered charms that were thrown into the lake to mollify them.

The disciples reported to Jesus that they found a man casting out demons using Jesus' name (Mark 9: 38-41). This man was using Jesus' name as a charm in the manner of every two-bit magician the first century ever produced. The disciples objected to this use of Jesus' name, but Jesus reassured them indicating that using his name would eventually have the effect of neutralizing the man. On the other hand, Jesus also warned that those who invoked his name would not necessarily enter the kingdom of heaven (Mat 7: 22).

In Acts 4: 1-12, Peter and John are arrested and questioned by the representatives of the religious establishment. When they are asked, 'By whose power or by what name' they were working, Peter responds that their work was done 'by the name of Jesus Christ' (Acts 4: 10). Acts 19: 11-20 recounts an episode in Ephesus in which Judean practitioners of magical arts are overpowered by an evil spirit when they misuse Jesus' name. Implicit in these episodes is the common presumption that a name was an effective charm against the power of demons. It should be noted that neither Peter nor Paul objected to that fundamental supposition or to the practice of invoking Jesus' name. They, too, assumed that names were, indeed, powerful devices to protect against malevolent forces.

From these examples, to say nothing of the many other instances in which the name of Jesus figured significantly in a story, it is evident that the idea that a name could be invoked as a charm against malevolent forces was widely accepted in the early church. Jesus himself keenly understood not only that his name could be used in such a way, but also that his name would be used inappropriately by others in the manner of the day. Thus, he warned against the mistaken assumption that the use of his name would guarantee membership in the kingdom of heaven.

Jesus certainly used the ordinary technique of invoking names as a way of controlling demons. The Gospel testimony is not that Jesus objected to the conventional practice of exorcism. Rather, he objected to the incorrect use of his name, as well as the use of other names, which he saw as inferior and consequently ineffective. At the bottom of Jesus' objection is his rejection of the Hellenistic assumption that the gods could be forced or manipulated for personal benefit. For most people, magic was a short cut to personal gain and through it the gods could be prompted to alter one's fate. Jesus did not question the power to alter fate. Rather, he rejected the concept that his power could be manipulated or controlled by others. One of the factors that distinguished Jesus from the many others who claimed to be in possession of metaphysical power is that Jesus carefully resisted being used in a simplistic manner by spiritual hucksters.

Beyond the popular practices of magic, the more conventional approach to the spiritual realm was through the many cults organized around specific deities. In the classical period of ancient Greece, gods were adopted by different cities. In the Hellenistic period, the concept of city gods gave way to a universalising tendency. The cult of a particular god would be transported across the Mediterranean region and observed in many localities. Local gods were given new names. The Greek Zeus was identified with the Egyptian Sarapis to create Zeus-Sarapis. The Greek goddess Artemis was identified with the Roman goddess Diana. Acts 19: 23-41 reflects the prominence this cult enjoyed in Ephesus. She is known there as Artemis of the Ephesians. Each city would have more than one temple.

The cults were known as 'mysteries'. The mystery was a sacred, secret ritual into which an individual was initiated for the purpose of being released from the powers and forces that controlled the world. Through initiation, the individual established a special relationship with the deity and the deity provided the specific benefits. These benefits were bestowed only upon those who were initiated, were the exclusive domain of the cult and could not be communicated to others. Participation in a mystery cult had social, as well as religious aspects. It often involved group dining and usually, the cult was responsible for the burial of its members. The language of the mysteries is even adopted by Paul who self-consciously possesses knowledge of a new one. To the Corinthians he writes, 'Behold, I reveal to you a mystery. We shall not all sleep. But we shall all be changed ...' (1 Cor. 15: 51) Paul's Corinthians were weaned in a spiritual environment saturated with mysteries and he uses the language they understand to introduce the secret that death is not the end of life. This mystery had the power of releasing the initiate from the power of death.

Typical of the mysteries is the cult of the god Dionysus. The story of Dionysus, much of which we know from Euripides' play *The Bacchae*, bears many features that were common to other cults and are reminiscent of stories usually associated with Jesus. Dionysus was the son of the god Zeus and a mortal mother. His birth occurred in Palestine in Scythopolis, one of the cities of the Decapolis. He was born in very unusual circumstances, was made to be immortal, and was visited by shepherds as an infant. Dionysus was identified in particular with wine making. Philo of Alexandria says of him that he is associated with merrymaking, banquets, festivals and galas. He was the first to cultivate grapevines and ferment grapes to make wine. Vineyards were said to be evidence of his presence and special favour. Pliny the Elder tells a legend of a spring that miraculously flowed with wine on special days associated with the deity. Pausanias relates that each year three empty jars were placed in a sealed room and were found to be full of fine wine the next day. Dionysus often appeared in the form of an animal. He was also understood to be present in wine. Thus, eating animal flesh and drinking wine was understood to be a way of identifying with the deity. Drinking wine was an important component of Dionysian worship, in which a state of ecstasy was induced through preliminary fasting, drinking and wild dancing. Our designation for a fraternity party as a 'bacchanalian event' derives from Dionysus' Latin name, Bacchus. Children were explicitly included in the Dionysian cult and stories of Dionysus' childhood are common in ancient frescos and mosaics.

The similarities between the cult of Dionysus and features of the stories so closely identified with Jesus can be jarring. Jesus, too, had a Divine father and mortal mother. He was born in unusual circumstances.

Luke tells the story of his being visited at birth by shepherds. John states that his first act of power was the act of changing water into wine. The inclusion of children in stories of Jesus and interest in stories of Jesus' childhood has Dionysian overtones.

Another prominent cult of a different sort was that of Asclepius. It was not a mystery cult in the strict sense, although it did function to release adherents from the dominion of the unseen powers. Rather it was a healing cult. It gained an enormous influence and lasted over 1,000 years, from the Classical Period of ancient Greece to the late Byzantine Period. When the Parthenon in Athens was being used as a church in the fifth century ADS, the sanctuary of Asclepius at the foot of the Acropolis continued to flourish. Over 300 Asclepion, healing centres associated with Asclepius, have been found around the Mediterranean Basin, including Corinth, Rome and Jerusalem. The ancient Greek word for 'doctor' is *Asclepiadae.* The symbol of Asclepius, the snake wrapped around a staff has become the universal symbol for pharmacies, not to mention the symbol of the American Medical Association. Hippocrates, who was considered to be the eighteenth successor to Asclepius, modelled his 'Hippocratic Oath' after the teachings of Asclepius. He was known as the god who cared for people, in contrast to the pantheon of gods who were involved with humankind in mischievous, capricious or malevolent ways. People feared other gods. They sought out Asclepius. It is not hard to speculate that early Christian writers were influenced by popular understandings of Asclepius when it came to portraying Jesus. In statues, he resembles Zeus, but he is always portrayed with a sympathetic and mild disposition. The story of Asclepius provides further impetus to speculation on the relationship between Asclepius and Jesus.

The story of Asclepius seems to be rooted in a historical figure. Homer knows of an ancient healer named Asclepius whose sons were also physicians. As the myth developed, several different stories accrued to it. Asclepius was the son of the god Apollo through his affair with a mortal woman, Coronis. He was born in highly unusual circumstances—a caesarean birth, the only known c-section in the ancient world.[3] As an infant child his life was threatened, but he was saved by Apollo's intervention. Healing had been one of Apollo's functions and he taught the healing arts to his son.

---

[3] Unusual circumstances surrounding the births of famous people was not at all unusual, however. Virginal conception was a popular method of differentiating the births of famous people. Perseus, Romulus, Alexander, the pharaohs and Augustus Caesar were all said to have been born of a virgin. Caesarean birth, in contrast, is attested only to the birth of Asclepius.

Asclepius learned the secret of life and death and performed a miraculous resuscitation of a dead man on whom he had pity. For this, he was killed by Zeus, but later was brought back to life. He was a hero who was known as saviour and over time, he was elevated to the status of a god.

The healing techniques of the cult of Asclepius developed over time. The longevity of the cult is a testament to the desire for health among people, but also to the effectiveness of the cures and the adaptability of the cult itself. Early in its history, cures were a function of divine intervention, because illness was understood as caused by gods or their emissaries. Later, however, under the influence of developments in Hellenistic science and the craft of healing, the cult adopted more natural remedies and favoured reasoned approaches to illness. Belief in supernatural causes of illness gave way to an understanding that illness had specific natural causes.

Excavations of Asclepion have revealed written testimonials to the god's success that often include descriptions of the cure. From these we know that illnesses were treated with a variety of techniques, including diet, exercise, massage, medicines, surgery and by inducing the proper mental outlook. At the entrance to the main Asclepion in Epidauros, an inscription was found which says, 'You must be purified before entering the sanctuary.' Much of the ceremony surrounding the cult produced the desired mental effect. Those who came to be healed were predisposed to the expected result. The centre included athletic fields, springs, baths, sleeping quarters, theatres, sometimes libraries and a sanctuary. Surgical tools are also included among the finds at Asclepion.

Offerings to Asclepius from thankful patients took the form of sacrifice, especially the sacrifice of a rooster. At the close of Plato's *Phaedo,* after Socrates drank the hemlock, his last words were, 'Crito, we owe a rooster to Asclepius. Pay it and do not neglect it.' Often, those who were healed left votive offerings as well as written testaments. These are sometimes discarded crutches, but more frequently they are terracotta representations of the body part that was treated. Hordes of these show the variety of illnesses treated, from infertility and erectile dysfunctions, to hearing and vision problems, to cysts, bone breaks and paralysis.

Parallels in the myth of Asclepius to stories told about Jesus, especially the story of Jesus' resuscitation of Lazarus (John 11), are as striking as parallels between Jesus and Dionysus. He had a heavenly father and a mortal mother. He was born in unusual circumstances and protected by god after birth. Most striking perhaps is Asclepius' return from death.

The similarities between the stories told about Dionysus, Asclepius and Jesus are not coincidental and introduce us to a very important element in understanding Christian origins. One of the features of Hellenistic rhetoric, i.e., the art of persuasion, is a technique called *synkrisis*. This is the process of comparing and contrasting one topic, person or value with another. When the Gospels writers composed their Gospels, they used the techniques of writing and persuasion that were standardized features in all writing in their day. They used language that people would understand and relate to. Evoking images associated with Dionysus and Asclepius, not to mention other gods, were ways to communicate that in the works of Jesus, God was present. Further, they were attempting to persuade their audiences, through comparison, that Jesus was superior to the cult figures they were well familiar with. No one would mistake their intention, because comparison was such a standard rhetorical device in ancient writing. A non-Israelite audience might miss certain elements of Jesus' Israelite background, but they would recognize the features of the Dionysus story and understand the author's purpose.[4] The use of these images helped communicate the meaning of Jesus' ministry beyond the bounds of Israel. To an audience accustomed to the process of renaming traditional gods and the blending of the stories of one cult with those of another, the device of comparison would seem to be a natural technique to introduce Jesus to a new audience.

While the similarities between the cults of the ancient world and the stories told about Jesus are inescapable, intriguing and important, *synkrisis* is more about contrasts than comparisons. It is hard to explain why more is made of the similarities than the differences, which are just as obvious and even more important. There is no question that early Christian writers and artists borrowed from mystery religions and other Hellenistic cults, not to mention the borrowing of specific ceremonial practices, such as meals and processions. The popular depiction of Mary holding the infant Jesus is too similar to statues of Isis holding the infant Horus to be coincidental. Even the date for the celebration of Jesus' birth is taken from the cult of Mithras who was born on 25 December.

Yet, the contrasts not the similarities with pagan cults are most important to early Christian writers. Their endeavour is always to portray Jesus as more powerful and in every way superior to gods associated with cults. While the early Christian witness adopted the language of salvation, the idea of salvation in early Christianity was quite different than that in popular mystery cults. For the members of the mysteries, salvation meant protection from elemental powers and the malevolent forces of the cosmos. In Christianity, salvation meant redemption from sin. Christian baptism was baptism of repentance, not protection from fate.

---

[4] Dionysus was well known to Israelites. He is mentioned in II Maccabees 3: 7 and III Maccabees 14: 33. Both Tacitus and Plutarch associated Yahweh with Dionysus so that non-Israelites were familiar with the God of Israel.

While resuscitations of the dead occur in various myths, there is nothing that approximates the resurrection of Jesus. Resurrection and resuscitation are two different things. Jesus' resurrection is unique. A resuscitation occurs when a corpse comes back to life. This is what happened to Lazarus (John 11) and this is what Asclepius experienced, along with a number of other gods. But it is clear from the early Christian witness that Jesus' resurrection is of an entirely different order. Paul is very clear that Jesus' body was not resuscitated. His concept of an afterlife has nothing to do with corporeal existence. He clearly distinguishes between the body that is sown and that which is to be (1 Cor. 15: 35-54). For Paul, resurrection is the mystery into which the baptized are initiated. It is not a secret, exclusive privilege in the domain of the cult, like other mysteries, but available to all, irrespective of their station, status, wealth or ethnic group.

The movement begun during Jesus' lifetime received its irresistible power and impetus from the decisive and hitherto unique event of Jesus' resurrection. Individuals who knew Jesus or knew of him experienced the event of this resurrection. That experience with the resurrected Lord occurred repeatedly and demanded communication to those beyond the original participants in the movement. This communication necessitated the use of standard devices, language and categories of understanding that were common in the ancient world. It is little surprise that the texts produced by the effort to communicate the good news relied on these techniques, because there was no alternative. Nor is it surprising that the early tellers of the Jesus story sought to compare and contrast the meaning and significance of Jesus with that of cult figures. These were revealed as impostors, but they commanded the attention of many adherents to their detriment and peril. Early Christian witnesses had no choice but to invoke the language that the people they hoped to reach would understand in order to communicate their message. But they did not lose sight of the uniqueness and impact of the event they were communicating. Christianity is the offspring of the ancient Hellenistic world and it bears a family resemblance to the religions that nurtured it, but it quickly became a distinct group differentiating itself from all others.

Chapter 6
PHARISEES, SCRIBES, SADDUCEES, BANDITS, PROPHETS, MESSIAHS, JEWS, JUDEANS, ISRAELITES, PAGANS, GOD-FEARERS, SAMARITANS, ESSENES, ZEALOTS, SICARISAMARITANS, ISRAELITES, JUDEANS, GOD-FEARERS AND PAGANS

To say that Jesus lived in a complex social environment is a monumental understatement. Acts 2 lists seventeen different ethnic groups that were among the people present in the upper room on the day of Pentecost. They are from all the regions of the Mediterranean basin. The Gospels depict Jesus as having close contact with people from Judea, Galilee, the regions of the Decapolis and beyond the Jordan River, Tyre and Sidon. They include people who were social outcasts, as well as well positioned people of influence. They were farmers, fishermen, and craftsmen, men and women and also Pharisees, centurions, lawyers, landowners and tax collectors. Paul, no less than Jesus, was familiar with people from an array of ethnic groups, religious affiliations, and social strata. He had close relations with Judeans and Greeks, slave and free, men and women. Like Jesus, he could call upon the resources of the wealthy, such as Chloe and her people (1 Cor. 1: 11), but also advocated for the lower classes. The ancient world was like a mosaic composed of interconnecting social *tesserae*. Without an appreciation for the sophistication of the first century social world, we cannot hope to understand the forces and influences with which Jesus and Paul interacted on a daily basis throughout their life.

It is important to stress the ethnic diversity that characterized the world of Jesus and Paul, especially in light of the common misconception, perpetuated by so-called experts, that Jesus' world was predominantly 'Jewish'.[1] Some posit strict separation between Israelites and non-Israelites and insist that Jesus' neighbourhood of lower Galilee was Jewish, while the region across the Jordan was Gentile.[2] Such a supposition, however, is supported neither by literary nor archaeological testimony. Indeed, Josephus

---

[1] Presently, I will expand on the meaning of the designation 'Jewish'.

[2] E.g., Bargil Pixner, *With Jesus Through the Galilee According to the Fifth Gospel,* Chorazin Publishing, Rosh Pina, 1992,. 17, 42-43; Charles R Page, *The Land and the Book,,*Abingdon Press, Nashville, 1993, 147, note 24, p.260.

states that Herod the Great encouraged Judeans to relocate to the region across the Jordan. John Hyrcanus attempted to ethnically cleanse the region of Galilee,[3] many non-Israelites lost their property when they fled, but their rights and property were restored by Pompey in 63 BC. It is impossible to determine demographic proportions of ethnic groups at the time of Jesus, but the literary testimony supports the impression that it was as diverse at that time as it had been throughout its history. Ignoring or suppressing knowledge of the ethnic diversity of Galilee at the time of Jesus obscures the relevance of Jesus' gospel in an ethnically diverse world such as our own. There never was a time when Galilee or Judea, to say nothing of the rest of the Mediterranean World, was 'ethnically pure'. The histories of non-Israelite peoples in Judea and Galilee are, for the most part, a forgotten chapter in the writing of biblical history.[4] Awareness of those histories contributes to making the preaching of Jesus all the more relevant to the modern reader.

We have abundant evidence of group formation in Jesus' day. Groupings of people occurred for many different reasons. There were professional guilds, trade associations and philosophical associations. There were affinity groups based on ethnic identity, religious sects and political parties. Oversimplification of the social scene in Jesus' day is a common pitfall.

We also have a wealth of information about the fundamental social values that helped maintain social cohesiveness. We know, on one hand, that the social values of the Early Roman Empire were firmly established from one end of the empire to the other. The same social values were operative from Spain to Syria. Scholars have produced an abundance of literature over the past thirty years on such social conventions as patron-client relations, the dynamics of honour/shame and friendship/enmity. All people, including Jesus and Paul operated within these social value systems.

On the other hand, we know the social environment also produced dissent. Factions developed within groups. These struggled for power. Groups splintered and new groups formed. Sometimes, when conflict was deep enough, open hostility occurred. Rome continually faced the necessity of maintaining stability by managing groups that competed against each other and sometimes with Rome itself. In the relatively rare and extreme cases when a group challenged the authority of Rome itself, as in the Judean rebellions, the challenge was forcefully, if not promptly, overcome. The phenomenon of dissent, however, some of which was well organized, some

---

[3] Josephus tells us (*Antiquities* 13.310) that Hyrcanus expelled Galilean non-Israelites, unless they agreed to undergo circumcision.

[4] See Keith Whitelam, *The Invention of Ancient Israel: the Silencing of Palestinian History,* Routledge, London, 1996.

of which was spontaneous, fractured and ineffective, is inconsistent with the popular impression that the Roman Empire was marked by wholesale repression and political intolerance. On the contrary, while individual and group liberties were always subordinate to the stability of the Empire, which was paramount, the diversity of dissent evident in the first century AD shows that Rome was required to adapt to local demands.

We have two primary sources for piecing together the social mosaic of first century Galilee and Judea. However, our sources present several distinct difficulties. The first source is material evidence derived from archaeological research. The second primary source is written records.

The first obstacle to face when handling our sources is the recognition that archaeology is extremely limited in its ability to help define and differentiate groups from each other. While groups of peoples often design characteristic features in their architecture, pottery, etc., at best, these help us establish broad group identifications over broad time periods. An archaeologist can help us distinguish between a water jug from the Early Bronze Age and one from the Hellenistic Period, but no one can tell the home of a Pharisee from that of a Sadducee by examining the foundations of their homes. The cistern of a Zealot is indistinguishable from the cistern of a member of the Sicarii. Archaeology is limited when it comes to defining social groupings in the first century AD.

On the other hand, archaeological excavation has uncovered cities, towns and villages, with their intricate infrastructure, the tools that were used to build them, the homes of those who used the tools, and the artefacts produced in a variety of different industries. From these, we can make educated judgements about the people who were employed in a variety of tasks with a high level of probability. It is obvious, for example, that the construction of Caesarea Maritima required a massive infusion of capital to employ architects, engineers, craftsmen and labourers. The city was massive in size, had intricate water supply and sanitation systems, a huge artificial harbour and the capacity to manage enormous commercial activity. This points to complex division of labour and specialization of tasks to say nothing of the economic and political conditions that are prerequisites to such a project. Not only did the construction project require a wide variety of skilled labourers, technicians and managers, these also had to be housed and sustained. The army of workers had to be fed and this points to the existence of an agricultural system capable of producing food for those who themselves could not produce their own. Moreover, it required a system of transportation and commerce. Thus, it is very safe to say that the first century world was made up of people who were engaged in a very wide variety of tasks.

Our written sources reinforce and enable us to elaborate this picture of enormous social sophistication. Literary sources provide a more fertile field for social investigations than archaeology. However, we must recognize that written sources also have characteristics that limit their usefulness. Written sources derive from the pens of a very small number of people, all of whom represent a select group within society, namely, those who are literate.[5] This means that information about the illiterate is mediated by the writings of the literate. Thus, while we can infer the existence of labourers, skilled workers, low level managers, farmers, bakers, merchants, artisans, etc. from our sources, they have not left a great amount of writings about themselves. There are some papyrus fragments that afford a glimpse into everyday life among middle level workers and their families and they are alluded to in literature, but almost all of our written sources derive from those in the upper strata of society.

The biases of the written sources must not be ignored. Josephus describes in copious detail the construction of the Temple in Jerusalem and he even mentions the number of workers the project required, but the workers are not allowed to speak for themselves. The Gospel writers mention farmers, shepherds, fishermen, tax collectors, merchants, labourers and soldiers, but the Gospel writers did not come from these groups. Thus, if we rely on written sources alone, we must admit that the picture we draw based on them is somewhat incomplete.

Another handicap in approaching the subject of the social environment on the Early Roman period is the simple recognition that much of our thinking is preconditioned by simplistic, outdated information. Consider, for example, the cliché uttered all too frequently and unconsciously by pastors and professors alike: 'If you want to understand Jesus, you have to understand Jesus' Jewishness'. This is repeated like a mantra in some circles, but no admonition is more misleading. A variation of this theme is offered by one noted scholar who begins his discussion with the statement, 'The first Christians were Jews.'[6] On the surface, this statement seems to go

---

[5] It is difficult to determine the level of literacy in first century Judea and Galilee. While we can posit with confidence that people in every segment of society spoke more than one language, speaking a language does not necessarily equate to the ability to read and write the language. On the other hand, the quantity and types of inscriptions found suggest that the ability to read and write at least one language was not restricted to the upper classes. For example, the Temple Mount inscription written in three languages warning pagans not to proceed into the inner precincts on the Temple compound was clearly intended to be read by anyone. This suggests an expectation that most people would be able to read at least one of the three languages of the inscription. *Ostraca* containing mundane messages passed from one soldier to another and between merchants and customers demonstrate that the ability to read and write extended beyond the boundaries of the upper classes.

[6] Henry Chadwick, *The Early Church: The Story of Emergent Christianity from the Apostolic Age to the Dividing of the Ways Between the Greek East and the Latin West*, London: Penguin Books, 1993, 1.

without saying, because it has been so consistently reinforced. Even those who know nothing else about Jesus think they know that he was born into a Jewish family in Judea. A superficial acquaintance with scripture reinforces the idea that the environment in which Jesus performed his earthly ministry was dominated by the traditions of first century Judaism and the customs of first century Jews. The meaning of Jesus' ministry is interpreted in the Gospels in terms which seem to be thoroughly Jewish.

On closer inspection, however, it turns out that the 'Jewishness' of Jesus is a fairly difficult phenomenon to figure out. Today, we use the term too loosely to apply it to the time of Jesus and we use it in a way that is quite different from its usage in the time of Jesus. A more careful approach to the question 'what is a Jew in the time of Jesus?' is called for.

First of all, a closer reading of scripture reveals that in the Gospels, the authors never depict Jesus referring to himself as a 'Jew'.[7] Second, although it may seem like a technicality, it is important to point out that the words, 'Jew' and 'Jewish' never occur in scripture.[8] One should not be surprised that *no* English words appeared in the earliest versions of the Bible. The English words 'Jew' and 'Jewish' are translations of the Greek words *Ioudaios* and *Ioudaioi*. It is clear however, that these Greek words had many more meanings than their common English translations admit to. For this reason, many scholars now avoid the customary translation of these words as 'Jew' and 'Jewish' in favour of 'Judean' and 'Judeans'.[9] K C Hanson and Douglas E Oakman state the matter thus, 'This term (Judean) is preferable to 'Jews' when speaking of the first century situation, since "Jews" has specifically "religious" connotations for modern readers, with different social indices.'[10]

---

[7] Paul's usage of the term Judean is unique (see Walter Gutbrod, 'Ioudaios', *Theological Dictionary of the New Testament, edited by Gerhard Kittle,* Wm B Eerdmans Publishing Co., Grand Rapids, MI, 1965, pp. 380-382.) He uses the term 'Judean' only when he is speaking to non-Judeans. He describes himself as a 'Hebrew' or as an 'Israelite'. (2 Cor. 11: 22, Rom. 11: 1, Phil. 3: 5)

[8] The ways in which the terms 'Jew' and 'Jewish' is an interesting study made more important by the casual way in which they are used by all too many. However, only a summary of the issues can be treated here.

[9] For example, Richard A Horsley, *Archaeology, History and Society in Galilee,* Trinity Press International, Valley Forge, PA, 1996, *Galilee: History, People, Politics,* Trinity Press International, Valley Forge, PA, 1995; Bruce J Malina, *The New Testament World: Insights from Cultural Anthropology,* Westminster/John Knox Press, Lousiville, KY, 1993.

[10] K C Hanson and Douglas E Oakman, *Palestine in the Time of Jesus: Social Structures and Social Conflicts,* Fortress Press, 1998, Minneapolis, MN, 176.

The phenomenon we know today as Judaism bears little resemblance to the religion of Judeans of the first century, so the use of the terms 'Jew', 'Jewish', and 'Judaism' in the context of the first century is misleading.[11] 'Judean' can have a variety of different meanings. It can refer to those who live in Judea, as opposed to Galileans or residents of other parts of Palestine.[12] It can refer to anyone with an ethnic connection to the people of Israel or a religious affiliation with Israel, irrespective of where they lived. It can refer, as it often does in the Gospels, to the religious authorities in Jerusalem.

Non-Israelites originally applied the term 'Judean' to the people of Israel. In its earliest stages of usage, it carried negative connotations, so its usage was resisted by Israelites, especially those resident in Judea and Galilee. When an Israelite such as Josephus applies the term 'Judean' to himself, it is because he is addressing a non-Israelite audience. Palestinian Israelites continued to avoid the use of the term 'Judean' in reference to themselves until after the time of Jesus. Their preferred self-designations are 'Israel', 'Israelite', and the lofty term 'Hebrew'.[13]

In the Gospels, the terms 'Israel' and 'Israelite' are used by Israelites to designate the people of God. The terms have no territorial connotations.[14] The region, as opposed to the people of the region, was referred to by the names of its various territories, such as Judea, Samaria, and Galilee. Non-Israelites had come to designate the area as 'Palestine'. The Greek historian Herodotus coined this term in the fifth century BC. Pliny the Elder uses it. The Emperor Hadrian applied the name *Provincia Palestina* to the territories of Judea, Samaria, and Galilee when he incorporated them into the empire in 135 AD. The term Israel, however, refers to Jesus' *people*, not his country. For example, he says of the centurion at Capernaum, 'Not even in Israel have I seen such faith.' (Lk 7: 9) In Matthew, he understands his mission to be to 'the house of Israel' (Mt. 10: 6, 15: 24).

---

[11] In *Early Judaism*, Prentice Hall, Upper Saddle River, NJ, 1997, Martin Jaffee acknowledges the distinction between modern Judaism and the religion of Judeans in the first century by distinguishing between 'Judaism' and 'Early Judaism'. Jacob Neusner differentiates between 'normative' and 'formative' Judaism.

[12] Scholars also use the term 'Palestinian' loosely, applying it broadly to people in an age when it only had reference to territory and applying to territory at a time well before the term was ever used to denote territory. Thus scholars speak of 'Palestinian' Judaism or 'Palestine' during the Iron Age. Both usages are anachronistic and misleading. An interesting and thorough discussion of the use of the terms 'Palestinian' and 'Jew' is contained in Duncan MacPherson, *A Third Millennium Guide to Pilgrimage to the Holy Land*, Melisende, London, 2000, 91-98.

[13] Walter Gutbrod, 'Ioudaios', *Theological Dictionary of the New Testament, edited by Gerhard Kittle*, Wm B Eerdmans Publishing Co., Grand Rapids, MI, 1965, 356-391.

[14] It is only occasionally used in the Gospels to refer to the *land*. When it does, the term 'land of' usually modifies it.

Israel in Jesus' day was the product of a wide range of influences. It had been developing for many centuries. It had undergone enormous transformation over the ages and was marked by broad diversity. So, to say that it is necessary to understand Jesus' *Jewishness* in order to understand Jesus is only true because it is vague. It is more misleading than helpful. The real question is 'what did it mean to belong to the House of Israel at the time of Jesus?'

The simple answer is that it meant identity with a particular people that self-consciously understood themselves to be related to their God, Yahweh, in a particular way. It is not correct to say that the Israelites were 'monotheists'. For one thing, the word does not occur in the Bible in any language and is not used in English until the seventeenth century. Thus, the use of the term, when applied to ancient Israel, is anachronistic. For another thing, the Israelites did, indeed, believe in the existence of more than one god. Yahweh was their tribal God, but there were rivals.

The Israelites disparaged the other gods in their writings, which pleased Yahweh, and occasionally worshipped them, which evoked Yahweh's wrath. Irrespective of Yahweh's changing temper, however, Yahweh was theirs and they were Yahweh's. The idea of *covenant* is central to understanding the people of Israel. They understood themselves to be chosen by God to stand in a special relationship to God. This 'chosenness' was refreshed and the covenant between God and Israel was renewed repeatedly. It was as central a concept to the Essenes as it was to Paul. In the words of institution at the Last Supper, Jesus also invoked this idea of covenant (Mark 14: 24).

The Israelites' self-consciousness as God's chosen people was the guiding principle in the writing of their sacred story. This story of the relationship between God and the people of Israel eventually formed what we know as the Hebrew Bible or the Old Testament. The ancient writings revered by Israel appealed to non-Israelites as well and the antiquity of the holy writings generated esteem among them. The narratives of the Hebrew Bible developed over a long period of time taking the form in which we receive them today in Mesopotamia between the fourth and second centuries BC. Over time, Jerusalem eclipsed other centres of power and became the ritual centre of Israelite religion as well as the locus of Israelite political power. The location of the cultic and political centre in Jerusalem cemented in the minds of non-Israelites the identification of the people of Israel with the territory of Judah. To outsiders, the people of Israel came to be called Judeans.

By the time Jesus was born, Jerusalem had been the political and religious focus of the Judeans for several hundred years. It was a destination

88

for periodic pilgrimages associated with festivals and all adult male Israelites were obliged to pay an annual tax to the Temple authorities. This was the half shekel tax that Jesus instructed Peter to pay for both of them from the shekel Peter would find in the mouth of the first fish he caught in the lake. (Matt 17: 24-27) Jerusalem had also become something of a religious curiosity for pagans as well. That pagans as well as Israelites frequented Jerusalem is well attested. Archaeologists have uncovered pagan ritual baths. The Gospels and other ancient literature testify that the city was saturated with Roman soldiers.

Beyond their special relationship to Yahweh and their identification as Judeans by outsiders, very little can be said to characterize *all* Judeans, unless it is that the people of Israel displayed a rich diversity. Their reverence for ancient writings was characteristic of Judeans and all other ancient peoples, but Israel did not agree on what books constituted its scriptures. Judeans outside Palestine considered the Septuagint to be the normative version of the Bible, but it is not clear that Judeans in Palestine used it. Samaritans, if they can be considered Israelites, accepted only the first five books of the Bible. Neither can it be said that the position of Jerusalem as cult centre was universally accepted among Israelites. The Essenes, for example, did not recognize the authority of the Jerusalem Temple cult. Thus, it is more productive to describe those groups we know to be part of Israel and attempt to place them on an informal continuum in relationship to each other instead of trying to identify Israel with any particular pattern of worship or norms of belief.

Before doing so, however, it is necessary to clarify a broader and more populous group to which I have already alluded. It is easy to cultivate the impression that Israelite culture was predominant in the ancient world, because scholars searching for the roots of Christianity tend to look first toward Israelite roots. This effort obscures the reality that Israelites represented a distinct minority throughout antiquity. It is even more erroneous to think of 'Christianity' as anything but a marginal presence until well after the first century AD. In fact, the dominant religious influence in the ancient world was that which came to be called 'pagan'. The term appears for the first time in Christian literature from the fourth century AD. As is so often the case, people outside the group coined and applied the label. It derives from the Latin word *paganus,* which means 'rustic', 'belonging to the country', or 'civilian'. It probably was used to denote those who had not become 'soldiers for Christ' through the ritual of baptism. Pagans represented the overwhelming majority of the population of the ancient world until the early fourth century AD when Constantine made Christianity the official state religion. Paganism persisted until much later, even to today. Indeed, Constantine's nephew, Julian, who succeeded Constantine, was baptized as an infant, but converted back to paganism as an adult, hence his nickname, 'Julian the Apostate'. Pagans also represent a huge and diverse group that cannot be adequately defined here. However, the diversity of their religious observances is well known.[15]

One group of pagans, on the periphery of Israelite society, is particularly interesting. Scholars refer to them as 'God-fearers'. The term appears in Josephus and is echoed in Luke and Acts. They were attracted to the values of Israelite religion as well as the spectacle of the city of Jerusalem. Toward the first century there was a drift toward the merging of multiple gods and their cults into one. Perhaps some pagans saw Israel's insistence on one God above all to the exclusion of others as the logical extension of this trend. Indeed, so enamoured with Israelite religion were some non-Israelites that they participated in the life of local synagogues even to the point of circumcision, although for obvious reasons, this seemed to many to be an extreme requirement. Short of undergoing circumcision, many non-Israelites participated in every other aspect of Israelite activity. The common belief that Jews kept strictly separate from non-Jews is a misconception. Josephus, who himself spent the last part of his life in close association with Gentiles, is well aware of the group called God-fearers. The Gospels and Acts presume an understanding that non-Israelites had close contact with Israelites. Indeed, the centurion in Luke 7 is probably a representative of this group. The elders of the Judeans approach Jesus on his behalf and say that he is worthy, loves the people, i.e., Israel and built their synagogue for them. He foreshadows the Gentile converts in Acts (cf. Acts 10) who are identified as devout and fearing God.[16]

It is interesting to note that this biblical testimony is supported by archaeological evidence as well. In the town of Akmonia in Asia Minor, an inscription was discovered in a synagogue building that dates to the middle of the second century. The inscription notes that Judean officials had restored the synagogue, but that a woman whose name was Julia Severa had built it originally. Another inscription from the same site identifies Ms Severa; whose name is as Latin as a name can get, as a Gentile. Specifically, she was a priestess in the cult of a pagan god. Clearly, Ms Severa was attracted to Judean religious practices and just as clearly the Judeans were not averse to her participation at least insofar as it involved patronage.

---

[15] See chapter 5, Religion in the Ancient World.

[16] When people say that the first Christians were Jews, they are on shaky ground in more than one sense. They are confusing the first followers of Jesus with 'Christians', a label that was never applied to anyone among the first two generations of Jesus' followers. Then, against all the biblical testimony that indicates that Israel rejected Jesus, they overlook the biblical testimony that the first to earn the label 'Christian' were pagan converts. (Acts 11: 26)

Another group at the blurred boundary of Israel is the Samaritans. Well known from the Gospels, they are not well understood. Unfortunately, their origins are obscured in a shroud of Israelite propaganda, in which they appear as outsiders, almost as outside as Gentiles. Josephus reports several separate incidents of open hostility between Judeans and Samaritans. The Gospels seem to corroborate this picture of tense, hostile relations between the two groups. The narrator of John points out that Judeans and Samaritans have no dealings (John 4: 9). In Matthew, Jesus forbids the twelve from entering any village or town of the Samaritans (Mt 10: 5). At other times, on the other hand, the Gospels suggest that Jesus was friendly toward the Samaritans. Samaritans are honoured in the parables of the Good Samaritan and the ten lepers (Luke 10: 29-37; 17: 11-19). In Acts, they are receptive to Philip's preaching and to the presence of Peter and John (Acts 8: 5-25). Josephus also states that the Romans attacked the Samaritans during the First Judean Revolt, indicating that the Romans considered the Samaritans to be in league with the Judeans. The Samaritans fought on both sides during the Bar Kochba Revolt. It is best to acknowledge that literary testimony does not adjudicate this question.

Scholars trace the root of the split between Judeans and Samaritans to the time of the Assyrian conquest of the northern kingdom of Israel. According to Judeans, the remnants of the Samaritans inter-married with foreign colonists. Samaritans, however, consider themselves to be descendents of the tribes of Ephraim and Manasseh. Further, they claim that the true locus for the worship of Yahweh is Mt. Gerazim in Samaria rather than in Jerusalem. Ezra 4 indicates a dispute between Judeans and Samaritans over the location of the Temple. It is probable that the historical tension between the two groups stems from this power struggle and ideological issues.

Like the Judeans, the Samaritans observed Passover, Pentecost and the feast of Booths. They considered Moses to be the only true prophet in Israel's history. They revered only the Torah, the first five books of the Bible. Their version of the Torah is some ways approximates the Septuagint, i.e., the Greek version of the Hebrew scriptures produced in Alexandria. Their writings reflect similarities to some of the Qumran material. Thus, they represent an interesting piece in the social mosaic of the ancient world. In so many ways, they are the duck-billed platypus of first century Palestine. Today, the Samaritans continue to maintain their own traditional rituals on Mt. Gerazim. There are about 300 remaining in the sect.

Until the discovery of the Dead Sea Scrolls, more was known about the Samaritans than about the Essenes, but scholars consider the Essenes to be closer to the core of the House of Israel. It is reasonable to wonder how this opinion would change if a cache of Samaritan writings were to be discovered in the Judean desert. Scholarly opinions often fill and are defined by vacuums in information.

Like the Samaritans whose cult centre was Mt Gerazim in Shechem, the Essenes at Qumran explicitly rejected the authority of the Temple cult, including its priesthood. They refused to sacrifice there and rejected the lunar-based calendar of the Temple cult, in favour of a solar calendar. In addition, they expressed their disdain for the Temple cult by referring to the High Priest as the Teacher of Wickedness. They oriented their graves away from Jerusalem, breaking with Israelite custom.

Until 1947 when the first scrolls were discovered in the foothills of the Judean Mountains at the northwest shore of the Dead Sea, the only knowledge of the Essenes was through scant references to them in Philo of Alexandria, Pliny the Elder and Josephus. There is no New Testament reference to Essenes. The discovery of the Dead Sea Scrolls and the excavation of the site of Khirbet Qumran have been a watershed in biblical scholarship, notwithstanding the accompanying sensationalized reports of scholarly intrigue, suppression of texts and Oliver Stone-like conspiracy theories. The texts fall into three general categories: 1) copies of the Old Testament that are to date the oldest manuscripts of the Old Testament in existence,[17] 2) rules pertaining to the community itself, 3) hymns and liturgical writings. For students of the New Testament, the scrolls represent a treasury of new information about one aspect of the world that forms the background of Jesus ministry and one aspect of Israel. We can only speculate, however, whether and in what ways the Qumran sect is reflective of first century Judean practice or thinking in general.

The Essenes at Qumran broke away from the Temple cult subsequent to the Hasmonean revolt against Antiochus IV. Favourable terms for the Hasmoneans led to the cessation of hostilities. The Hasmoneans were given the office of the high priest, even though they were not from the appropriate line. Consequently, the Essenes rejected the Hasmonean High Priest and withdrew to Qumran. There they cultivated grain, produced medicines from the minerals around the Dead Sea and produced copies of sacred texts. This latter occupation was not only a livelihood, but also a form of devotion.

Scholars debate the extent to which the Essenes isolated themselves,[18] but they deliberately gave up of material comforts as a form of self-purification in preparation for the coming of the Lord. Their Manual of

---

[17] Gabriel Barkay discovered the oldest fragment of an OT text in tombs in the Hinnom Valley in 1988.

[18] That Rome ultimately attacked them suggests at least that the Romans were considered to be implicated in the revolt. The discovery of a scroll on Masada that was produced at Qumran, however, is not the smoking gun it might seem to be.

Discipline cites Isaiah 40: 3 as their *raison d'être*. It also identifies the study of the Law as their 'way' or 'path'. They self-consciously considered themselves to be a righteous remnant waiting for God's decisive action to vindicate his faithful. Their writings are distinctly 'apocalyptic'. They looked at the world as a field of struggle between God and the forces of evil. Humanity was divided into these two opposing camps. Ultimately and imminently, God would act to restore righteousness.

Similarity in language and the presumed geographical proximity between the Qumran community and the area of John the Baptist's activity leads many to posit a connection between the two.[19] The Gospels also identify John with Isaiah 40: 3. John's reference to Jesus' baptism with spirit and fire (Luke 3: 16) seems to be paralleled in the Essenes' Manual of Discipline where 'water', 'holy spirit', 'spirit of truth', and God's refining power are mentioned as part of God's activity to prepare his community. The Damascus Document[20] states, 'He made known his holy spirit to them through his messiahs' (Damascus Rule 2: 12).

Supposed connections between the Essenes and John the Baptist, however, are highly speculative. Still, the literature from Qumran gives us a valuable window into the first century world. The Essenes give us one more view of the diversity of the House of Israel.

It is not far fetched to consider the Essenes a protest group of sorts, but they remained well within socially accepted standards of expressing dissent. Josephus, who states that he spent time among the Essenes, speaks glowingly of them. He identifies them as one of three or four[21] 'schools' or 'sects' or 'philosophies' of the Judeans, thus according them official status of sorts. Given his usual posture against anyone who would upset the social apple cart, it is a safe conclusion that the Essenes were not in any way social or political revolutionaries. They clearly registered dissent from the Jerusalem authorities, but their dissent did not approach violent rejection. Indeed, many Essenes continued to live in various villages and towns of Judea.

Protest was an integral part of ancient life as much as it is part of modern life. Groups and individuals were accustomed to asserting their interests and scrambling for power. The Essenes reflect one way in which groups differentiated themselves from one another in the normal process of social change.

The authorities of established Israel are represented in the Gospels

---

[19] E.g., John Fitzmyer, *The Dead Sea Scrolls and Christian Origins,* 2000.

[20] This document, pieced together from fragments found in cave 4, is one of the sectarian documents that were intended for use within the Qumran community. It includes sectarian rules and displays some of the theological presuppositions of the community.

[21] His interpretation is inconsistent in *The Wars* and in *The Antiquities.*

as the Pharisees and Sadducees, along with groups loosely referred to as scribes, chief priests, tax collectors, soldiers and Herodians. Together, these groups make up the 'establishment' against which opposition groups dissent. Although the Gospels tend to blur the boundaries of these groups, depicting them as a united front arrayed against Jesus and his followers, more careful reading of the biblical texts, supplemented by Josephus shows that they were distinct groups that often competed against each other. In the matrix of first century society, however, all of these groups make up the ruling class and their assorted partners. It is tempting to think of them as the 'bourgeois' of the ancient world, but the modern conception of a social pyramid does not fit the ancient world very well. The modern concept of a middle class is anachronistic if applied to the ancient world.

It is better to conceptualise ancient society as consisting of two classes—the ruling class and the production class. The latter would make up at least two-thirds of the total population and would include farmers, craftsmen, labourers, and merchants. This class is composed of many different groups that produced goods of various kinds.

The ruling class maintained power, order, and stability. Its role was to organize and protect society so that the production class would be able to produce enough to sustain itself and generate a surplus to sustain the rulers. The ruling class maintained its position through a complicated system of patronage, backed up by an effective tax system and a strong military.[22]

To put a complicated process in crude and simplistic terms, Rome won its position through the successful exercise of power, i.e., a combination of political savvy and military force. It maintained power by conveying authority to those who would loyally protect its interests. These 'clients' or 'retainers' gained position, wealth, and honour to the degree that they were able to return honour, maintain order and command the loyalty of the production class. They were dependent upon their patrons, but above the production class. For example, Rome was a patron of Herod the Great, bestowing power upon him. Herod returned honour, maintained order and stability, protected the production class and created conditions that would increase production. He guaranteed productivity and the wealth that came with it. He accomplished these things by patronizing others who returned loyalty and helped maintain stability and guarantee productivity.

Within this class of rulers, power groups emerged. In first century

---

[22] The military itself was a complex organism. A popular metaphor for the military was the body and its parts. It was not a class in itself, but a group within a class. While it served the interests of the ruling class, its constituents came from various strata of society, including the gentry on one hand and workers and farmers on the other. Roman citizenship required military service.

Judea, the Pharisees and Sadducees are among the chief power groups, but there were many, many others. When the system worked well a sort of symbiotic social equilibrium was reached. Rome protected the borders, stability prevailed, productivity led to general low level prosperity among the producers, and various power groups promoted and protected various interests. When taxation became excessive, when the rulers were inept, when external or internal forces threatened stability, when natural disasters stressed productivity, the system broke down, dissent rose and sometimes rebellion broke out. The ruling class hated rebellion. Rebellion is not good for business. The rulers did whatever it could to make sure rebellion did not happen. The groups that made up the ruling class were continually jockeying for better position and competing with one another to advance their specific interests.

The Pharisees and Sadducees are the best known of the power groups in first century Judea. Josephus described the Pharisees and Sadducees as distinct 'philosophies', just as he did the Essenes. In spite of the negative impression the Gospels give, to be counted among the Pharisees was not something to be ashamed of. The Gospels highly polemical language is a reflection of the depth of conflict between the early churches and their adversaries among the Judean ruling parties. Relying on the Gospels to understand the Pharisees, scribes and Sadducees is like relying on one estranged partner in a divorce for a characterization of the other. Paul claims to be a Pharisee (Phil 3: 5), as does Josephus. These groups were not universally disliked and, indeed, were supported by the production class.

Josephus indicates that the Pharisees were the most influential power group. They believed in life after death and were known for their interpretation of the law. Aside from what he explicitly says, it is clear from his descriptions of their roles that they functioned as an interest group with its own programme for religious and social organization. The same can be said for the Sadducees, who were a priestly caste made of members of the aristocracy. They rejected the idea of life after death. Both groups favoured the status quo, both benefited from favoured positions in society and neither was particularly hostile to Roman rule.

At times, however, circumstances became intolerable. When conditions deteriorated enough, the ruling parties would face social unrest. Sometimes, the ruling parties organized this unrest. At one point, Josephus identifies the leaders of such movements as members of the Pharisees.[23] Various programs for change were promoted, including direct appeal to Rome for assistance or, when that failed, open resistance.

---

[23] *Antiquities*, vol. XVIII.1-27.

Josephus identifies a number of resistance movements. These have been analysed[24] from sociological perspectives and can be broken down into two general categories. First, charismatic figures developed and led loosely organized rural movements made up of members of the production class. These charismatic leaders claimed to be or were labelled as *messiahs* or *prophets*. It is clear that Israelite culture preserved such traditions. Such movements developed from the popular, rural discontent that rose and fell depending on social and economic conditions. However, they were not well organized, they did not have coherent platforms of social reform and they were not successful.

Another reflection of the mood of social protest consists of better organized movements of social reform led by members of the ruling classes that advanced coherent platforms and were much more successful. The two groups that Josephus identifies as 'the fourth philosophy' and the Sicarii fall into this category. He also makes reference to 'the Zealots', a group he singles out for special opprobrium. Josephus labels social dissident groups variously as brigands, bandits and thieves.[25] Together, these groups represent the worst of Judean society. It is important to point out, first of all that they are, in fact, distinct groups. Scholarly discussion of these groups is imprecise, following the imprecision of ancient authors who also confuse the groups with one another. It is usual to lump them together, even though Josephus, our only source, clearly distinguishes them.

Dissident groups are interesting and important to understand from the perspective of New Testament study, because they were active from time to time during the first century and thus provide a backdrop to the life of Jesus. Further, the Sicarii were active when the traditions about Jesus were taking shape. The Gospels were written in the immediate aftermath of the First Judean Revolt, at precisely the same time that Josephus was writing his history *The Wars of the Judeans*. Just as Josephus had an interest in differentiating deviant rebel groups from upright Judeans who were loyal to Rome and worthy subjects, so the nascent Jesus movement did not want to be identified in any way with a failed rebellion or the groups that advocated rebellion. Apologetics, i.e., defence of his people, was one motivation for Josephus' writing. The Gospels writers also had an apologetic interest.

The Zealots are singled out as the worst of the worst, but Josephus' mention of them is fleeting. Indeed, his vague references to them are disproportional to the mountain of scholarly material dedicated to them. The

---

[24] Richard A Horsley. *Bandits, Prophets, and Messiahs*, 1988, and *Jesus and the Spiral of Violence*, 1987.

[25] By the time he did his writing, Josephus had come to hate dissent, even though he says that he, himself, led the Judean forces in Galilee against Rome.

confusion about their identity is due to the similarity between them and other dissident groups, such as the Sicarii and the fourth philosophy. There is a family resemblance among them and Josephus understands them all to be representative of seditious groups, varying only in the severity of their actions. Clearly, Josephus includes the Zealots along with the Sicarii and the 'fourth philosophy' as perpetrators of grave social offences. Just as clearly, he differentiates all three and puts the Zealots in a class by themselves. All the more surprising in light of this is the fact that scholars usually blur the three into one group.

The Zealots were not a social protest group. They did not have a clear programme for social reform. They came into existence in the period of social dislocation during and in the wake of Rome's suppression of the First Judean Revolt. Rome's tactics in suppressing rebellion cannot be termed enlightened. The legions did not employ surgical strikes to minimize collateral damage. When they encountered resistance they followed a scorched earth policy.[26] In the aftermath of Roman action, there was tremendous hardship, a breakdown of civil order and a consequent rise in banditry and petty thievery. Josephus' identifies the Zealots with bandits and brigands, i.e., common outlaws and thugs, who emerge from the countryside. The implication is that they took advantage of the breakdown in stability to profit personally. Unlike the fourth philosophy and the Sicarii, however, they did not represent a cohesive movement of social protest.

According to Josephus, the fourth philosophy was founded about fifty-five years before the outbreak of the First Judean Revolt. Thus, it was part of the social fabric at the time of Jesus' early adulthood and perhaps during the early years of his ministry.[27] Luke's Gospel situates Jesus' birth during the time of Quirinius, the governor of Syria (Luke 2: 2). Luke specifically mentions an enrolment, which was an action instituted in order to raise taxes.[28] Luke clearly intends his readers to understand Jesus' birth against the background of Roman Imperial history in general and the issue of tax

---

[26] It is a mistake to presume that all Judeans opposed Rome. Many towns and cities preferred capitulation to destruction. Some, like Sepphoris, refused to participate in the revolt against Rome and pledged allegiance in exchange for favourable terms and treatment.

[27] There is no reason to cling to the conventionally held position that Jesus' ministry lasted only three years. That belief is based on the record of the Synoptic Gospels and presumes that their understanding of history and chronological exactness is similar to ours in the twentieth century. It is hard to explain how a ministry of only three years would have resulted in so many widely dispersed communities, along with strong traditions so soon after Jesus' death.

[28] Typical of Hellenistic historians of the first century, the exact date of Jesus' birth was not important to Luke. The period of Quirinius rule does not match the date of Jesus birth.

assessment in particular. Josephus associates the beginning of the fourth philosophy with Quirinius, mentions an assessment of property for tax purposes and identifies tax resistance as one of the fourth philosophy's foundational principles. He says that Judas the Galilean, a teacher who is mentioned in Acts 5: 37 in association with a census, and a Pharisee whose name was Saddok, led the fourth philosophy. There is no hint in Josephus that the fourth philosophy advocated violence. Theirs was a form of social resistance that appears to have been well within the bounds of what Rome considered legitimate social expression and tolerated. It was led by members of the privileged classes and had a coherent ideology. There is no clear link between the fourth philosophy and the revolt fifty-five years later, but Josephus says that their ideology infected the populace, that it was intrusive and that it sowed the seeds of strife and trouble. The fourth philosophy does not appear again in Josephus' writings, but the descendents of one of its founders do.

The Sicarii took their name from their weapons of choice—long daggers they hid under their garments. The literal translation of 'Sicarii' is 'ones who carry daggers'. They embodied the principles of tax resistance that were associated with the fourth philosophy and thus were arrayed against Rome. They engaged in stealthy acts of selective violence as well. While their enemy was Rome, their primary targets were fellow Judeans of the ruling class. Their strategy was to terrorize their wealthy countrymen, who benefited most from Roman rule, in order to persuade them to desert their Roman patrons. They mounted raids on the property of the wealthy, launched kidnappings for ransom—usually the release from prison of their own members—and engaged in assassinations. They operated in urban settings, emerging suddenly and seemingly out of nowhere. Once their operation was complete, they melted back into the crowds. According to Josephus, they were notorious for their outrages against Judeans and he tells numerous stories about their treachery. Josephus does not conceal his contempt for the Sicarii. Once the revolt against Rome broke out, the Sicarii did not participate in it, but withdrew to the mountain fortress of Masada, from which they launched operations against nearby Judean villages. Their occupation of Masada and their ultimate demise there is the climax of Josephus' defence of his people to the Roman public.

Contemporary retelling of the Masada story badly distorts it. This distortion is a gross violation of Josephus. It obscures his purpose and prevents current day readers of the Gospels from gleaning important insights about the Gospels through the reading of Josephus.

The popular fiction about Masada has obvious contemporary meaning for the people of the modern state of Israel. It has taken on a life of its own, notwithstanding its morbid overtones. It refers to the deaths of the 'Zealots' as collective suicide, when Josephus describes it as mass murder. It misidentifies the Sicarii as Zealots and characterizes their actions as heroic, noble and worthy of emulation. By contrast, Josephus, our only source, intended his readers to understand that the Sicarii were despicable, cowardly traitors whose treachery against their own people was the reason for the destruction of the Temple. The device Josephus uses to achieve this understanding is the story of their self-sacrifice at Masada. It is a motif that is attested four times in Josephus' own writings and sixteen times in Hellenistic literature. It always functions to show that those who are taking their own lives recognize the futility of their ambitions, admit that they were wrong to advance on their ambitions and accept God's judgement against them. They get what they deserve. In Josephus, the motif functions to exonerate both the people of Israel in the eyes of the Roman public and Rome from any agency in the destruction of the rebels. In Josephus, the Sicarii are the scapegoat, not the heroes.

Josephus' accounts are obviously biased in favour of the ruling classes. He is beholden to his Roman patrons. He disdains anyone who represents a challenge Roman rule. Nonetheless, he portrays Judean society as complex and diverse. The groupings of people he identifies, with the exception of the Essenes, are also mentioned in the Gospels. Jesus' disciples include people from different stations in the social order, including members of the ruling class (tax collectors) and those among the producing class (fisherman). Lists of the disciples also identify dissidents, such as Simon the Zealot (Luke 6: 15).

It is quite possible that another notorious member of Jesus' disciples was involved in social dissent. The name of Judas Iscariot is often understood as referring to Judas' village of origin, i.e., Judas who is from Scariot. The problem with this interpretation is that there is no evidence that there was such a village. On the other hand, if the Latin word *Sicarii,* which is a plural form, were to be translated into Aramaic, the language of the people of Judea, it would be rendered *Sicariot.* Judas behaves in a manner strikingly similar to the Sicarii. He betrays a fellow Judean on the night of Passover (compare the Sicarii massacre of 700 Judeans on the night of Passover at En Gedi) and then, when he realizes that his cause was misguided, takes his own life.

In any case, the social world described by Josephus is, to a large extent assumed by the authors of the Gospels. The ministry of Jesus and the Gospel message is presented against the background of a complex, vibrant society in which dissent was expressed in a variety of ways and in which groups asserted their interests in an effort to gain greater advantage. It is tempting to see Jesus as member of one or the other group and scholars identify him with a number of different groups. While exact identification is not possible, at least we can see how easy it was for Jesus to have been confused with any of several different groups.

Chapter 7
THE SEARCH FOR
THE HISTORICAL JESUS

In the weeks approaching Easter over the past few years, the national print media re-enacted a curious ritual. On the covers of *Newsweek*, *Time* and *US News* and *World Report* a surprising cover boy has been featured—none other than Jesus of Nazareth. In recent years, National Public Radio has featured stories about him. He was the subject of a popular Public Broadcasting Company series called 'From Jesus to Christ'. The occurrence of these news stories illustrates how popular the so-called quest for the historical Jesus has become throughout society. The discerning reader should be wary, however. As a journalist for *The Boston Globe* once told me, 'There is a reason why they are called news *stories*.'[1]

The academic community also dedicates an enormous amount of scholarly attention to the question and quest of the historical Jesus. Indeed, no other topic in biblical studies attracts as much popular or academic attention. Given the arcane nature of most biblical scholarship, it is amazing that research attracts any popular attention at all. At the annual convention of The Society of Biblical Literature, which attracts over 8,000 participants from the academic community each year, lectures pertaining to the search for the historical Jesus attract more participants than those of any other subject. The subject has produced some of the best scholarship over the past 40 years, as well as some of the worst. Honours in the latter category must go to the members of the quasi-academic association known as The Jesus Seminar who *cast votes* to determine the authenticity of the words of Jesus in the Gospels.[2]

---

[1] Ethan Bronner, Middle East Bureau Chief for *The Boston Globe*, in a personal interview, Jerusalem, 10 June 1996.
[2] Robert W Funk, Roy W Hoover, The Jesus Seminar, *The Five Gospels: the Search for the Authentic Words of Jesus: New Translation and Commentary*, Macmillan, New York, 1993.

The Word of God and the world of the Bible

All but laid to rest by Albert Schweitzer in 1906, the quest for the historical Jesus was resurrected by Ernst Kasemann's essay, 'The Problem of the Historical Jesus' in 1953. Then in 1959, James Robinson published his book *A New Quest of the Historical Jesus*.[3] Over the past twenty years, popular interest was fuelled by the sensational pronouncements of The Jesus Seminar. Today, scholarly and popular passions are equally excited. It is rare when the popular imagination is aroused by biblical scholarship, so the phenomenon deserves attention.

Interest in the person of Jesus of Nazareth in and of itself is not new, of course. Although Christians consider the Bible as a whole to be scriptural, the New Testament is often considered a primary source. Marcionism, the ancient belief that belief in Jesus as Christ rendered the Hebrew scriptures obsolete, was declared to be heretical by the early church. However, it is, unfortunately, not entirely extinct. The Gospels are often given an unofficial status of supremacy among books of the New Testament. Some Christian denominations formalize this unofficial status in the liturgy by standing when the Gospel lesson is read. Others express their heightened esteem for the Gospels in the liturgy by reading the Gospel lesson last when there are also readings from the Epistles and the Old Testament.

The special status accorded to the Gospels is due to the role of Jesus in Christianity. He is not only the subject of faith, but the object of faith as well. Without Jesus there is no Christianity. The Gospels preserve what seem to be biographical details about Jesus' life and ministry, so they take on an air of primacy. The words attributed to Jesus in the Gospels are, to some people, the most important parts of all. Some versions of the Bible differentiate the words of Jesus from other verses in the Gospels with red lettering.

The Gospels and the words of Jesus, however, are both compelling and mysterious objects of study. Not only their profound message, but also their peculiarities attract attention and generate speculation. This interest is not unique to the modern era. By the middle of the 2nd century AD, Marcion and others noted that the Gospels showed signs of modification by editors.[4] Tatian noticed that the accounts of Jesus in the Gospels were not uniform, but rather presented different details, perspectives and understandings of what is important about Jesus' life and ministry. This observation led him to produce the first *Gospel harmony*. A harmony of the Gospels is produced when elements of the four Gospels are distilled and brought together to form

[3] James McConkey Robinson, *A New Quest of the Historical Jesus*, SCM Press, London, 1959.
[4] Text and redaction criticism are both discusses in chapter 2.

one harmonious account. The presumption in any of many Gospel harmonies throughout the ages is that agreement among the four Gospels proves the truth of the Gospels.[5] Clement of Alexandria, writing around AD 200 noticed obvious differences between the Gospel of John and the other three Gospels, which are referred to as *the Synoptic Gospels*, because they share so much in common.[6] Augustine of Hippo was also aware of difficulties reconciling the various Gospel accounts of the ministry of Jesus and produced a harmony of his own early in the 5th century AD.

That the Gospels present different pictures of the life and ministry of Jesus when read superficially and literally is beyond dispute. John puts the episode of the cleansing of the Temple at the beginning of Jesus' ministry while the synoptics understand it as part of Jesus' final days. In Matthew, the Holy Family is in residence in Bethlehem when Jesus is born, while in Luke, they travel from Nazareth to Bethlehem on account of a census ordered by Caesar Augustus. In Matthew, Joseph brings his wife and child Jesus to Egypt to escape persecution by Herod. From Egypt, they travel directly to Nazareth. By contrast, in Luke, the Holy Family is not threatened by anyone and they return directly to Nazareth. Neither Mark nor John shows the slightest interest in Jesus' birth or childhood.

Disparities among the various Gospel accounts prompt examination. Examination breeds speculation. If the Gospels are biographies of Jesus and they do not agree about key details of Jesus' life, does this mean that one is 'right' and another 'wrong?' Do the Gospels represent different perspectives on Jesus that are meant to be blended into a composite picture? If they are intended to be biographies, which one is the most accurate?

Aside from questions arising from the various Gospel accounts themselves about the life and ministry of Jesus, as historical knowledge increases, certain details about the Gospel reports seem dubious. For example, while the census ordered by Caesar Augustus at the time of Jesus' birth is well known from the Gospel of Luke, it is not mentioned anywhere else in historical records.[7] Moreover, neither Judea nor Galilee was under Roman rule at the time of Jesus' birth, so Caesar Augustus would not have had jurisdiction to order such a census in those regions.

As historical information accumulates, some details in the Gospels are cast into question. Inquiring minds are then set to investigation and speculation. The motives for investigation can be to uncover the truth and

---

[5] This assumption is misguided and misleading.

[6] The word *synoptic* is derived from Greek and literally means 'view together'.

[7] Josephus reports a census taken during the time of Quirinius, governor of Syria, but the period when Quirinius was assigned to Syria does not correspond to the time of Jesus' birth.

corroborate the veracity of the Gospel records or it can be a cynical attempt to expose faith as vacuous and the Gospels as fictitious. The results can be both alarming and inspiring. To many, the critical examination of the Bible is sacrilegious. Modern scholarship is often criticized as undermining faith. To others, faith without the application of reason is incredulous. In either event, the search for the historical Jesus springs from widespread recognition that the information we have about the person of Jesus of Nazareth is not uniform and is difficult to reconcile. Because he occupies such an important position in the faith of millions of people and in world history, scholars throughout history applied their inquiring minds to the question, 'who really was Jesus?'

Albert Schweitzer is popularly remembered for his missionary work in Africa, but in 1906, he wrote a landmark book called *From Reimarus to Wrede*.[8] It came to be known as *The Quest for the Historical Jesus*. Until its publication, scholars had been trying to reconstruct an accurate picture of the life of Jesus. Schweitzer's book was a history of this effort, as well as a report of his own attempt.

The search for the historical Jesus as it is known today began in the age of Enlightenment. People understood humanity to be endowed with reason. They believed that humanity had the ability to uncover ultimate truth. They understood that God was freely accessible through intuition and the exercise of the mind. It was inevitable that this spirit of free inquiry would be applied to religion and the Bible. Enlightenment scholars inferred that the Gospel accounts represented not only historical details about Jesus' ministry and life, but also a fair amount of material contributed by those who compiled the Gospels, including perhaps some early church dogma. In the spirit of the Enlightenment, dogma—both ancient and modern—came under scholarly scrutiny. Deism, the popular religious philosophy of the Enlightenment, advocated religious tolerance and free access to God through intuition.

One of the first to express questions about the historical Jesus was Hermann Reimarus (1694-1768), a German scholar who insisted that true faith can only be gained through natural insight and not through church dogma and institutions. The authority of the Church was subject to question and critique. Another German scholar of the Enlightenment, Johann Semler, argued for complete academic freedom. As dogma came under scrutiny, traditional teachings about Jesus also were being examined in light of the growing awareness that the Gospel pictures of Jesus were stylised, domesticated and served the purpose of the magisterial Church. Trust in dogma gave way to trust in the ability of reason or natural insight to uncover religious truth.

---

[8]   Albert Schweitzer, *The Quest for the Historical Jesus: a Critical Study of its Progress from Reimarus to Wrede*, Macmillan, New York, 1910.

Scholars employed the historical-critical method to reveal the history of the development and transmission of the Gospel texts, instead of relying on the authority of the church. What emerged was the understanding that the Jesus who appears in the Gospels is a stylised and domesticated Jesus who may not bear much resemblance to the historical Jesus of Nazareth. At the time, any challenge to the authority of the institutional church was risky, so some scholars published their work on the subject pseudonymously. Gottwald Lessing, for example, published some of the work of Reimarus under a pseudonym. Good thing, too, because the work was immediately condemned.

By the 19th century, the critique of the Gospel reports was sharpened even further. In 1835, David Friedrich Strauss wrote *The Christ of Faith and the Christ of History*,[9] in which he questioned the historical value of every verse of the Gospels. Instead of understanding the Gospels as historical biographies, he suggested that it was not important that the Gospels be historically accurate. To him, the important element is that within the person of Jesus of Nazareth, God has penetrated human history. He proposed to understand the Gospels as witnesses to the faith of the disciples and early church. He introduced the idea that the Gospels were *myths* preserving early beliefs in Jesus that form the basis of Christian faith.

While it is easy to understand that Strauss's views would be received as a challenge and as a threat to faith, his ideas are surprisingly contemporary. Today, we are experiencing a revival in our understanding of *myth*.[10] It is no longer understood as contrary to truth, but part and parcel with the deepest and most profound kind of truth. Strauss displayed both the promise and the pitfalls of scholarship. He could be seen as a threat to established religion. Others would see him as a champion of faith, establishing a foundation for faith that includes intelligence. On the one hand, we see in Strauss one of the fundamental errors of the search for the historical Jesus, namely the idea that there is a difference between the 'Christ of faith' and the 'Jesus of history'. On the other hand, we see an ability to avoid one of the glaring pitfalls of the current search for the historical Jesus. He ascribed to Jesus attributes that he did not himself possess.[11]

One of the first to travel to the Holy Land to conduct 'research' on the background of Jesus was Ernst Renan (1823-1892). He wrote a biography

---

[9] David Friedrich Strauss, *Der Christus des Glaubens un der Jesus der Geschihcte,* trans. Leander E Keck, Fortress Press, Philadelphia, 1977.

[10] While the word *myth* conjures impressions of falsehood and fairytale, properly understood *myth* is a story containing a truth so profound that it cannot be expressed in propositional form. Thus, the truth being expressed requires the vehicle of a story.

[11] As I will show, one of the problems with the so-called *new quest* for the historical Jesus fails in this important regard.

of Jesus called *The Life of Jesus.*[12] A product of the time, it envisioned Jesus
as a preacher of liberal, progressive, 19th-century morality. As a rationalist,
Renan looked for explanations in nature for any miracle stories that seemed
far-fetched. He believed that increased understanding of natural geographical
phenomena in Palestine would yield understanding of the stories told about
Jesus in the Gospels. He believed that the stories of the Bible should be in
harmony with the 19th-century rational understanding of the natural world.
The attempt to explain certain miracle stories in terms of natural phenomena
continues today.

Others who visited the Holy Land to advance their understanding
of the Bible and the life of the historical Jesus included missionaries such as
the American Edward Robinson, who is popularly known for his archaeological
research. Like all missionaries in the 19th century, Robinson engaged in a
variety of fields of research including identifying places mentioned in the
Bible. He is credited for identifying the remains of a monumental archway on
the Temple Mount from the time of Jesus. Visitors were drawn to the Holy
Land in the 19th century, like many today, to seek the historical Jesus in
geography and archaeology.

19th-century scholarship on the historical Jesus was very
productive. Many scholars contributed to the shape of the modern search
for the historical Jesus. Johanness Weiss produced a 'life' of Jesus,
anticipating the modern proliferation of scholarly pictures of the historical
Jesus. Karl Schmidt proposed that the Gospels be understood as theological,
literary devices rather than as history. Wilhelm Wrede asserted that the
framework of the Gospel of Mark was constructed by its author to suit his
purpose. He claimed that it is not an historical outline.

Albert Schweitzer favoured an image of Jesus as an eschatological
prophet of the coming new kingdom. He concluded, however, that the efforts
over the previous 200 years to peel off the layers of faith tradition in order to
discover the 'real' Jesus had come to naught. He thought that there simply
was not enough reliable information about the historical Jesus to construct
a biographical image of Jesus.

The first stage of the search for the historical Jesus lasted through
the 19th century and yielded important discoveries that have become
normative ideas in contemporary biblical scholarship. For instance, the idea
that the Gospels are based on written sources that were based on oral sources
gained wide acceptance. This is the almost unchallenged view today. Further,
scholars came to understand that the Gospels represent *traditions about*
Jesus deriving from the early church, not life stories of Jesus deriving from

[12] Ernst Renan, *The Life of Jesus*, The Modern Library, New York, 1927.

eyewitnesses. In the Gospels, church *kerygma*, i.e., proclamation, is embedded in the accounts about Jesus.

Still, the absence of hard historical data doomed the search. The experience of World War I produced wide spread pessimism throughout Western civilization and undermined scholarly confidence in the ability to uncover absolute truth. Scholars gave up the hope of distinguishing the historical Jesus from the Christ of faith.

Less than a century later, though, the latest quest for the historical Jesus is in high gear again. Since the time that Schweitzer put the old quest to rest in 1906, a number of important collections of ancient manuscripts were discovered, such as the Nag Hammadi library and the Dead Sea Scrolls. These provide new data that bring fresh air to the musty corridors of history. Certainly we have a much better picture of Christian origins today than the ones scholars concocted 100 years ago. New techniques of historical research also raise hopes that the dim shadow of the historical Jesus can be brought into the light of day. But has the new search really shed the liabilities of the old one?

The revived quest for the historical Jesus, inaugurated by Kaseman and Robinson, builds on the earlier scholarship, but has the advantage that today there are more source materials—thanks to new archaeological discoveries. Still, advanced data does not guarantee advanced scholarship. It seems as though the scholars of the 'new' search stumble where their forebears did. Scholars of the new search have produced a wide variety of pictures of Jesus, many closely resembling their artists. This shows how difficult it is to come up with a definitive one. Indeed, one of the most striking features of the renewed search for the historical Jesus is the absolute lack of any consensus among historical Jesus scholars about the figure of the historical Jesus itself. Scholars variously describe Jesus as a 'marginal Jew' (Meier), a major figure in mainstream Jewish thought (Vermes), a 'revolutionary peasant' (Crossan), an exorcist (Twelftree), a teacher of Wisdom (Borg), a wandering cynic philosopher (Mack), an eschatological prophet (Koester) and, among other things, a rabbi from the Hillelian school of Pharisaic Judaism.

Harvard's Helmut Koester, one of the giants of contemporary New Testament scholarship, sums up the problem with such a proliferation of portraits of Jesus. He puts the matter this way, 'The fallacy of the modern quest is that scholars only see in Jesus things that they themselves believe.'[13] The modern 'pictures' of Jesus often bear a remarkable resemblance to their makers, like so many self-portraits. Would the historical Jesus really think like us? Did the historical Jesus conform to the values and conduct of those

---

[13] Lecture at Harvard Divinity School, 29 September 1995.

around him? James D G Dunn remarks, 'The Jesus of cheap scholarship, the Jesus-as-I-personally-like-to-imagine-him, has been zealously promoted through the past decade like a fizzy new drink.'[14] When our personal pictures of Jesus become too familiar, when we are too comfortable with the Jesus that we have fashioned in our minds, when our images of Jesus too nearly conform to our own values, then the Jesus of *our* faith ceases to be the universally reforming, transforming person he most probably was. A Jesus—historical or not—who does not lead us out of comfortable complacency, who does not prod us, call us, inspire us to deeper, higher and broader understandings of our purpose in the world, is not a Jesus worth walking with. The conspicuous lack of consensus among scholars about Jesus and the convenient way in which impressions of Jesus reinforce personal preferences are sure signs that the pursuit for the historical Jesus is deeply flawed. A closer examination of the new quest is in order.

Geza Vermes is a leading biblical scholar and a recognized authority on the Dead Sea Scrolls. He is also a well-known advocate of the scholarly attempt to recover the 'historical Jesus' from the 'Christ of faith'. Typical of those involved in historical Jesus scholarship, he presumes that the Christ of faith obscures the Jesus of history. In an article in the 17 August 1999 edition of *The Jerusalem Report,* he describes his method. Starting from the saviour figure of Jesus contained in the decrees, councils and dogma of the Catholic Church, he says:

> ... I intend to move backwards: from the Fourth Gospel, to the Acts of the Apostles, to the beginning of Christian preaching but still far below the level of dogmatic Christianity. Then there are the first three gospels, the synoptic gospels, where you begin to see the historical figure ... And then the final step would be to try to go beyond the gospels to discover the mysterious figure that is already to some extent elaborated and stylized even in the earliest stages of Christian tradition.

Vermes illustrates an array of presuppositions that are adopted in nearly all historical Jesus scholarship without critical examination. At its root is the assumption that there is a difference between the Jesus of history and the Jesus who is presented in the Gospels and the traditions of the Church. Considered logically, if this is presumed as a premise, then of course it will be

---

[14] Luke Timothy Johnson, *The Real Jesus: The Misguided Quest for the Historical Jesus and the Truth of the Traditional Gospels*, HarperSanFrancisco, San Francisco, 1996, front matter.

found in the conclusion.

Next, Vermes assumes that the Jesus of history can be discovered by peeling off the layers of tradition that have accrued in the development of the Gospels. He assumes that later developments in the tradition are less historically reliable than earlier ones. His task, thus, is to peel off these later layers as one would peel off the layers of an onion or, in the manner of an archaeologist, to dig deeper into the underlying strata. Such an approach carries obvious problems. Vermes expresses the supposition that the synoptic Gospels, 'where you begin to see the historical figure' are more historically reliable than John. There is no rule, however, that later developments in the Gospel tradition, such as the Gospel of John, have less reliable historical data than earlier ones.[15] It is very possible that there are details in the Gospel of John that preserve a more accurate historical picture than any of its Gospel predecessors. Scholars make a similar assumption when they presume that the sources used by Matthew and Luke contain more historically reliable data than their Gospels. This presumption cannot be proved.

That texts should be treated like archaeological tells is not unique to Vermes. A leading historical Jesus scholar recently produced a book entitled *Excavating Q: The History and Setting of the Sayings Gospel*.[16] Widely accepted, yet unexamined, the process of 'onion-peeling' literary texts to derive historical truth is a presupposition that merits closer inspection.

Vermes confidently asserts his plan to dig even deeper than the earliest written sources about Jesus, i.e., '… beyond the gospels …' At this stage, which all historical Jesus scholars aspire to reach, scholarship is 100 percent speculation. Even when the tools of the historical-critical method are applied to the texts and are successful in discerning traces of early layers of the development of the narrative tradition, we are entitled to only the most tentative positions and qualified conclusions. Leaving aside for a moment the reality that historiography is never about objective Truth, historical Jesus scholarship at this stage is about plausibility and possibility more than probability. Getting beneath the Gospel testimony about Jesus is conjectural at best.

Finally, Vermes presumes that even the 'elaborated and stylised' picture of Jesus contained in the earliest traditions about Jesus is less valuable

---

[15] Although there is no scholarly unanimity on the subject, the consensus is overwhelming that John is the last of the four Gospels to have been written. Mark is considered to be the earliest of the four Gospels and Matthew and Luke are held by most scholars to have been written at roughly the same time, about ten years after Mark and about 15 years prior to the writing of John. This is the position that I take.

[16] John Kloppenborg Verbin, *Excavating Q: The History and Setting of the Sayings Gospel*, Augsburg Fortress Publishers, Minneapolis, 2000.

than the *actual* Jesus, i.e., the person of Jesus of Nazareth. This latter belief is, perhaps, the most questionable of all the unexamined assumptions resident in any quest for the historical Jesus. Is the historical Jesus the subject of anyone's faith? Do we encounter the historical Jesus in our faith walks or do we encounter the resurrected Christ?

In his book, *The Real Jesus: The Misguided Quest for the Historical Jesus*,[17] Luke Timothy Johnson forcefully challenges the assumptions of those, like Vermes, who suppose that the recovery of the 'historical' Jesus is both possible and desirable. Johnson points out that historical Jesus scholarship is characterized by mistaken assumptions about what history actually is, reckless inferences from 'historical' data, and dubious conclusions.

What is missing from the search? For one thing: data. Notwithstanding significant advances in biblical criticism and astounding archaeological discoveries, the pool of evidence has not grown enough to yield reliable conclusions about the historical Jesus. Notwithstanding the discoveries at Nag Hammadi and Qumran in the mid 1940s, our information about the time of Jesus in general and the person of Jesus in particular is too limited to yield confident conclusions about him. In the case of the former, most scholars agree that the writings from Nag Hammadi date to the 2nd century AD at the earliest.[18] In the case of the Qumran texts, while they provide new insight into one group of Judeans at the time of Jesus, they do not enable us to draw conclusions about Jesus himself. The multiplication of mutually incompatible scholarly pictures of Jesus testifies to the failure of the new quest. If the evidence were so much more advanced in this century than in either of the previous two, we would not have the phenomenon of so many diverse images of the historical Jesus.

Beyond the problem of historical data, however, is a more difficult challenge to the attempt to formulate a picture of the historical Jesus. Even if sufficient data were available to us, recovering the 'historical' Jesus could never attain the level of arrogant confidence displayed by many historical Jesus scholars, because the process of historiography never results in objective knowledge. Many historical Jesus scholars overlook the obvious reality that the process of historical thinking always involves a subject, namely the historian. No historian can escape his or her own culturally conditioned prejudices, assumptions and biases. It is not desirable to do so. Indeed, the idea that 'objective truth' is itself possible to discover and desirable to pursue is a culturally conditioned notion. All modern efforts to

---

[17] Johnson, *The Real Jesus: The Misguided Quest for the Historical Jesus and the Truth of the Traditional Gospels*.

[18] A few, such as Harvard's Helmut Koester, favour a date as early as the middle of the first century AD.

uncover the historical Jesus, from the 18th century to the present day, are marred by the imposition of modern intellectual prejudices on 1st-century documents.

Be this as it may, we can advance toward an understanding of who Jesus of Nazareth was. Not even radical categorical doubt can doom us to total ignorance. However, we must distinguish between those things that are knowable beyond the shadow of a doubt and those things about which we can only conjecture, even when our conjectures have higher levels of probability.

There are two categories of general sources about Jesus. The first is our general knowledge about his world. The second is written testimony, including the Gospels. We can draw general conclusions with either absolute certainty or an extremely high level of probability based on what we know about his world. And we can draw conclusions with greater or lesser degrees of certainty from written sources, as well.

On the subject of Jesus' birth, we have an example of a biographical detail about which we can be reasonably, but not entirely certain. It is more likely than not that Jesus was born in Bethlehem as the written testimony states. There is, of course, reason to speculate that Matthew and Luke posited the birth of Jesus in Bethlehem to accomplish the goal of indicating that Jesus was an heir to David. However, it is not likely that they would have come up with the same mechanism to accomplish the same goal independently of one another, unless there was a tradition circulating that Jesus was indeed born there. Far more likely it is that they knew the freely circulating tradition about Jesus' birth in Bethlehem and found it convenient to use it to emphasize the more important truth that Jesus was in the royal lineage, an heir to the throne at least in some sense.[19]

We can know that Jesus of Nazareth was the product of complex cultural and diverse social environments, because we know he was from Galilee and this is the sort of environment that Galilee was in the Early Roman Period. We know that he would have been exposed to lifestyles identified with both rural village life and urban city life. He would have been exposed to a wide variety of ethnic groups. We know this, because the early written testimony about him identifies him with the village of Nazareth. Nazareth was a small village situated within four miles of Sepphoris, dependent upon

---

[19] Birth details were not a necessary part of Hellenistic historiography. A gospel could be complete with them. The authors of Mark and John, for instance, got by nicely without any infancy narratives at all. Matthew and Luke included this material to make a point. It was the point that mattered, not its historicity. If it were historically correct, that was a bonus.

Sepphoris and its commercial activity for everything. Both Nazareth and Sepphoris were within a few miles of one of two major superhighways, i.e., the Via Maris. The region of the lower Galilee was well known as a place of great cultural diversity (Isaiah 9: 1). There is no known instance of a person in the ancient world being identified with a town (Saul of Tarsus, Mileto of Sardis, Nicalaus of Damascus, John of Gishala, Philo of Alexandria), unless that person was indeed from that town in some sense.[20] Thus, Jesus was either born in Nazareth or he had enough experience in Nazareth to earn the designation 'of Nazareth' in his proper name. In either case, there is no reasonable way that he could have had that kind of experience without being exposed to the world around Nazareth, unless he was like the man in Plato's Allegory of the Cave and no witness suggests that Jesus was a hermit.

Regarding details of Jesus' physical features, traits normally associated with modern biographies, we know very little about Jesus. We do not know what he looked like. All modern representations of Jesus are based on artists' interpretations. He could have been from any of several race categories. His ethnic group, Israelite, did not rule out his being either what we would call African or Caucasian. Israelites could be either or both. Preoccupation with skin colour is a modern not an ancient distinction. We know that the ancient world was racially diverse, although racial characteristics do not seem to have been important.[21] From mosaics, statues, frescos and funerary art, we get a picture of the Early Roman Period as one in which what we would refer to as racial groups were widely dispersed.

Neither do we know how Jesus wore his hair. The Gospels of Matthew and Mark picture John the Baptist as an ascetic of sorts, a Nazerite, to be exact and depict his clothing. They include this information only because it is relevant to understanding John in a certain light. Luke obviously does not share the interest in characterizing John in this way, because he does not include that detail about him. If it is an accurate historical detail, then it is probable that John was not clean-shaven, because Nazerites displayed their station in life by not shaving or cutting their hair. If Jesus was a member of the Nazerites or another group, such as the Cynics, then he also

---

[20] The question of birth in a particular place based on that place being part of a person's proper name is another question. The fact that Jesus is universally identified with Nazareth, when his proper name occurs suggests to some scholars that Jesus was born there. If he were born in Bethlehem, one would expect that he would be called *Jesus of Bethlehem*. However, no one has studied the question enough to conclude that the designation of a place name in a person's proper name implies birth in that place and geographical mobility is well attested in the Early Roman Period. No one can rule out the sort of relocation posited in both Luke's and Matthew's infancy material.

[21] Ethnic distinctions, on the other hand, were very important.

might have let his beard and hair grow. But it is not likely that he was a member of either of these groups, because he does not display other characteristics associated with them. Thus, we can conjecture that Jesus was clean-shaven like every other Hellenised male in his day. The only times in any early Roman art when a male is depicted other than clean-shaven is when that male is in a period of grief. At such times, it was customary for men to refrain from shaving. Jesus probably was clean-shaven and wore his hair short, except when he was grieving.

But how do we know that Jesus was a Hellenised male? We know this with a high degree of probability from our two sources: what we know generally about Jesus' world and what we know specifically from written sources. It is abundantly clear from all historical data, archaeological and literary, that Judea and Galilee were thoroughly Hellenised by the time Jesus lived.[22] Even small Galilean towns such as Bethsaida and Capernaum were Hellenised. Excavations revealed that their streets were laid out according to the Hippodamian plan, i.e., typical of Hellenistic and Roman city plans. Big cities, such as Sepphoris and Jerusalem were built with all the typically Hellenistic architectural features: theatres, baths, stoa, agora, etc.[23] Coins in common usage were minted with Greek lettering. At least fifty percent of all inscriptions from the Early Roman Period were written in Greek. The Gospels, which were written in Greek, depict Jesus as having conversations with people from a wide variety of ethnic groups. This could only be accomplished by speaking Greek. There is never a suggestion that Jesus employed a translator and it is highly doubtful that Pontius Pilate, to name but one of Jesus' interlocutors, spoke Aramaic.[24] All relevant literary sources presume Jesus used Greek and was familiar with Greek styles, customs and culture.

Jesus' station in life is a subject on which there is no consensus. There is no archaeological evidence to establish his socio-economic status. There are no inscriptions with his name in them. No one erected a statue to him. Aside from Christian literature, there is little literary testimony about Jesus, but there is some.[25] These references indicate, however, only that people outside the movement that developed around Jesus noticed the

---

[22] See Martin Hengel, *The Hellenization of Judaea,* 1989; *Judaism and Hellenism,* 1974.

[23] See above, 'From Alexander to Jesus'.

[24] Aramaic was Jesus' native language.

[25] Josephus, the Roman historians Seutonius and Tacitus, the Roman governor Pliny the Younger, and the satirist Lucian of Samosata refer more or less obliquely to Jesus. Of these, Josephus refers directly to Jesus. 'Now there was about this time Jesus, a wise man, if it be lawful to call him a man, for he was a doer of wonderful works—a teacher of such men a receive the truth with pleasure. He drew over to him both many of the Jews, and many of the Gentiles. He was Christ; and when Pilate, at the suggestion of

movement itself. Christian literature is the best literary source for information about Jesus' role in life, but we must draw inferences from it.

The testimony from early Christian literature suggests that Jesus came from the class of his society that sociologists call the 'retainer' class, i.e., a class of people who were connected with the ruling class through employment or other functions. He is repeatedly called 'Rabbi'. Rabbis were educated, a characteristic of those on higher rungs of the social ladder. He was skilled in arts of speaking, persuasion and healing. He was well acquainted with Israelite sacred writings and was accustomed to disputation concerning their interpretation. These arts and skills were studied and taught in schools, suggesting further that Jesus was educated. The Gospels continually present Jesus as being connected to the Pharisees. Not only does he continually get invited to eat with them he also discourses with them. Both activities reflect some type of collegiality. Further, the nature of these discourses is reflected in the Gospels. The types of engagement on issues they depict suggest he was well acquainted with the techniques of disputation. Even the sharp disagreements he has with the Pharisees suggests collegiality as well. That he has a network of friends with important assets and the influence to call upon these as resources further suggests someone whom is highly esteemed. He is at home in other peoples' houses and he can call upon friends to supply lodging and a place for meals. He is sought out by people of high standing. 'Friendship' and the conventions associated with it occupy a prominent position in the Gospel narratives. Clearly, Jesus has accumulated enough good will from these friends that he can cash in some social chips to his advantage when necessary. These actions are in complete conformity with his society's conventions of friendship and suggest a person from a relatively high level of society.

Sometimes, the popular tradition that Jesus was the son of a carpenter is taken as a sign that Jesus came from the class of artisans. Aside from this being inconsistent with the way in which Jesus is depicted in the Gospels, this is not a safe assumption. First of all, the Greek word, *tekton,* which is usually translated as 'carpenter' does not mean 'carpenter' at all, but artisan. Further the expression, 'son of a *tekton* (artisan, Mt. 13: 5)' was

---

the principal men amongst us, had condemned him to the cross, those that loved him at the first did not forsake him, for he appeared to them alive again the third day, as the divine prophets had foretold these and ten thousand other wonderful things concerning him; and the tribe of Christians, so named from him, are not extinct at this day.' Josephus, *Antiquities of the Jews,* book 18, chapter 3. 3, trans. William Whitson, *The Works of Josephus,* vol. IV, Baker Book House, Grand Rapids, MI, p.11.

a colloquial expression used to designate a particularly wise person.[26] The metaphorical use of *tekton* is attested in the Talmud and if this usage was current in the 1st century then the tradition that Jesus was the son of an artisan in a literal sense may have to be put to pasture.

Those who insist that Jesus was a peasant leader of a peasant movement have yet to explain whom in 1st-century Palestine would have paid any attention to a peasant who preached wisdom? There is no example in any ancient source of a peasant who started a lasting movement of any kind.[27] Peasant movements were decidedly poorly organized. They lacked skilled leadership. They did not have coherent ideologies and they were conspicuously short-lived. Nothing about the movements that developed around the figure of Jesus remotely resembles the profile of a peasant movement. The Gospel evidence is that Jesus included people from different social groups and all stations on the social ladder and the Gospel testimony does not suggest that Jesus' movement took root among peasants—even though peasants were a constituency of that movement. People like Lazarus, Nicodemus and Joseph of Arimithea were situated socially somewhere among the upper thirty percent of society. Jesus' own disciples included skilled workers and at least one person who was part of the ruling apparatus, namely Matthew, the tax collector. Tax farmers were not drawn from the peasantry. No peasant would be invited to eat at any Pharisees home. No peasant would be approached in the manner the elders of the Judeans approach Jesus on behalf of the centurion at Capernaum (Luke 7: 1-10). When we add the testimony of Paul's letters, written twenty years earlier than the earliest Gospel, we get a clear picture showing that the earliest churches for which we have evidence were urban and included members from high strata of society. How would a peasant from a class-conscious society have appealed to such high-ranking people? In Jesus' world, pedigree mattered.

Beyond a bare sketch of Jesus we can mine other fragments of historical bedrock from the New Testament texts. I take it that these fragments are more important than the sketches we are able to draw.

Many historical Jesus researchers believe that the most historically reliable texts of the Gospels are those parts of the texts that are identified as 'sayings' of Jesus. Scholars often refer to a 'sayings source'. This is believed to have been a source that circulated orally before being committed to writing.

---

[26] David Flusser, *Jesus*, Herder and Herder, New York, 1969, p.20;

[27] The best study on peasant movements is *Bandits, Prophets, and Messiahs* by Richard Horsley. He identifies several peasant movements during the 1st century AD, points out that none of these were able to articulate coherent ideologies or policies for social change and concludes this failure is precisely the cause of their ineffectiveness.

It included proverbial wisdom sayings, allegories, parables and prophetic sayings, such as the beatitudes.[28] This source is usually designated 'Q', and it was a primary source that was used by Matthew and Luke. This source only exists as a part of those Gospels, but I agree with the scholarly consensus that it circulated prior to the Gospels and represents an early stratum in the development of the Gospels. However, I do not agree that Q provides us a direct, clear view of the historical Jesus or the words of the historical Jesus. No one can determine to what extent those who compiled these sayings acted upon them. Q scholars now say that Q had two different stages in its development, thus acknowledging a degree of early editorial activity. It is very possible that the sayings source accurately remembers the original words of Jesus, but we have no evidence for it prior to its appearance in the Gospels of Matthew and Luke, *ca.* AD 85.

More important, however, I believe that there is an even older, more reliable layer of textual evidence for the historical Jesus. This material is from the passion narratives, the *traditions* about the Last Supper preserved in Paul's Letter to the Corinthians, the words of Jesus contained in those traditions and those contained in Mark's story of the Last Supper. This is where one can almost hear Jesus' voice. The core of the passion narratives preceded the sayings source.[29]

There are two occasions where Paul cites 'a tradition' that he received and handed over to the Corinthians (1 Cor. 11: 23, 15: 3). Both instances are related directly to Jesus' passion. Both recitations of the tradition are clearly brief repetitions of it. In each case, much information is left out, but Paul's citation of these traditions presumes acquaintance with a longer version of them. He cites brief formulas that encapsulate the traditions, not the traditions themselves. The traditions he cites, thus, circulated in a larger context of story and ritual. Since this is a tradition that Paul received, we know that already before the time Paul is writing, the earliest church placed the fact of Jesus' death in the context of Israel's scripture and understood his death in specific theological terms. It understood that Jesus 'died for our sins in accordance with the scriptures' (1 Cor. 15: 3). The broader context of the tradition is alluded to clearly in Paul's recitation of the tradition. It is closely linked to the Israelite scriptures, especially Isaiah 53. It is rooted in a ritual act that Jesus himself instituted, namely the giving and receiving

---

[28] See Burton Mack, *The Lost Gospel,* 1993.

[29] These biblical traditions are paralleled in a non-biblical source, called the *Didache.* The *Didache* is an ancient source. Eusebius mentions it in his list of apocryphal New Testament texts. Clement of Alexandria cites it as scripture. Its name derives from the subtitle of one of its manuscripts, 'The teaching of the Twelve'.

of bread and the cup.

The story of Jesus' death and resurrection, not any of his teachings is the heart of the oldest tradition. It is a new story that is tied to the ancient story of Israel. It is formalized and made repeatable in ritual. Embedded in this tradition are the words of Jesus, 'This is my body which is given for you. Do this in remembrance of me ... This cup is the new covenant in my blood. Do this as often as you drink it, in remembrance of me' (1 Cor. 11: 24-25). These words go back farther and with more certainty than any of the sayings of Jesus contained in the Q document.

The words of Jesus quoted in the tradition Paul cites refer to a 'new covenant in my blood'. It is 'new' only in contrast to the covenant between God and Israel. It is 'new', because it was never done before, even though the language of covenant is old and familiar and rooted in an esteemed history. Paul adds the words, 'For as often as you eat this bread and drink the cup, you proclaim the lord's death until he comes' (1 Cor. 11: 26). 'Until he comes' is distinctly ominous, foretelling a future event.

Mark's retelling of the same tradition is almost the same as Paul's. It also quotes Jesus and refers to the 'covenant' sealed in blood (Mark 14: 24). It also looks forward to a future event. 'I will not drink it until that day when I drink it in the new kingdom of God' (Mar 14: 25). In both contexts, the tradition of Jesus' death is ritualised, tied to Israel's history through language and understood as having future significance.

In the ancient world, the association of a specific ritual with an ancient, venerated tradition is the common pattern in establishing new communities. It occurs at the founding of new peoples. The rituals in Olympia and Delphi were closely connected with Homeric stories to create a new self-consciousness as *Hellenes,* i.e., Greeks. Virgil's epic *Aeneid* was linked to the rituals of the emperor's personal cult to become the new story of the Roman people. The retelling of the Exodus story in association with the ritual of Passover served to constitute the people of Israel and is another obvious parallel.

In Corinth, Paul reinforced the connection between the eucharistic ritual and the story of Jesus not for the purpose of starting a new *religion*, but for the purpose of giving identity and cohesiveness to a new *people*. Paul did not set out to create a new social group—one more square in the social mosaic. The Jesus movement was not meant to be another new cult, one more among a smorgasbord table of cults. It was meant to be an entirely new order of community, an entirely new *people*. This is why the Gospels depict him so clearly redefining the terms of social, ethnic and family relationships. Had the early followers of Jesus, already constituting themselves as distinct communities within twenty years of his death and resurrection, wanted to establish themselves as religious cults, they would have chosen language that was distinctly religious. But their terminology, e.g., *ekklesia* (church), *euangelion* (gospel), *huiou tou theou* (son of god), *soter* (saviour), etc. is drawn not from the religious culture of their day, but from the political culture. Paul's rhetorical choices of metaphors for the church are also drawn from a pool of images, ideas and analogies that were commonly used to define political entities. For example, his use of the metaphor of the body and its parts was a common illustration for the people of Rome and the Roman legion. He simply transfers stock language from the political arena to the church. He is aware that the founding of this new people is rooted in Jesus' own institution of the ritual we call the Lord's Supper. He is also aware that this ritual was part of a larger context of meals establishing community. This context derives from the ministry of Jesus himself.

All evidence suggests that the act of sharing meals (and pointing forward to a new era—as in the constitutive rituals of the Hellenistic world) was an integral part of Jesus' ministry. Paul presumed knowledge of this. It is corroborated by Mark's account of the institution of the Lord's Supper, which quite possibly precedes the compilation of the sayings source, Q.

One of the presuppositions of much historical Jesus research, as I pointed out above, is that layers of interpretation obscure the identity of Jesus of Nazareth. According to this view, the early church distorted Jesus' identity by wrapping their information about Jesus in a theological package. Jesus, as he appears in the Gospels, is a 'stylised' and 'elaborated' Jesus, not the *true* Jesus. In such a view, there is a contrast between the historical Jesus and the Christ of Faith. It presumes that the Gospels are less reliable than the hypothetical Q document in reconstructing the historical Jesus.

I contend that the Christ of faith is rooted in the historical Jesus, i.e., there is clear continuity between the words and ministry of Jesus and accounts of Jesus in the Gospels and in Paul's first letter to the Corinthians. The most reliable evidence we have is not about who Jesus was, but rather about what he did.

This is not to say that there is no distinction between Jesus of Nazareth, whose ministry inspired the movement that became Christianity, and the figure of Jesus that is elaborated in scripture and tradition—what has come to be called the Christ of faith. Nor does it discredit the scholarship of many fine, conscientious scholars. The search for the historical Jesus, has yielded deep insights and added to our collective knowledge about the sociological, cultural, political and religious milieu of 1st-century Palestine.

My point is simply that the Gospels contain more historically reliable information than many scholars give them credit to contain. The popularity and sensation associated with the contemporary search for the historical

Jesus should not be equated with truth. Much of the best-known Jesus research has exploited and reinforced the popular thirst for sensation. *Newseek, Time* and *US News and World Report* are just a few of the 'news' outlets that have jumped on the opportunity to publish sensational conclusions without caring much to apply critical questions. The Jesus Seminar is subject to this same criticism. It generates a lot of heat, but does not cast much light on the subject. It is long on sizzle, but short on steak. And, it is particularly misleading. The absence of critical scholarship in the search for the historical Jesus is one of its dubious distinctions.

What difference does the scholarly search for the historical Jesus make to faith? None. In the end, the search for the historical Jesus, properly understood, is distinct and only tangentially related to the subject of Christian faith. The Christ of faith and the historical Jesus are two separate figures notwithstanding the continuity between them. No one worships Jesus of Nazareth. On the contrary, the Risen Christ is the centre of Christian faith and the object of worship. What is preserved in Paul's letters, the Gospels and Acts, the rest of the New Testament canon and the traditions of the church is, thankfully, not merely an historical record. Rather it is the record of the encounter between people of faith and the living Lord, the Risen Christ. Those who have experienced this encounter know that it *is* historical. It occurs in time and space over and over again. Moreover, this encounter is as real as real ever gets.

Appendix 1
ANCIENT TEXTS

The following texts are provided to give the reader experience with ancient texts. These are just a sampling of texts that historians use to reconstruct the past. They are particularly germane to the study of biblical history. I am grateful to Harvard University Press for permission to reprint copyright translations.

Assorted letters, notes, petitions revealing aspects of daily life

The following texts should be read with an interest in gleaning bits of information about daily life in the ancient world. The assortment of texts makes reference to relations between men and women, between parents and children, between workers and employers, attitudes about marriage and divorce, and also gives insights into such mundane topics as clothing and dinner parties. These texts were discovered in Oxyrhynchus, Egypt during excavations of graves, stores and garbage dumps. They provide a valuable window into the lives of every day people.

A Marriage contract, ca. AD 260 (Papyri, *A S Hunt, 1932*):

For good fortune. Aurelia Thaesis daughter of Eudaemon and of Herais, of Oxyrhynchus, acting with Aurelius Theon also called Nepotianus and however he is styled, has given her daughter Aurelia Tausiris in marriage to Aurelias Arsinous son of Tryphon and of Demetria, of the said city, as husband, to whom the said giver brings as the dowry of her said daughter the bride in common gold on the Oxyrhynchite standard a necklace ... with a stone, weighing without the stone 13 quarters, a brooch with 5 stones set in gold...a pair of earrings with 10 pearls;...and questioned concerning the aforesaid dowry by the giver of the bride, Aurelia Thaesis, the bridegroom Aurelius Arsinous acknowledged that he had received the full number at the aforesaid weight and valuation. Wherefore let the parties to the marriage live together blamelessly, observing the duties of marriage, and let the bridegroom supply his wife with all the things necessary in proportion to his means. But if—which heaven forbid—owing to disagreement a separation takes place between the parties, the bridegroom shall restore to the giver of the bride ...the aforesaid dowry in full within sixty days ... If at the time of the separation the bride is pregnant, the bridegroom shall give her for the expenses of her confinement 40 drachmae ... I Aurelia Thaesis, have given my daughter in marriage to the abovementioned Arsinous ... I, Aurelius Theon also called Nepotianus, acted with her and wrote on her behalf, as she is illiterate. I, Aurelius Arsinous, have received the aforesaid dowry, and if—which heaven forbid—a separation takes place, I will restore it as stated above, and in answer to the formal questions I have given my consent.

*A divorce agreement, ca. AD 305 (*Papyri, *A S Hunt, 1932):*

... Soulis, grave digger, of the toparchy of Kusis, to Senpsais daughter of Psais and of Tees, grave digger, of the same toparchy, greeting. Since through some evil spirit it has come about that we have separated from each other in respect of our common wedded life, I, the aforesaid Soul, herewith acknowledge that before sending her away I have received in full all the objects given to her by me ... that she is free to depart and marry whom she chooses; and I, the aforesaid Senpsais, acknowledge that I have received in full from him, the aforesaid Soul, all that was given to him by the dowry ... we will not henceforth take proceedings against each other about any matter at all of any kind ... because the separation is absolute. This deed of separation, written in duplicate and signed, shall be valid and guaranteed as if deposited in a public record office, and in answer to the formal question I have given my assent.

*A letter from a wife to her husband, 168 BC (*Papyri, *A S Hunt, 1932):*

Isias to her brother Hephaestion greeting. If you are well and other things are going right, it would accord with the prayer which I continually make before the gods. I myself and the child and all the household are in good health and think of you always. When I received your letter from Horus, in which you announce that you are in detention in the Serapeum in Memphis, for the news that you are well I straightaway thanked the gods, but about your not coming home, when all the others who had been secluded there have come, I am ill pleased, because after having piloted myself and your child through such bad times and been driven to every extremity owing to the price of corn I thought that now at least, with you at home, I should enjoy some respite, whereas you have not even thought of coming home nor given any regard to our circumstances, remembering how I was in want of everything while you were still here, not to mention the long lapse of time and these critical days, during which you have sent us nothing. As, moreover, Horus, who delivered the letter has brought news of your having been released from detention, I am thoroughly ill pleased. Notwithstanding, as your mother also is annoyed, for her sake as well as for mine please return to the city, if nothing more pressing holds you back. You will do me a favor by taking care of your bodily health. Goodbye. Year 2, Epeiph 30. Addressed to Hephaestion.

*From Sarapion to his brothers 154 BC (*Papyri, *A S Hunt, 1932):*

Sarapion to his brothers Ptolemaeus and Apollonius greeting. If you are well, it would be excellent. I myself am well. I have made a contract with the daughter of Hepserus and intend to marry her in the month of Mesore. Please send me half a chous of oil. I have written to you to let you know. Goodbye. Year 28, Epeiph 21. Come for the wedding day, Apollonius. Addressed to Ptolemaeus and Apollonius.

*A letter from a husband to his wife, 1 BC (*Papyri, *A S Hunt, 1932):*

Hilarion to his sister Alis very many greetings, likewise to my lady Berous and Apollinarion. Know that we are still in Alexandria. Do not be anxious; if they really go home, I will stay in Alexandria. I beg and entreat you, take care of the little one, and as soon as we receive our pay I will send it up to you. If by chance you bear a child, if it is a boy, let it be, if it is a girl, cast it out. You have said to Aphrodisias "Do not forget me.' How can I forget you? I beg you then not to be anxious. The 29th year of Caesar, Pauni 23. Deliver to Alis from Hilarion.

*A letter of commendation, AD 25 (*Papyri, *A S Hunt, 1932):*

Theon to the most honored Tyrannus very many greetings. Heraclides, the bearer of this letter, is my brother, wherefore I entreat you with all my power to take him under your protection. I have also asked your brother Hermias by letter to inform you about him. You will do me the greatest favor if you let him win your approval. Before all else I pray that you may have health and the best of success, unharmed by the evil eye. Goodbye. To Tyrannus the diocetes.

*A letter from a son to his mother, second century (*Papyri, *A S Hunt, 1932):*

Antonius Longus to Nilous his mother very many greetings. I pray always for your health; everyday I make supplication for you before the lord Serapis. I would have you know that I did not expect that you were going up to the metropolis; for that reason I did not come to the city myself. I was ashamed to come to Karanis, because I go about in filth. I wrote to you that I am naked. I beg you, mother, be reconciled to me. Well, I know what I have brought on myself. I have received a fitting lesson. I know that I have sinned. I heard from ... who found you in the Arsinoite nome, and he has told you everything correctly. Do you know that I would rather be maimed than feel that I still owe a man an obol? ... Addressed to Nilous his mother from Antonius Longus her son.

*From an agent to his employer, second century (*Papyri, *A S Hunt, 1932):*

... stream, and the entrance and exit for all the workmen is by the side way; but when we bring the work to a happy conclusion, then the roof also will be made secure. The stair has been balustered and the portico will have a balustrade made for it along with that of the small dining hall. The beams of the windows of the large dining hall have today been partly fixed. The second water cooling closet is to be roofed tomorrow ... I have sent to you the account from the beginning ...to be submitted to your guardian in order that he ... may feel no suspicion with regard to the account ... I pray that I may see you my lord enjoying further advancement and solid prosperity. Goodbye, my lord.

*To Zenon from a housepainter, ca. 255 BC (*Papyri, *A S Hunt, 1932):*

Memorandum to Zenon from Theophilus the ... About the work in the house of Diotimus; for the portico (I undertake) to have the cornice painted with a purple border, the upper part of the wall variegated, the lower course like vetch seed, and the pediment with circular veining, providing myself with all the materials, for 30 drachmae. For the dining room with seven couches, I will do the vault according to the pattern which you saw, and give the lower course an agreeable tint and paint the Lesbian cornice, providing myself with all the materials, for 20 drachmae. And for the dining rooms with five couches, I will paint the cornices, providing myself with all materials, for 30 drachmae. The sum total is 53 drachmae. But if you provide everything, it will come to 30 drachmae. Goodbye.

A list of Zenon's clothes, ca. 257 BC (Papyri, A S Hunt, 1932):

Zenon's trunk in which are contained: 1 linen wrap, washed; 1 clay colored cloak, for winter, washed, and 1 worn, 1 for summer, half worn, 1 natural colored, for winter, washed, and 1 worn, 1 vetch colored, for summer, new; 1 white tunic for winter, with sleeves, washed, 1 natural colored, for winter, with sleeves, worn, 1 natural colored, for winter, worn, 2 white, for winter, washed, and 1 half worn, 3 for summer, white, new, 1 unbleached, washed; 1 coarse mantle; 1 summer garment, white, washed, and 1 half worn; 1 pair of Sardian pillow cases; 2 pairs of socks, clay colored, new, 2 pairs of white, new; 2 girdles, white, new. Addressed: From Pisicles, a list of Zenon's clothes.

A Wine bill of a social club, second century (Papyri, A S Hunt, 1932):

Hathur 17. For the funeral feast of Kalatutis: 1 six chous jar of wine 2000 drachmae, 6 dinner loaves 190 drachmae, total 2190 drachmae. 22 persons present, of whom 18 were members and 4 were guests ... total 22 at 100 drachmae each, 2200 drachmae ...

A toll receipt, AD 75 (Papyri, C C Edgar, 1934):

Sarapion has paid the one percent tax for toll dues of the Oasis upon one ass-load of barley and one ass-load of garlic. The 2nd year of Vespasianus the lord, seventh day of Mecheir.

A complaint to the police of a household robbery, AD 28-9 (Papyri, C C Edgar, 1934):

To Serapion, chief of police, from Orsenouphis son of Harpaesis, notable of the village of Euhemeria in the division of Themistes. In the month Mesore in the past 14th year of Tiberius Caesar Augustus I was having some old walls on my premises demolished by the mason Petesouchus son of Petesouchus, and while I was absent from home to gain my living, Petesouchus in the process of demolition discovered a hoard which had been secreted by my mother in a little as long ago as the 16th year of Caesar, consisting of a pair of gold earrings weighing 4 quarters, a gold crescent weighing 3 quarters, a pair of silver armlets of the weight of 12 drachmae of uncoined metal, a necklace with silver ornaments worth 80 drachmae, and 60 silver drachmae. Diverting the attention of his assistants and my people he had them conveyed to his own home by his maiden daughter, and after emptying out the aforesaid objects he threw away the box empty in my house, and he even admitted finding the box, though he pretends that it was empty. Wherefore I request, if you approve, that the accused be brought before you for the consequent punishment. Farewell.
Orsenouphis, aged fifty, scar on left forearm.

*From Demophon to Ptolemaeus, ca. 245 BC (*Papyri, *Hunt & Edgar, 1932)*

Demophon to Ptolemaeus greeting. Send me by hook or crook the flute player Petous with both the Phrygian and the other flutes; and if any expenditure is necessary, pay and you shall recover from me. Send me also Zenobious the effeminate dancer with a drum and cymbals and castanets, for the women want him for the sacrifice; and let him be dressed as finely as possible. Get the kid also from Aristion and send it also to me. And if you have arrested the slave, hand him over to Semptheus to bring to me. Send me also as many cheeses as you can, empty jars, vegetables of all sorts, and any delicacies that you may have. Goodbye. Put them on board with policemen who will help to bring the boat along. To Ptolemaeus.

*Letter from a strategus about tax-farmers, ca. late 1st century AD, (*Papyri, *C C Edgar, 1934):*

Paniscus …, strategus of the Oxyrhynchite nome, to Asclepiades, royal scribe of the same nome, greeting. When at the auction of taxes held by me and you in the presence of the customary officials, the farmers of the sales tax and the record-office tax refused to bid, on the ground that they were incurring serious losses, and seemed likely to abscond, I wrote as we decided to his excellency the praefect on the matter. Now he replied to the effect that I should examine the former leases and lighten the burden of the tax farmers as much as possible in order to avoid a flight of persons engaged by force, and I have already sent you a copy of his letter for your information, adding that in your absence, as the contracts had not been taken up by the tax farmers nor were any new bidders coming forward in spite of repeated proclamations, I had taken written oaths of the farmers of the sales tax and the record office-tax ...

*Account of Public Games, ca. 2nd century AD (*Papyri, *Hunt & Edgar, 1932):*

Of this sum there were paid on Mecheir 23: to an actor 496 drachmae, to a Homeric reciter 448 drachmae, and for music ... drachmae, to a dancer 1[.]4 drachmae ... Received from the exegetes 42 drachmae, from the cosmetes 53 drachmae ½ obol, total 500 drachmae 1 obol. Of this sum there were paid out: to image bearers of the god Nile 20 drachmae, to the image bearers of the gods 56 drachmae, to grooms 16 drachmae, to 14 temple slaves 84 obols, for the voyage of the temple slaves 20 obols, to a crier 9 drachmae, to a trumpeter 4 drachmae, to the boys for breakfast 6 obols. To ... pancratiast, ... drachmae, to ..., competitor, ... drachmae, to ..., boxer, ...

*Emancipation of a slave, ca. AD 100 (*Papyri, *Hunt & Edgar, 1932):*

The 10th year of the emperor Caesar Domitianus Augustus Germanicus,...at Oxyrhynchus in the Thebiad, before three agoranomi, all called Psammis. Achilleus, aged about 20 years, of medium height, with fair complexion, long face, and a scar in the middle of his forehead, and Sarapas, aged about ... years, of medium height, with fair complexion, long face, and scar on his left ..., both sons of ... have set free under sanction of Zeus, Earth, and Sun, by deed drawn up in the street, the third part which they jointly own of a female slave who has already been freed as regards the other two thirds, namely Apollonous, aged about 26 years, of medium height, fair complexion, long face, and a scar on the right foot; ... the sum payable in respect of the third part now being freed consists of a fee of ... drachmae 4 obols of coined silver and of the ransom paid to Achilleus and Sarapas ... I, Achilleus, with my brother Sarapas, have emancipated the third part of the slave Apollonous, and I have received the ransom, 200 drachmae of silver...

Imperial edicts and proclamations

*Two edicts of Germanicus, AD 19 (*Papyri, C C Edgar, 1934):

Proclamation of Germanicus Caesar, son of Augustus and grandson of the deified Augustus, proconsul. [Being informed that in view of my visit] requisitions of boats and animals are being made and that quarters for lodging are being occupied by force and private persons intimidated, I have thought it necessary to declare that I wish neither boat nor beast of burden to be seized by anyone except on the order of Baebius my friend and secretary, nor quarters to be occupied. For if it is necessary, Baebius himself will allot the quarters fairly and justly; and for boats of animals which we requisition I command that hire be paid in accordance with my schedule. Those who disobey I desire to be brought before my secretary, who will himself either prevent private persons from being wronged or report the case to me. And I forbid beasts of burden to be forcibly appropriated by those who meet them traversing the city; for this is nothing but an act of open robbery.

Proclamation of Germanicus Caesar, son of Augustus, procunsul. Your goodwill, which you display on all occasions when you see me, I welcome, but your acclamations, which for me are invidious and such as are addressed to gods, I altogether deprecate. For they are appropriate to him who is actually the savior and benefactor of the whole human race, my father, and to his mother, my grandmother. But our position is…their divinity, so that unless you comply with my request, you will compel me to appear in public but seldom.

*Letter of Claudius to the Alexandrians, AD 41(*Papyri, C C Edgar, 1934):

Proclamation by Lucius Aemilius Rectus. Seeing that all the populace, owing to its numbers, was unable to be present at the reading of the most sacred and most beneficent letter to the city, I have deemed it necessary to display the letter publicly in order that reading it one by one you may admire the majesty of our god Caesar and feel gratitude for his goodwill towards the city. Year 2 of Tiberius Claudius Caesar Augustus Germanicus Imperator, the 14th of Neus Sabastus.

    Tiberius Claudius Caesar Augustus Germanicus Imperator, Pontifex Maximus, holder of the Tribunician Power, consul designate, to the city of Alexandria greeting…your ambassadors, having delivered to me the decree, discoursed at length concerning the city, directing my attention to your goodwill towards us, which from long ago, you may be sure, had been stored up to your advantage in my memory; for you are by nature reverent toward the Augusti, as I know from many proofs, and in particular have taken a warm interest in my house, warmly reciprocated, of which fact (to mention the last instance, passing over the others) the supreme witness is my brother Germanicus addressing you in words more clearly stamped as his own. Wherefore I gladly accepted the honours given to me by you, though I have no weakness for such things. And first I permit you to keep my birthday as a dies Augusti as you have yourselves proposed … (*a long list of honors is identified*) … But I deprecate the appointment of a high priest to me and the building of temples, for I do not wish to be offensive to my contemporaries, and my opinion is that temples and such forms of honor have by all ages have been granted to the gods alone … *(instructions concerning granting rights of citizenship, administering the temple of Augustus, a proposal to establish a local senate)* …

As for the question which party was responsible for the riots and feud (or rather, if the truth must be told, war) with the Jews … I was unwilling to make a strict inquiry, though guarding within me a store of immutable indignation against whichever party renews the conflict; and I tell you once for all that unless you put a stop to this ruinous and obstinate enmity against each other, I will be driven to show what a benevolent prince can be when turned to righteous indignation. Wherefore once again I conjure you that on the one hand the Alexandrians show themselves forbearing and kindly towards the Jews who for many years have dwelt in the same city, and dishonor none of the rites observed by them in the worship of their god, but allow them to observe their customs as in the time of the deified Augustus, which I also, after hearing both sides, have sanctioned; and on the other hand I explicitly order the Jews not to agitate for more privileges than they formerly possessed, and not in the future to send out a separate embassy as if they lived in a separate city, a thing unprecedented, and not to force their way into … games … If desisting of these courses you consent to live in mutual forbearance and kindliness, I on my side will exercise a solicitude of very long standing for the city … Farewell.

Correspondence and a treatise revealing aspects of the craft of letter writing

The following texts give us information about the craft of writing.

Cicero lived between 106 and 44 BC At the age of fifteen he went to Rome where he studied rhetoric under the orator Crassus. He also studied law and philosophy. He was fluent in Greek and became a master of rhetoric, writing a number of books on the subject. He was a member of the senate and a was personally acquainted with the most powerful figures in Roman history, including Julius Caesar, Pompey and Octavian. We know more about Cicero than any other figure in antiquity, thanks to his prolific writing.

*Cicero, To Quintas, (*Letters to His Brother Quintas, *2.12b.1.Williams, 1926):*

For this letter I shall use a good pen, well-mixed ink, and ivory polished paper too. For you write that you could hardly read my last letter, but for that there were none of those reasons which you suspect my dear brother. I was not busy, nor upset, nor angry with someone, but it is always my practice to use whatever pen I find in my hand as if it were a good one.

*Cicero, To Atticus (*Letters to Atticus, *337. XII.45, Shackleton Bailey,1999):*

After you left I had a visit from Lamia who brought me a letter sent to him by Caesar. It was dispatched earlier than the one brought by Diocares, but it states clearly that he will be home before the Roman Games…

*Cicero, To Atticus (*Letters to Atticus, *326.XIII.19, Shackleton Bailey,1999):*

My clerk, Hilarus, had just left (28 June) with a letter for you from me when a courier arrived with your letter of the previous day, in which I am particularly glad to read that our dear Atticus asks you not to fret…

*Cicero: To Atticus (*Letter to Atticus, *426.XVI.15, Shackleton Bailey,1999):*

You must not suppose that it is out of laziness that I do not write in my own hand—and yet upon my word that is exactly what it is.

*Apprenticeship to a shorthand writer, AD 155 (*Papyri, *A S Hunt, 1932):*

Panechotes also called Panares, ex-cosmetes of Oxyrhynchus, through his friend Gemellus, to Apollonius, writer of shorthand, greeting. I have placed with you my slave Chaerammon to learn the signs which your son Dionysus knows, for the period of two years from the present month Phamenoth of the 18th year of Antoninus Caesar the lord, for the fee agreed upon …the remaining 40 drachmae you will receive at the end of the period when the boy can read and write from prose of all kind without fault…

*Pliny the Elder on the process of making paper (*Natural History, *XIII.21.68-26.83, Rackham, 1944):*

> *Pliny the Elder was born in Italy ca. 23 BC He went to Rome at a very early age and after serving in the army and studying law, he devoted himself to scholarly study. He published many volumes that have been lost. His thirty-seven volume work* Natural History *is the only work of his to survive. It is a treatise on geography and earth sciences and gives us insight into how the physical world was understood at the time of Jesus. His interest in natural phenomena led him to study the eruption of Mt. Vesuvius. Unfortunately, he got too close and was overcome by noxious fumes. He died in AD 79.*

We have not yet touched on the marsh plants nor the shrubs that grow by the rivers. But before we leave Egypt we shall also describe the nature of papyrus, since our civilization or at all events our records depend very largely on the employment of paper. According to Marcus Varro we owe the discovery of paper to the victory of Alexander the Great, when he founded Alexandria in Egypt, before which time paper was not used. First of all people used to write on palm leaves and then on the bark of certain trees and then afterwards folding sheets of lead began to be employed … Subsequently, also according to Varro, when owing to the rivalry between King Ptolemy and King Eumenes about their libraries Ptolemy suppressed the export of paper, parchment was invented in Pergamum; and afterwards the employment of the material on which the immortality of human beings depends spread indiscriminately.

Papyrus then grows in the swamps of Egypt or else in the sluggish waters of the Nile where they have overflowed and lie stagnant in pools not more than three feet in depth …

Papyrus grows also in Syria on the borders of the lake … It has recently been realized that papyrus growing in the Euphrates near Babylon can also be used in the same way for paper; nevertheless up to the present the Parthians prefer to embroider letters upon cloths.

The process of making paper from papyrus is to split it with a needle into very thin strips as wide as possible, the best quality being the center of the plant...the first quality used to be called 'hieretic paper' and was in early times devoted solely to books connected with religion, but in a spirit of flattery it was given the name of Augustus, just as the second best was called 'Livia' after his consort, and thus the name 'hieretic' comes down to the third class ...

Paper of all kinds is 'woven' on a board moistened with water from the Nile, muddy liquid supplying the effect of glue. First an upright layer is smeared on to the table, using the full length of papyrus available after the trimmings have been cut off at both ends, and afterwards cross strips complete the lattice work. The next step is to press it in presses, and the sheets are dried in the sun and then joined together, the next strip used always diminishing in quality down to the worst of all. There are never more than twenty sheets in a roll ...

Roughness is smoothed out with a piece of ivory or a shell, but this makes the lettering apt to fade, as owing to the polish so given the paper does not take the ink so well, but has a shinier surface ...

The common kind of paste for paper is made of fine flour of the best quality mixed with boiling water with a very small sprinkle of vinegar; for carpenter's paste and gum make too brittle a compound. But a more careful process is to strain the crumb of leavened bread in boiling water; this method requires the smallest amount of paste at the seams, and produces a paper softer than linen. But all the paste used ought to be exactly a day old—not more nor yet less. Afterwards the paper is beaten thin with a mallet and run over with a layer of paste, and then again has its creases removed by pressure and is flattened out with the mallet. This process may enable records to last a long time; at the house of the poet and most distinguished citizen Pompanius Secundus I have seen documents in the hands of Tiberius and Gaius Gracchus; while as for autographs of Cicero, of his late Majesty Augustus, and of Virgil, we see them constantly.

Texts on geography and history

The following texts provide information about history. Pliny's 37 volume treatise Natural History *is an invaluable source that describes geography and natural phenomena. Josephus' two major works,* The Wars of the Judeans *and* The Antiquities of the Judeans *are our best source of information about events in Palestine between the Hasmoneans and the First Judean Revolt.*

*Pliny the Elder on the region of Palestine (*Natural History, *V.13-16, Rackham, 1944):*

The next country on the coast is Syria, formerly the greatest of lands. It had a great many divisions with different names, the part adjacent to Arabia being formerly called Palestine, and Judaea, and Hollow Syria, then Phoenicia and the more inland part Damascena...

At Ras Straki, 65 miles from Pelusium, is the frontier of Arabia. Then begins Idumaea, and Palestine at the point where the Serbonian Lake comes into view ... Further along the coast is the region of Samaria, the free town Ascalon, Ashdod, the two towns named Iamnea, one of them inland; and the Phoenician city of Joppa ... Next Apollonia, and the Tower of Strato, otherwise Caesarea, founded by King Herod, but now the colony called Prima Flavia established by the Emperor Vespasian; this is the frontier of Palestine ... After this comes Phoenicia, and inland Samaria; the towns are Naplous ... Sabustieh on a mountain...

Beyond Idumaea and Samaria stretches the wide expanse of Judaea. The part of Judaea adjoining Syria is called Galilee, and that next to Arabia and Egypt Peraea. Peraea is covered with rugged mountains and is separated from the other parts of Judaea by the river Jordan. The rest of Judaea is divided into ten Local Government Areas in the following order: the district of Jericho, which has numerous palm-groves and springs of water, and those of Emmaus, Lydda, Joppa, Accrabium, Jufna, Timnath-Serah, Beth-lebaoth, the Hills, the district that formerly contained Jerusalem, by far the most famous city of the East and not of Judaea only, and Herodium with the celebrated town of the same name.

The source of the river Jordan is the spring of Panias from which Caesarea described later takes its second name. It is a delightful stream, winding about so far as the conformation of the locality allows, and putting itself at the service of the people who dwell on its banks, as though moving with reluctance toward that gloomy lake, the Dead Sea (Latin: Asphaltiten), which ultimately swallows it up, its much prized waters mixing with the pestilential wasters of the lake and being lost. For this reason at the first opportunity afforded by the formation of the valleys it widens out into a lake usually called the Sea of Gennesareth. This is 16 miles long and 6 broad, and is skirted by the pleasant towns of Bethsaida and Hippo on the east, El Kerah on the south (the name of which place some people also give to the lake), and Tabariah with its salubrious hot springs on the west. The only product of *Asphaltites* is bitumin, the Greek word for which gives it its name. The bodies of animals do not sink in its waters, even bulls and camels floating; this has given rise to the report that nothing at all can sink in it. It is more than 100 miles long, and fully 75 miles broad at the broadest part but only 6 miles at the narrowest. On the east it is faced by Arabia of the nomads, and on the south by Machaerus, at one time next to Jerusalem the most important fortress in Judaea. On the same side there is a hot spring possessing medicinal value, the name of which, Callirroe, itself proclaims the celebrity of its waters.

On the West side of the Dead Sea, but out of range of the noxious exhalations of the coast, is the solitary tribe of the Essenes, which is remarkable beyond all the other tribes of the world, as it has no women and has renounced all sexual desire, has no money, and has only palm trees for company. Day by day the throng of refugees is recruited to an equal number by numerous accessions of persons tired of life and driven thither by the waves of fortune to adopt their manners. Thus through thousands of ages (incredible to relate) a race in which no one is born lives on forever: so prolific for their advantage is other men's weariness of life!

Lying below the Essenes was formerly the town of En Gedi, second only to Jerusalem in the fertility of its land and in the groves of palm trees, but now like Jerusalem a heap of ashes. Next comes Masada, a fortress on the rock, itself also not far from *Asphaltite*. This is the limit of Judaea.

Adjoining Judaea on the side of Syria is the region of Decapolis, so called from the number of its towns, though not all writers keep to the same towns in the list; most however include Damascus, with its fertile water-meadows that drain the river Chrysorroe, Philadelphia, Raphana (all these three withdrawn toward Arabia), Scythopolis (formerly Nysa, after Father Liber's nurse, whom he buried there) where a colony of Scythians are settled; Gadara, past which flows the river Yarmuk; Hippo mentioned already, Dion, Pella rich with its waters, Galasa, Canatha. Between and around these cities run tetrarchies, each of them equal to a kingdom, and they are incorporated into kingdoms—Trachonitis, Panias (in which is Caesarea with the spring mentioned above), Abila, Arca, Ampeloessa, and Gabe.

From this point we must go back to the coast and to Phoenicia ... Then comes Cape Carmel, and on a mountain the town of the same name, formerly called Acbatana...the river itself flows out of the marsh of Cendebia at the foot of Mount Carmel. Close to this river is Ptolemais, a colony of the Emperor Claudius, formerly called Acce ...

Josephus was born ca. AD 39. He died ca. AD 100. His writings, which were written in Rome under the patronage of several emperors and their wives, are an invaluable resource in reconstructing the history of Palestine at the time of Jesus and also for becoming acquainted with the purpose of writing at that time.

*Josephus on the attack on En Gedi by the Sicarii (*Wars, *Book IV.401-404, Thackeray, 1997):*

And now a fourth misfortune arose, in order to bring our nation to destruction. There was a fortress of very great strength not far from Jerusalem, which had been built by our ancient kings, both as a repository for their effects in the hazards of war, and for the preservation of their bodies at the same time. It was called Masada. Those that were called *Sicarii* had taken possession of it formerly, but at this time they overran the neighboring countries, aiming only to procure to themselves necessaries; for the fear they were then in prevented their further ravages. But when once they were informed that the Roman army lay still, and that the Jews were divided between sedition and tyranny, they boldly undertook greater matters; and at the feast of unleavened bread, which the Jews celebrate in memory of their deliverance from the Egyptian bondage, when they were sent back into the country of their forefathers, they came down by night, without being discovered by those that could have prevented them, and overran a certain small city called Engaddi:—in which expedition they prevented those citizens that could have stopped them, before they could arm themselves, and fight them. They also dispersed them, and cast them out of the city. As for such as could not run away, being women and children, they slew of them above seven hundred. Afterward, when they had carried every thing out of their houses, and had seized upon all the fruits that were in a flourishing condition, they brought them into Masada. And indeed these men laid all the villages that were about the fortress waste, and made the whole country desolate; while there came to them every day, from all parts, not a few men as corrupt as themselves. At that time all the other regions of Judea that had hitherto been at rest were in motion, by means of the robbers. Now as it is in a human body, if the principal part be inflamed, all the members are subject to the same distemper; so, by means of the sedition and disorder that was in the metropolis, had the wicked men that were in the country opportunity to ravage the same. Accordingly, when every one of them had plundered their own villages, they then retired into the desert; yet were these men that now got together, and joined in the conspiracy by parties, too small for an army, and too many for a gang of thieves: and thus did they fall upon the holy places (11) and the cities; yet did it now so happen that they were sometimes very ill treated by those upon whom they fell with such violence, and were taken by them as men are taken in war: but still they prevented any further punishment as do robbers, who, as soon as their ravages [are discovered], run their way. Nor was there now any part of Judea that was not in a miserable condition, as well as its most eminent city also.

Josephus Wars on defense of Masada by the Sicarii (Wars, Book VII.253, Thackeray, 1997):

...This fortress was called Masada; and the Sicarii who occupied it had at their head a man of influence named Eleazar. He was a descendent of the Judean who, as we have previously stated, induced multitudes of Judeans to refuse to enroll themselves, when Quirinius was sent as censor to Judea. For in those days the Sicarii clubbed together against those who consented to submit to Rome and in every way treated them as enemies, plundering their property, rounding up their cattle, and setting fire to their habitations; protesting that such persons were no other than aliens, who so ignobly sacrificed the hard-won liberty of the Judeans and admitted their preference for the Roman yoke. Yet, after all, this was but a pretext, put forward by them as a cloak for their cruelty and avarice, as was made plain by their actions. For the people did join with them in their revolt and take part in their war with Rome, only, however, to suffer at their hands still worse atrocities...The Sicarii were the first to set the example of this lawlessness and cruelty to their kinsmen ...

The Roman general advanced at the head of his forces against Eleazar and his band of Sicarii who held Masada, and, promptly making himself master of the whole district, established garrisons at the most suitable points, threw up a wall around the fortress, to make it difficult for any of the besieged to escape, and posted sentinels to guard it ... Having completed these preliminary arrangements, Silva turned his attention to the siege, which demanded great skill and severe exertion, owing to the strength of the fortress, the nature of which was as follows.

A rock of no slight circumference and lofty from end to end is abruptly terminated on every side by deep ravines, the precipices rising sheer from an invisible base and being inaccessible to the foot of any living creature, save in two places where the rock permits no easy ascent. Of these tracks one leads from the Lake Asphaltites on the east, the other, by which the approach is easier, from the west. The former they call the snake, seeing a resemblance to that reptile in its narrowness and continual windings...On this plateau the high priest Jonathan first erected a fortress and called it Masada; the subsequent planning of the place engaged the serious attention of King Herod ...

But the stores laid up within would have excited still more amazement, alike for their lavish splendour and their durability. For here had been supplied a mass of corn, amply sufficient to last for years, abundance of wine and oil, besides every variety of pulse and piles of dates. All these, Eleazar, when he with his Sicarii became through treachery master of the fortress, found in perfect condition...

Silva ... ordered his troops to throw up an embankment. Working with a will and a multitude of hands, they raised a solid bank...on top of it was constructed a platform of great stones fitted closely together...The engines in general were similar to those first devised by Vespasian and afterwards by Titus for their siege operations; in addition a sixty-cubit tower was constructed entirely cased in iron, from which the Romans made volleys of missiles from numerous quick-firers and ballistae quickly beat off the defenders on the ramparts and prevented them from showing themselves. Simultaneously, Silva, having further provided himself with a great battering-ram, ordered it to be directed without intermission against the wall, and having, though with difficulty, succeeded in effecting a breach, brought it down in ruins. The Sicarii, however, had already hastily built up another wall inside, which was not likely to meet with a similar fate from the engines; for it was pliable and calculated to break the force of the impact...Observing this, Silva, thinking it easier to destroy this wall by fire, ordered his soldiers to hurl at it showers of burning torches. Being mainly made of wood, it quickly caught fire, and from its hollow nature becoming ignited right through blazed up in a volume of flame. At the first outbreak of the fire, a north wind which blew in the faces of the Romans caused them an alarm ... and almost reduced them to despair. Then suddenly the wind veering, as if by divine Providence, to the south and blowing with full force in the opposite direction, wafted and flung the flames against the wall, which now through and through was all ablaze. The Romans, thus blessed by God's aid, returned rejoicing to their camp, with the determination of attacking the enemy on the morrow; and throughout that night they kept stricter watch lest any of them should secretly escape.

However, neither did Eleazar himself contemplate flight, nor did he intend to permit any other to do so. Seeing the wall consuming in the flames, unable to devise any further means of deliverance or gallant endeavor, and setting before his eyes what the Romans, if victorious, would inflict on them, their children, and their wives, he deliberated on the death of all. And judging as matters stood, this course the best, he assembled the most doughty of his comrades and incited them to the deed by such words as these...

'Long since, my brave men, we determined neither to serve the Romans nor any other save God, for He alone is man's true and righteous Lord; and now the time has come which bids us verify that resolution by our actions. At this crisis let us not disgrace ourselves; we who in the past refused to submit even to a slavery involving no peril, let us not now, along with slavery, deliberately accept the irreparable penalties awaiting us if we are to fall alive into Roman hands. For as we were the first of all to revolt, so are we the last in arms against them … we ought to have read God's purpose and to have recognized that the Judean race, once beloved of him, had been doomed to perdition … did we forsooth hope that we alone of all the Jewish nation would survive and preserve our freedom, as persons guiltless towards God and without a hand in crime— we who were the instructors of the rest? Mark, now, how He exposes the vanity of our expectations, by visiting us with such dire distress as exceeds all that we could anticipate … we have been deprived, manifestly by God himself, of all hope of deliverance. For it was not of their own accord that those flames which were driving against the enemy turned back upon the wall constructed by us; no, all this betokens wrath at the many wrongs which we madly dared to inflict on our countrymen. The penalty of those crimes let us not pay to our bitterest foes, the Romans, but to God through the act of our own hands …'

He would have pursued his exhortation but was cut short by his hearers, who, overpowered by some uncontrollable impulse, were all in a haste to do the deed. Like men possessed they went their way, each eager to outdo his neighbor … In the end not one was found a truant in so daring a deed: all carried through their task with their dearest ones…then having chosen by lot ten of their number to dispatch the rest, they laid themselves down each beside his prostrate wife and children, and, flinging their arms around them, offered their throats in readiness … These, having unswervingly slaughtered all, ordained the same rule of the lot for one another, that he on whom it fell should slay first the nine and then himself last of all…Finally, then, the nine bared their throats, and the last solitary survivor, after surveying the prostrate multitude … then collecting his strength drove his sword clean through his body and fell beside each family. They died in the belief that they had left not a soul of them alive to fall into Roman hands; but an old woman and another, a relative of Eleazar … with five children, escaped by concealing themselves in the subterranean aqueducts, while the rest were absorbed in the slaughter. The victims numbered nine hundred and sixty, including women and children, and the tragedy occurred on the fifteenth of the month Xanthicus.

Josephus on the four philosophies. Antiquities *VIII.1-27*

Quirinius, a Roman senator who had proceeded through all the magistracies to the consulship and a man who was extremely distinguished in other respects, arrived in Syria, dispatched by Caesar to be governor of the nation and to make an assessment of their property ... Quirinius also visited Judea, which had been annexed to Syria, in order to make an assessment of the property of the Jews and to liquidate the estate of Archelaus. Although the Jews were at first shocked to hear of the registration of the property, they gradually condescended...But a certain Judas, a Gaulanite from a city named Gamala, who had enlisted the aid of Saddok, a Pharisee, threw himself into the cause of rebellion. They said that the assessment carried with it a status amounting to downright slavery, no less, and appealed to the nation to make a bid for independence ... Since the populace, when they heard their appeals, responded gladly, the plot to strike boldly made serious progress; and so these men sowed the seed of every kind of misery ... They sowed the seed from which sprang strife between factions and slaughter of fellow citizens ... In this case certainly, Judas and Saddok started among us a fourth philosophy; and when they had won an abundance of devotees, they filled the body politic immediately with tumult, also planting the seeds of those troubles which subsequently overtook it, all because of the novelty of this hitherto unknown philosophy that I shall now describe.

The Jews, from the most ancient of times, had three philosophies pertaining to their traditions, that of the Essenes, that of the Sadducees, and, thirdly, that of the group called the Pharisees ... The Pharisees simplify their standard of living, making no concession to luxury. They follow the guidance of that which is their doctrine has selected and transmitted as good ... They show respect and deference to their elders...they do not deprive the human will of the pursuit of what is in man's power...They believe that souls have the power to survive death and that there are rewards and punishments under the earth ... eternal imprisonment is the lot of evil souls, while the good souls receive an easy passage to a new life...

The Sadducees hold that the soul perishes along with the body. They own no observance of any sort apart from the laws; in fact, they reckon it a virtue to dispute with the teachers of the path of wisdom that they pursue. There are but few men to whom this doctrine has been made known, but these are men of the highest standing. They accomplish practically nothing, however. For whenever they assume some office, though they submit unwillingly and perforce, yet submit they do to the formulas of the Pharisees, since otherwise the masses would not follow them.

The doctrine of the Essenes is wont to leave everything in the hands of God. They regard the soul as immortal and believe that they ought to strive especially to draw near to righteousness. They send votive offerings to the temple, but perform their sacrifices employing a different ritual of purification. For this reason they are barred from those precincts of the temple … they are of the highest character, devoting themselves solely to agricultural labor … Moreover, they hold their possessions in common and the wealthy man receives no more enjoyment from his property than the man who possesses nothing. The men who practice this way of life number four thousand. They neither bring wives into the community nor do they own slaves, since they believe that the latter practice contributes to injustice and that the former opens the way to a source of dissension…

As for the fourth of the philosophies, Judas the Galilean set himself up as leader of it. This school agrees in all other respects with the opinions of the Pharisees, except that they have a passion for liberty that is almost unconquerable, since they are convinced that God alone is their leader and master. They think little of submitting to death in unusual forms and permitting vengeance to fall on kinsmen and friends if only they may avoid calling any man master…

Josephus makes three important and controversial references to Jesus Christ, John the Baptist and James, the brother of Jesus. These are our earliest non-Christian references to either of the three.

Josephus' comments about Jesus the Christ. Antiquities of the Judeans, *LCL XVIII.63-64, LCL 1963 (Whitson XVIII.3.3), translation my own:*

And about this time there was Jesus, a wise man, if he should be called a man, for he did wonderful works, a teacher of those men who accept the truth gladly. He attracted many of the Judeans and many of the Greeks. He was the Christ. And when he was accused by the leading men among us, Pilate condemned him to the cross, he was not forsaken by those who first loved him. For he appeared to them on the third day having life again, the prophets of God having prophesied these and many other marvelous things about him. And to this day, the tribe of Christians, so called after him, have not disappeared.

Josephus' account of John the Baptist. Antiquities of the Judeans, *LCL XVIII.113-117, LCL 1963, (Whitson XVIII5.2), translation my own:*

But to some of the Judeans it seemed that the destruction of the Herodian army by God was righteous vengeance on account of John who was called the Baptist. But Herod had him killed even though he was a good man and exhorted the Judeans to lead righteous lives toward each other and piety toward God and to be baptized, for this was necessary if the baptism was to be acceptable to God, not just for the purification of just some sins, but a consecration of the body, presuming that the soul was already cleansed by righteousness. So when many others were drawn to him because they were attracted by the hearing of his words, Herod feared that his words might incite the crowds to rebellion for it seemed that they would do whatever he said and he decided that it would be better to strike first than to wait for a rebellion ... though he was sent to Machaerus as a prisoner ... and put to death, the Judeans considered the destruction of Herod's army God's vindication of John.

Philosophical treatises and texts from religious cults, sects:

The following texts help us understand the religious and philosophical outlook of the ancient world.

*A petition to an oracle, first century AD (*Papyri, *C C Edgar, 1934):*

O Lord Sarapis, beneficent one. Say whether it is fitting that Phanias my son and his wife should not agree now with his father, but oppose him and not make a contract. Tell me this truly. Goodbye.

*An application for employment in the office of prophet, AD 146 (*Papyri, *C C Edgar, 1934):*

Copy. To Tiberius Claudius Justus, administrator of the private account, from Pakebkis, son of Marsisouchis, exempted priest of the famous temple of Soknebtunis also called Cronus and the most great gods, which is situated in the village of Tebtunis in the division of Polemon in the Arsinote nome. I wish to purchase the office of prophet in the aforesaid temple, which has been offered for sale for a long time, on the understanding that I shall ... and carry the palm branches and perform the other functions of the office of prophet and receive in accordance with the orders the fifth part of all the revenue which falls to the temple, at the total price of 2,200 drachmae instead of the 640 drachmae offered long ago by Marsisouchis son of Pakebkis, which sum I will pay, if my appointment is ratified, into the local public bank at the customary dates; and I and my descendents and successors shall have the permanent ownership and possession of this office for ever with all the same privileges and rights, on payment (by each one) of 200 drachmae for admission. If therefore it seem good to you, my lord, you will ratify my appointment here in the city upon these terms and write to the strategus of the nome about this matter, in order that the due services of the gods who love you may be performed. The fifth share of the proceeds which falls to me, as aforesaid, after deducting expenses is 50 artabae of wheat, 9 5/8 artabae of lentils, 60 drachmae of silver. Farewell. The 10th year of the Emperor Caesar Titus Aelius Hadrianus Antoninus Augustus Pius, Tubi 10.

*Concerning and auction of priestly offices, AD 197 (*Papyri, C C Edgar, 1934):*

Claudius Diognetus, imperial procurator and deputy-chief-priest, to the strategus of the Panopolite nome greeting. Copies of two letters written to me by Saturninus, secretary of the chief priest, concerning Pekusis, son of Psenthermouthus, priest, who has paid the price of an office of stolistes amounting to 100 drachmae and extra charges, and Heremiphis son of Sisois, priest, who has paid the price of another office of stolistes amounting to 100 drachmae and extra charges, in both cases to Metiochus, oeconomus of our most godlike lord and Emperor Severus Pertinax, are appended to my present letter. Take steps on your part along with the royal scribe to put the offices up to auction and, if no one bids higher, to hand them over to them, but not for a price inferior to the valuation or to the sum paid for the offices on other occasions. I pray for your health. Year 5, Pachon 29.

From Apollonius to his Father Ptolemaeus, ca. 152 BC (Hunt & Edgar, 1932)

Apollonius to his father Ptolemaeus greeting. I swear by Serapis that if I had not a little compunction, you would never have seen my face again; for you utter nothing but lies and your gods likewise, for they have plunged us into a deep mire in which we might die, and when you have a vision that we are to be rescued, we sink outright. Know that the runaway will try to prevent us

The Word of God and the world of the Bible

remaining in the place; for because of us he has suffered a loss of 15 talents. The strategus is coming up tomorrow to the Serapium and will spend two days in the Anubieum drinking. Never again can I hold up my head in Tricomia for shame that we have given ourselves away and been deluded, misled by the gods and trusting in dreams. Farewell. To Ptolemaeus greeting. A reply to the soothsayers.

*Josephus' reference to the Temple Mount warning to non-Israelites (*War, *vol. V.193, Thackeray,1997):*

Proceeding across towards the second court of the temple, one found it surrounded by a stone balustrade, three cubits high and of exquisite worksmanship; in this at regular intervals stood slabs giving warning, some in Greek, some in Latin characters, of the law of purification, to wit that no foreigner was permitted to enter the holy place, for so the second enclosure of the temple was called ...

*Temple Mount warning inscription, discovered 1871(*Inscriptiones, *Dittenberger, 1960):*

No man of another nation to enter within the fence and enclosure round the temple. And whoever is caught will have himself to blame that his death ensues.

The Dead Sea Scrolls, The Community Rule, 1 QS 5: 1-10 (Vermes, G. 1995):

And this is the Rule for the men of the Community who have freely pledged themselves to be converted from all evil and to cling to all His commandments according to His will.

They shall separate from the congregation of the men of injustice and shall unite, with respect to the Law and possessions, under the authority of the sons of Zadok, the Priests who keep the Covenant, and of the multitude of the men of the Community who hold fast to the Covenant. Every decision concerning doctrine, property, and justice shall be determined by them. They shall practice truth and humility in common, and justice and uprightness and charity and modesty in all their ways ...

The Dead Sea Scrolls, The Community Rule, 1QS 8:1-19 (Vermes, G. 1995):

And when these become members of the community in Israel according to all these rules, they shall separate from the habitation of ungodly men and shall go into the wilderness to prepare the way of him; as it is written, *Prepare in the wilderness the way of ... make straight in the desert a path for our God* (Is. 40: 3). This is the study of the law which he commanded by the hand of Moses, that they may do according to all that has been revealed from age to age, and as the prophets have revealed by his holy spirit.

The Dead Sea Scrolls, The War Rule, 1 QM 1: 1-11 (Vermes, G. 1995):

For the M[aster. The Rule of] War on the unleashing of the attack of the sons of light against the company of the sons of darkness, the army of Satan: against the band of Edom, Moab, and the sons of Ammon, and [against the army of the sons of the East and] the Philistines, and against the hand of the Kitim of Assyria and their allies the ungodly of the covenant

The sons of Levi, Judah, and Benjamin, the exiles in the desert, shall battle against them in ... all their bands when the exiled sons of light return from the Desert of the Peoples to camp in the Desert of Jerusalem; and after the battle they shall go up from their...

*Plato, The Allegory of the Cave (*Republic, *VII,)*

> *Plato lived in the early fifth century BC. He was a student of Socrates, who appears in many of his works, and a teacher of Aristotle. His allegory of the cave illustrates fundamental suppositions about the universe, as well as encapsulating Plato's doctrine of knowledge. For Plato, the material world is unreal. Only the world of ideas, symbolized by the sun in the allegory, has ultimate value. Knowledge of ideas is therefore considered to be superior to knowledge about nature, which Plato considers to be on the level of opinion.*

... Picture men dwelling in a sort of subterranean cavern with a long entrance open to the light on its entire width. Conceive them as having their legs and necks fettered from childhood, so that they remain in the same spot, able to look forward only, and prevented by the fetters from turning their heads. Picture further the light from a fire burning higher up and at a distance behind them, and between the fire and the prisoners and above them a road along which a low wall has been built, as the exhibitors of puppet-shows have partitions before the men themselves, above which they show the puppets ...

... See also, then, men carrying past the wall implements of all kinds that rise above the wall, and human images and shapes of animals as well...do you think that these men would have seen anything of themselves or of one another except the shadows cast from the fire on the wall of the cave that fronted them? ... do you not think that they would suppose that in naming the things that they saw they were naming the passing objects? ... Then in every way such prisoners would deem reality to be nothing else than the shadows of the artificial objects ...

Consider, then, what would be the manner of the release and healing from these bonds if...something of this sort were to happen to them: When one was freed from his fetters and compelled to stand up suddenly turn his head around and walk and to lift up his eyes to the light, and in doing all this felt pain and, because of the dazzle and glitter of the light, was unable to discern the objects whose shadows he formerly saw, what do you suppose would be his answer if someone told him that what he had seen before was all a cheat and an illusion, but that now, being nearer to reality and turned toward more real things, he saw more truly? ... do you not think that he would be at a loss and that he would regard what he formerly saw as more real than the things now pointed out to him?...

... And if someone should drag him thence by force up the ascent which is rough and steep, and not let him go before he had drawn him out into the light of the sun, do you not think that he would find it painful to be so haled along, and would chafe at it, and when he came out into the light, that his eyes would be filled with its beams so that he would not be able to see even one of the things that we call real?...

... Then there would be need for habituation, I take it, to enable him to see the things higher up. And at first he would most easily discern the shadows and, after that, the likenesses or reflections in water of men or other things, and later, the things themselves, and from these he would go on to ponder the appearances in the heavens and heaven itself, more easily by night, looking at the light of the stars and the moon, than by day the sun and the sun's light...

... And so, finally, I suppose, he would be able to look upon the sun itself and see its true nature, not by reflections in water or phantasms of it in an alien setting, but in and by itself in its own place … And at this point he would infer and conclude that this it is that provides the seasons and the courses of the year and presides over all things in the visible region, and is in some sort the cause of all things that they had seen.

Ancient texts' bibliography

A S Hunt & C C Edgar, trans. *Selected Papyri, Vol. I & II*. Cambridge: Harvard University Press, 1932, 1934.

Cicero. Letters to Atticus. *Translated by D.R. Shackleton Bailey, Cambridge:* Harvard University Press, 1999

Cicero. *Letters to His Friends*. Translated by W.G. Williams. Cambridge: Harvard University Press, 1926.

Cicero. *Letter to His Brother Quintas, vol. II,12b.1*. Translated by W.G. Williams. Cambridge: Harvard University Press, 1953.

Dittenberger, Wilhem, trans. *Orientis Graeca Inscriptiones Selectae, 598*. Hildesheim: G. Olms, 1960.

Josephus. *The Antiquities of the Jews, vol. XVIII*. Translated by L. Feldman. Cambridge: Harvard University Press, 1965.

Josephus. *The Jewish Wars, vol. IV & VII*. Translated by H. St. J. Thackeray. Cambridge: Harvard University Press, 1997.

Pliny the Elder. *Natural History, vols. V & XIII*. Translated by H. Rackham. Cambridge: Harvard University Press, 1944.

Plato. *The Republic*. Translated by Paul Shorey. Cambridge: Harvard University Press, 1980.

Vermes, Geza. *The Dead Sea Scrolls in English*. London: Penguin Books, 1995.

Appendix 2
CHRONOLOGICAL CHARTS AND TABLES

1. Table of Archaeological and Historical Time Periods:

Period	*Approximate dates*
Paleolithic Age (old stone age)	1,000,000 – 15,000 BC
Mesolithic (middle stone age)	15,000 – 8,000 BC
Neolithic (new stone age)	8000 – 4000 BC
Chalcolithic (copper age)	4000 – 3200 BC
Bronze Age	3200 – 1200 BC
Early Bronze	3200 – 2000 BC
Early Bronze I	3200 – 3000 BC
Early Bronze II	3000 – 2700 BC
Early Bronze III	2700 – 2300 BC
Early Bronze IV	2300 – 2000 BC
Middle Bronze	2000 – 1550 BC
Middle Bronze I	2000 – 1750 BC
Middle Bronze II	1750 – 1550 BC
Late Bronze	1550 – 1200 BC
Late Bronze I	1550 – 1400 BC
Late Bronze II	1400 – 1200 BC
Iron Age (Israelite)	1200 – 536 BC
Iron Age I	1200 – 900 BC
Iron Age II	900 – 536 BC
Persian Period	536 – 332 BC
Classical Greece	500 – 332 BC
Hellenistic Period (Palestine)	332 – 63 BC

Hellenistic Period (Greece)	332 – 146 BC
Roman Period (Palestine)	63 BC – AD 325
Roman Period (Greece)	146 BC – AD 325
Early Roman (Palestine)	63 BC – AD 135
Early Roman (Greece)	146 BC – AD 135
Late Roman	AD 135 – 325
Byzantine Period	AD 325 – 638
Islamic Period (Palestine)	AD 638 – 1917
Ummayad Period	AD 638 – 744
'Abbasid Period	AD 744 – 1099
Crusader Period	AD 1099 - 1187
Ayyubid Period	AD 1187 – 1291
Fatamid and	
Mamluk Periods	AD 1291 - 1517
Ottoman Period	AD 1517 – 1917
British Mandatory Period	AD 1917 – 1948

2. Chronology of Mediterranean, Near Eastern and Israelite History (according to the biblical narrative) to the time of Jesus (all dates BC and most others are approximate)

Date

3000 – 2100	Old Egyptian Kingdom (the age of great pyramids)
2800 – 2360	Sumer
2600	Gilgamesh Epic written
2360 – 2180	Akkadian dynasty
2100 – 1800	Middle Egyptian Kingdom
	Babylonian Empire
1800 – 1700	Abraham migrates to Canaan
	The time of the Patriarchs
1750	Code of Hammarabi
	Joseph
1800 – 1100	New Kingdom, (the age of Luxor)
	Assyrian Empire
1750 – 1550	Hyksos rule in Canaan

147

The Word of God and the world of the Bible

1700 – 1250	Israel in Egypt
1700 – 1400	Minoan Civilization
1550 – 1400	Egyptian rule in Canaan
1400 – 1150	Mycenean Civilization
1379 – 1362	Amenophis IV (Akhenaten)
1250	Ramses II
	Moses and the Exodus
1200	Israelite conquest/settlement of Canaan
1200 – 1100	Period of the Judges
1100 – 930	Period of the United Monarchy (Saul, David and Solomon)
930 – 722	divided Kingdoms (Judah and Israel)
722	Assyrian conquest of Israel
605 – 562	Nebuchadnezzar II
586	Babylonian Conquest, destruction of the Temple
586 – 536	Babylonian Captivity
559 – 530	Cyrus the Persian
536	Persian conquest of Babylon
	Release of Judeans from captivity
	Restoration of the Temple
525	Ezra and Nehemiah
490	The Battle of Marathon
480	The Battle of Salamis
479	Athenenian/Spartan defeat of Persians
479 – 433	Golden Age of Pericles
433 – 404	The Peloponnesian War
358 – 336	Philip II Macedonia
338	Philip II triumphs over Athens and its allies
336	Alexander assumes Macedonian throne
333	Alexander defeats Persian King Darius
332	Alexander conquers Palestine
323	The death of Alexander
	Egypt and Palestine under the Ptolemies
	Greece under the Antigonids
	Syria under the Seleucids
264 – 241	First Punic War (Rome-Carthage)
218 – 201	Second Punic War (Rome-Carthage)
200	Septuagint translated
198	Palestine under Seleucids
197	Roman defeat of Philip V of Macedonia in Thessaly
175 – 163	Antiochus IV Epiphanes
168	Macedonia becomes a Roman province

166 – 160	Maccabean Revolt
164	Rededication of the Temple
166 – 63	Hasmonean Dynasty
160 – 142	Jonathan
148	Roman defeat of Greece (Achaia)
146	Destruction of Corinth by Rome
142 – 134	Simon (Hasmonean dynasty)
134 – 104	John Hyrcanus (Hasmonean dynasty)
104 – 103	Aristobulus I (Hasmonean dynasty)
76 – 76	Alexander Jannaeus (Hasmonean dynasty)
86	Roman defeat and destruction of Athens
69 – 63	Aristobulus II (Hasmonean dynasty)
63	Pompey conquers Syria and Palestine
63 – 37	Hasmonean-Herodian Civil War
48	End of Roman Republic
46	Corinth rebuilt as a Roman colony
44	Assassination of Julius Caesar
41	Battle of Philippi
	Octavian, Marc Antony defeat Brutus, Cassius
37	Herod assumes Judean throne
31	Battle of Actium
	Octavian's defeat of Marc Antony
28	Octavian accepts title of Augustus
	Roman Imperial Period begins
20	Herodian reconstruction of Jerusalem begins
6	Birth of Jesus
4	Death of Herod the Great

3. Early Roman Emperors (dates after Augustus are AD)

27 BC – AD 14	Augustus
14 – 37	Tiberius
37 – 41	Caligula
41 – 54	Claudius
54 – 68	Nero
68 – 69	Galba
69 – 79	Vespasian
79 – 81	Titus
81 – 96	Domitian
96 – 98	Nerva

The Word of God and the world of the Bible

98 – 117	Trajan
117 – 138	Hadrian

4. Governors of Palestine (all dates AD)

6 – 8	Coponius
9 – 12	Ambibulus
12 – 15	Annius Rufus
15 – 26	Valerius Gratus
26 – 36	Pontius Pilatus
36 – 37	Marcellus
44 – 46	Cuspius Fadus
46 – 48	Tiberius Alexander
48 – 52	Ventidius Cumanus
52 – 60	Antonius Felix
60 – 62	Pordius Festus
62 – 64	Albinus
64 – 66	Gessius Florus

5. Chronology of the Kings of Israel and Judah (all dates are BC and approximate)

The United Monarchy

Saul	1050 - 1000
David	1000 – 965
Solomon	965 – 930

The Divided Kingdoms

Israel		*Judah*	
930 – 910	Rehoboam	930 – 907	Jeroboam
910 – 908	Abijam	907 – 906	Nadab
908 – 867	Asa	906 – 883	Baasha
867 – 845	Jehoshaphat	883 – 882	Elah
845 – 840	Jehoram	882 – 871	Zimri
840 – 835	Athaliah	882 – 871	Omri

835 – 798	Joash	871 – 851	Ahab
798 – 770	Amaziah	851 – 850	Ahaziah
770 – 730	Uzziah	850 – 842	Jehoram
758 – 743	Jotham	842 – 814	Jehu
730 – 727	Ahaz	814 – 800	Jehoahaz
727 – 698	Hezekiah	800 – 784	Jehoash
698 – 642	Manassah	784 – 748	Jeroboam
642 – 640	Amon	748	Zechariah
639 – 609	Josiah	748	Shallum
609	Jehoahaz	747 – 737	Menahem
608 – 598	Jehoiakim	737 – 735	Pekahiah
597	Jehoiachin	735 – 733	Pekah
596 – 586	Zedikiah	733 – 724	Hoshea

Appendix 3
GLOSSARY

Afro-Syrian Rift Valley: a 4,000 mile long geological feature that stretches from northern Syria to Mozambique and include the Hula Valley, the Sea of Galilee, the Jordan River Valley, the Dead Sea, and the Gulf of Aqaba.

Agora: Greek for marketplace, it was a standard feature in the Hellenistic city.

Apocalypticism: the name of a world-view that originated in ancient Persian religion and is expressed in some Christian and Jewish literature. Apocalypticism can be loosely characterized as a belief in two distinct cosmic powers, one good and the other evil. These powers compete for control of the world. History is interpreted in light of the struggle between the two. Present suffering is usually understood as a part of the cosmic Divine plan and recompense for suffering is guaranteed in the future coming age. The present age, under the sway of the cosmic evil power, will soon be replaced by the coming, eternal and perfect age under the command of God. The coming age will be a new creation. It will occur suddenly, imminently and be accompanied by earthly upheaval mirrored in heavenly events such as lightning, thunder, dramatic comets and spectacular celestial and planetary displays. Even though the new age is imminent, no one knows exactly when it will occur.

Apocalyptic literature uses striking astral, animal and numerical imagery. It is highly symbolic and usually includes predictions of dire woes for those who oppose the coming age. It is often ascribed to the vision of a particular person and is often written pseudonymously. The Book of Revelation is a stunning example of Christian Apocalypticism, although it does not strictly conform to the details of written apocalyptic. Apocalyptic literature is also found in the Gospels (Mark 13), the Qumran literature and the Book of Daniel, among many other examples dating to the Late Hellenistic and Early Roman Periods. Indeed, Apocalypticism has continued to be popular in Christian belief to the present day.

The Apocrypha: the seventeen books of the Septuagint or Greek version of the Hebrew Scriptures. Martin Luther considered these books non-canonical, because they were not in current usage by contemporary Jews and he excluded them from the Protestant Canon. These books are considered canonical by Roman Catholics and were included in Jerome's Latin translation of the Bible, called the Vulgate.

Aramaic: one of several Semitic languages known to be in usage in Jesus' day. It was the language of the Persian Empire and was the universal language until Greek replaced it during the Hellenistic Period. It was Jesus' mother tongue.

Armageddon: one of the most well known references to the valley of Jezreel comes from the Revelation of John (16: 14-21) which prophecies that a place called Armageddon will host the armies of all the world on the day of the ultimate battle between the forces of good and evil. 'Armageddon' is a Greek form of 'Har Megiddo,' which in Hebrew means the 'hill of Megiddo.' By the time of the writing of the Apocalypse of John, it had been called the battleground of the nations for many generations, it had been a host to the armies of conquering powers for millennia and its reputation had spread throughout the known world. In modern times, the armies of Napoleon and Allenby fought major battles there. General George Patten is said to have dreamt of staging tank battles there!

Augustus Caesar: the adopted nephew of the Roman dictator Julius Caesar, he was named in Caesar's will as his successor. His full name was Gaius Julius Caesar Octavianus. In 30 BC at Actium, he defeated the navy of Marc Antony who had been his ruling partner for a number of years. He was elected Augustus in 27 BC by the Roman Senate. He outwardly observed republican forms, but he possessed enormous power. When Jesus was born, he was the undisputed ruler of the Mediterranean world. His rule was known in official propaganda as one of great prosperity and stability. He self-consciously understood that his reign was pivotal in Roman history and he took credit for the transformation of the empire for which others gladly credited him as well. He is reported to have remarked, 'I found Rome made of brick and left it made of marble.' He carefully cultivated popular support through his personality cult and was understood to possess divine powers. An inscription celebrating his birthday in the year 7 BC reads as follows: 'it is hard to say if the birthday of the most divine Caesar is more joyful or more advantageous; we may rightly regard it as the beginning of all good things, if not in the world of nature, yet in advantage; everything was deteriorating and changing into misfortune, but he set it right and gave the whole world another appearance...The birthday of the god was the beginning of the good news to the world on his account.' The comparison to Mark 1: 1 is obvious. No one should fail to understand that the gospel writers, especially Luke, very deliberately intended to contrast the reign and majesty of Jesus with that of Augustus.

The Babylonian Exile: a fifty-year period in Israelite history that began in 586 BC when the Babylonian King Nebuchadnezzar sacked Jerusalem (2 Kings 10-17). This period marks a turning point in Israelite history. All of the books of the Hebrew Scriptures were given their final form after this event. All the records of Israel's self consciousness as a people are from after this period. From Babylon all of Israel's outstanding literature was written (e.g., Psalm 137). In Babylon, the identification of Israel as *Judean* developed. From the perspective of the non-Israelites, people from *Judah* were Judeans.

Bethlehem: a city in the West Bank, biblical Judah, best known as the birthplace of Jesus and for the stories associated with Jesus' birth. Its history is much older. Popularly believed to come from Hebrew, meaning 'house of bread,' (Arabic= house of meat) its name derives from that of a Canaanite god, Lahmi who was worshipped there. It is the scene of the story of Ruth whose liaison with Boaz is prominently mentioned in the genealogy of Jesus in Matthew's gospel (Mt 1:5). Rachel's tomb is found there and the prophet Samuel bestowed religious significance on the town by sacrificing there (I Samuel 16: 5) The birthplace of King David, Bethlehem became known by New Testament times as the city of David (Luke 2: 4,11).

Bethsaida: located today on the eastern shore of the River Jordan about one mile north of the Sea of Galilee in occupied Syria, in Jesus' day it was situated on the Jordan's western shore. Earthquakes changed the course of the river. The Gospels tell us that Bethsaida, which means house of the fishermen, was the home of Philip, Simon and Andrew. It is mentioned more often in the gospels than any other town except Jerusalem and Capernaum. Along with Capernaum and Chorazin, it was cursed by Jesus (Mt 11: 21) for the refusal of its inhabitants to respond favorably to Jesus' preaching and mighty works. Its ruins bear silent testimony to the power of Jesus' curse. Archaeologically considered, it is important because it is the only site in Palestine where the 1st century remains are on the top of the tel. Excavations reveal a village laid out along Hellenistic lines with a north-south running Cardo Maximus and an east-west oriented Decamanus. Of particular interest is the house of the fisherman, so named because artefacts discovered in it included fishing implements, along with a wine cellar. Excavations also show that the site was occupied by the Early Bronze period.

Bronze Age: an archaeological period generally considered to begin 3200 BC and end 1200 BC. It is divided into three sub-periods: Early, Middle and Late. Each of these is further subdivided.

Byzantine Period: an historical period (325-638 AD) starting when Constantine moved the Roman capital to Byzantium.

Caesarea Maritima: one of Herod the Great's most spectacular building accomplishments, it is located on the Mediterranean coast of the Plain of Sharon. Herod built the city over smaller settlements dating back to the Phoenicians in order to provide his kingdom with a port. It was also the seat of his institutions of civil administration. When Judea was incorporated into the Roman Empire as a province, it was the seat of the Roman governor. Among the interesting archaeological artefacts discovered there is the Pilate Stone, the only extant inscription that refers to Pontius Pilatus.

Since Judea had no natural port, Herod ordered his engineers to build an artificial one. According to Josephus, when it was completed it was large enough to protect 1,000 ships and rivalled Piraeus, the port of Athens in size. The harbour was named Sebastos in honour of Augustus Caesar. The construction of the harbour required the use of *hydraulic cement* that hardens on contact with water. Marine archaeologists discovered the foundations of the harbour in sixty feet of water. Its breakwaters, upon which wharves were constructed stretch six hundred fifty yards from the shore and are two hundred feet wide. Other engineering marvels at Caesarea Maritima include the water and sewage systems, designed to provide the city of 50,000 inhabitants with water and carry off its waste.

Caeserea Maritima grew to about 250,000 inhabitants during the Byzantine Period. During that time, it was an important centre of Jewish learning and early Christianity. It boasted a world-famous library. Origen, the church father and Eusebius, the 4th century church historian both lived there.

Biblical references to Caesarea Maritima are concentrated in the Book of Acts. Philip preached there (Acts 8: 40), the centurion Cornelius became the first gentile to convert to Christianity there (Acts 10, 11), Paul embarked from there to go to Tarsus (Acts 9: 30) and to Rome after his trial before Agrippa (Acts 25-27). He had a hearing before Festus and Felix there as well (Acts 23: 23; 25: 12).

Canon: a rule or standard. In the context of biblical studies, the canon is the collection of writings that is deemed to be authoritative. The process of the canonization of the New Testament took place over several centuries. In this process, authorities eliminated many books that had been held to be scripture by one group or another. Today, the criteria that were used are not entirely known and there is no unanimity among Christians about which books should be included. The result, however, is the canon of the New Testament. For Protestants, it includes the books of the Hebrew Bible in a rearranged order. For Catholics, the canon includes these books as well as those of the Apocrypha, which were in the Greek Septuagint.

Capernaum: a village located on the northern shore of the Sea of Galilee, it is mentioned in association with Jesus more often in the Gospels than any city except Jerusalem. It is located on the Via Maris. Jesus situated his Galilean ministry here probably because of its proximity to that major highway. The gospels testify that Jesus was active here. He healed Peter's mother-in-law (Mk 1: 29-31), raised the paralytic man (Mt. 9: 1-8), healed the Centurion's servant (Lk. 7: 1-10) and called the disciples Matthew, James and John (Mt. 9: 9). Visitors to Capernaum, one of the most frequently visited sites in the Holy Land, are usually told that the prominent 4th century AD limestone synagogue is built over the 1st century AD foundations of the synagogue in which Jesus taught. However, the archaeologist never identified the 1st century foundations as those of a synagogue and the consensus among contemporary scholars is that synagogues were not *buildings* in Palestine in the 1st century. Excavations revealed the 1st century streets, residential areas, a Roman bath and garrison, a number of flour mills that were manufactured there, the harbour, wharves and fish ponds. One particular room in a residential area is designated the house of Peter's mother-in-law. A modern structure used for mass and devotion is situated over the foundations of a 5th century, octagonal church. This structure is built around and over a 4th century church. The centre of this 4th century church is a simple room from the 1st century. When it was excavated, plaster from its walls showed evidence of early veneration of the room in association with Jesus.

Central Highlands (the Hill Country): to the east of the coastal plain, this north-south running ridge of rugged mountains rises to heights of about 3,000 feet. Until the introduction of water collection systems in the Late Bronze Age, settlement was sparse and restricted to areas with natural water supplies. Settlement increased during the Iron Age when the region was populated by a wide variety of Canaanite peoples.

Since it does not possess extraordinary natural mineral resources and is off the beaten trade track, societies developed on the Central Highlands relatively unmolested. Occasionally, however, major powers, such as Babylon, Assyria, Greece and Rome were prompted to pacify the area.

The mountains are made of limestone that decomposes into rich soil and from the Iron Age to the present, the region supported farming and grazing. Vineyards, olives, and a variety of grains flourish there. The mountains are important from the point of view of rainfall, serving as huge watersheds for the coastal plain to the west and the rift valley to the east. The western slope of the Central Highlands receives abundant rainfall. However, the average annual rainfall drops precipitously as storms lose intensity moving from the central ridge toward the east. Within two miles of the ridge, the average amount of annual rainfall drops 50 percent. Consequently, the ridge constitutes a geographical boundary between the well-watered settled farming territory to the west and the semi-arid grazing territory to the east.

The depth of the Rift Valley to the east exaggerates the ruggedness of the mountains. Within fifteen miles moving in an easterly direction, the mountains drop from an elevation of about 3,000 feet above sea level to 1,300 feet below sea level at the Dead Sea.

The Coastal Plain: a north-south running strip of land hugging the shore of the eastern Mediterranean Sea. It is blessed with exceptionally fertile alluvial soil that was washed down from the mountaintops and deposited on the plain. It also has an abundance of springs and a very high water table that makes possible the construction of wells. This combination of factors led to the growth of permanent agricultural settlements and sophisticated civilization from the earliest of times. It is on this coastal plain that the population density has been highest throughout history.

Cosmology: from Greek words *cosmos,* meaning 'world,' and *logos,* meaning 'word, reason.' Cosmology is the study of the nature of the world or universe and the theories, principles and assumptions about it.

The Dead Sea: one of two inland bodies of water in Palestine (the other is the Sea of Galilee), it is located at the deepest part of the Afro-Syrian Rift Valley, 1,300 feet below sea level. It is about thirty miles long by fourteen miles wide and about eighty miles in circumference. It has been known for its mineral content throughout history. These minerals have been mined for medicines, cosmetics and for use in embalming. Today it is best known for its peculiar buoyancy—it is impossible to sink in its waters. This effect is due to its high salt content, thirty times higher than that of seawater. It is also known for its slimy texture, its stench and its annoying stinging effect.

The Dead Sea Scrolls: one of two treasuries of ancient texts discovered in the mid-1940s that provide biblical scholars with enormous new material for research. The Dead Sea Scrolls were discovered in 1947 in caves on the northwest shore of the Dead Sea. The legendary stories told about the discovery of the scrolls are testimony to the fertility of the human imagination. In fact the true story is interesting enough, if not quite as colourful as the apocryphal ones.

Bedouin boys who were exploring/playing in the caves in the vicinity of Khirbet Qumran while grazing their sheep stumbled upon them and brought them to their encampment. Realizing from their prior experience in archaeological excavation that they were artefacts of interest to antiquities dealers, the Bedouin elders brought them to a dealer in Bethlehem. They were sold subsequently to Professor E.L. Sukenik of the Hebrew University and the Syrian Orthodox Metropolitan of Jerusalem, Athanasius Samuel. The Syrian scrolls were eventually smuggled to the United States. They were put on sale through an advertisement in the Wall Street Journal and were purchased by agents for the newly established State of Israel for $250,000 in 1954. They were added to the Hebrew University collection.

After the war of 1948 in which Israel was established, excavations of the caves near Khirbet Qumran began under the auspices of the Jordanian Department of Antiquities and the Ecole Biblique in Jerusalem. Over the next few years, excavations of the nearby ruins of Qumran commenced as well. By the end of the decade, eleven caves had yielded the treasures they had concealed for 2,000 years.

Altogether, the discovery and excavation of the library of Qumran are watershed events in biblical scholarship. Scholars now have a vast new collection of literature dating to the time of Jesus. About half of the library consists of copies of books of the Hebrew scriptures. Until their discovery, the oldest Old Testament manuscripts dated to the 10th century AD. The remaining scrolls provide invaluable insights into the intertestamental period and life at the time of Jesus.

Parallels between the community that produced the Dead Sea Scrolls, John the Baptist and Jesus are hard to resist. However, such parallels are based on apparent similarities between words and habits that may be purely coincidental. Be this as it may, much Holy Land speculation takes place in a Disneyland atmosphere. Good stories always take priority over facts, so imaginative theories abound that John and/or Jesus were members of the Qumran community.

The Decapolis: from the Greek words *Decca* and *polis* meaning 'ten cities,' the Decapolis was a confederation of about ten cities which, except for Scythopolis (Beth She'an), lay on the eastern bank of the Jordan River, between modern Amman and Damascus, both of which were members. Scholars are not certain now that the Decapolis was an economic league. It may have been an administrative association of cities. Nor is it certain that it included ten cities, as its name suggests. Pliny the Elder acknowledges that other authors list more. The Gospel of Mark (5: 20, 7: 31) states that Jesus travelled through the region of the Decapolis. It is certain that he passed through Scythopolis, because it is a major junction of the Via Maris and on the way between Galilee and Jerusalem. Hippos is situated on the eastern shore of the Sea of Galilee, within easy reach of Capernaum by boat or by foot. Gadera is equally close, located south of the Sea of Galilee a few miles. It is not unlikely, however, that he visited Jerash (ancient Gerasa, Mark 5: 1) as well and no one can rule out broader peregrinations.

Egeria: a pilgrim who travelled from her home in Western Europe to the Holy Land on a four year pilgrimage (AD 380-384). She was a member of a religious order of some kind and is often referred to as a nun. She kept a careful journal that survives and provides invaluable information about the Holy Land, from Egypt to Asia Minor during the times she travelled. Thus, from her journal, one of the few surviving written sources from that time, we know what holy sites had been identified and were being shown to pilgrims. We also know what she understood by pilgrimage. Her journey was a deeply religious event in her life that was marked by investigation of biblical places, worship with indigenous Christians and prayer.

The Epic of Gilgamesh: the oldest heroic literary epic in the history of any culture. It is one of the oldest narratives known, its earliest versions dating to the Middle Bronze Age (2500 BC). It was composed in Ancient Sumer in Mesopotamia. Gilgamesh is a royal figure who is formed from the dust of the earth. He is an urban dweller who grapples with the inevitability of death. His companion, Enkidu, is a semi-wild man whose origin is the desert. The story of their creative, competitive relationship is symbolic of one of the mighty themes of ancient Near Eastern literature: the struggle between urban and desert society. It shares this theme with the Bible. Other common themes include the relationship between the gods and the ruler, the story of a great flood and the agency of the gods in creating humanity.

Essenes: often identified with the authors of the Dead Sea Scrolls and the inhabitants of the community at Qumran, the Essenes were a group of

Israelites who broke away from the Temple cult in Jerusalem in the immediate aftermath of the Hasmonean Revolt. A minority opinion among scholars is that the Qumran community was not Essenes, based on the simple fact that the word 'Essene' does not occur in the Dead Sea Scrolls. The authors of the Dead Sea Scrolls did not refer to themselves as Essenes, but rather as *covenanteers*. Nonetheless, the evidence overwhelmingly supports the identification of the Qumran community as Essenes. In addition to the Dead Sea Scrolls themselves, Philo of Alexandria, Josephus, and Pliny the Elder provide literary sources about the Essenes. Pliny was aware of an Essene community in the wilderness near the northeast shore of the Dead Sea. Josephus provides information about the lifestyle of the Essenes that is mostly supported by the information from the Dead Sea Scrolls themselves.

After rejecting the authority of the Jerusalem Temple cult, the Essenes separated themselves from the mainstream of Israelite society for the purpose of purifying themselves in advance of the expected apocalypse. According to their own accounts, they went into the desert in order to maintain ritual purity so that they would be born as a new Israel in the last days. They consciously identified with Isaiah 40: 3-5 in that their life in the desert was for the purpose of 'preparing the way of the Lord.' Parallels to John the Baptist are tempting, but should be resisted. Josephus identifies them as one of several 'sects' of the Judeans. The information from Josephus and Philo that they lived in many villages and towns, cultivated intimate fellowship, held property in common, shared communal meals, and entered into a sort of voluntary poverty is supported by the Qumran writings.

Form criticism: one ingredient of the historical critical method. It is a type of biblical scholarship in which the scholar identifies 'forms' within the biblical text. Different types of writings occur in different forms. The letter is different from the legal code. Identifying the form helps determine how a particular passage should be understood.

Gadara: one of the cities of the Decapolis, located several miles south of the Sea of Galilee on the eastern bank of the Jordan river. It is identified with modern Umm Qeis in Jordan. Some of the best biblical manuscripts identify the demoniac in Mark's story (Mark 5: 1-20) as a Gaderene. According to Josephus, Gadara was a cultural and political centre in the late Hellenistic and Early Roman Periods. The poet, Meleager, the Cynic philosopher, Mennipus, and the rhetorician Philodemus all hailed from there. The presence of such a rich locus of culture illustrates the extent to which the region of Galilee had been Hellenized and the sort of cultural influences to the people of Galilee had been exposed.

The Garden of Gethsemane: derived from the Aramaic word meaning *olive presses*, it is located on the lower part of the western slope of the Mount of Olives. It is across the Kidron Valley (John 18: 1) from the Old City of Jerusalem, directly opposite the Golden Gate. All the Gospels locate Jesus' arrest there. Today, two sites are set apart by tradition as the spot where Jesus prayed and was arrested. Both places have been venerated since antiquity. On one spot, the Basilica of the Agony or Church of All Nations receives over a million pilgrims a year. In its garden are ancient olive trees said to be over two thousand years old.

Galilee: a region of Northern Israel. Of all the regions of the Holy Land, none is more significant in terms of understanding the history of New Testament times and particularly the gospels than the region called Galilee. Derived from the Hebrew word 'galil' which means 'circle,' the Galilee is the region in northern Israel/Palestine where Jesus was born, spent his formative years and most of his earthly ministry. Upper Galilee is mountainous. Lower Galilee tends toward gentle hills and wide plains.

Additionally, the region was known for its fertility and, because it receives generous amounts of rainfall, its abundant agricultural productivity. Josephus says, 'The soil is universally rich and fruitful, full of plantations of trees of all sorts...' Thus, it was prized throughout history as an important agricultural centre, as well as a strategic region control of which was vital for international trade and the wealth and prosperity it yielded. Consequently, the Galilee was a region through which peoples from all over the known world travelled.

Gospel: one of several genres of literature found in the New Testament, the term is most often identified with the first four books of the New Testament, Matthew, Mark, Luke and John. Christian Gospels represent a distinct literary form that contain elements of other genres, such as the Hellenistic *Romance*. The term *gospel* has no antecedent in Israelite religious usage. In fact, the term is drawn from the political milieu of the Hellenistic and Early Roman Periods. Before it was used in association with the life and ministry of Jesus it was widely understood to refer to the announcement of the birth of a new political ruler. For example, an inscription celebrating the achievements of the Emperor Augustus Caesar refers to Augustus' birth as, '...the beginning of the good news to the world on his account.' Quite possibly, the term gospel was applied to the ministry of Jesus by followers who deliberately sought to contrast the power of Jesus and his heavenly reign with that of the secular, political ruler of the Mediterranean world.

Gospel Harmony: an attempt to reconcile the various accounts of Jesus' life and ministry into one coherent and uniform biography.

The Gospel of Thomas: a collection of 114 sayings of Jesus discovered in 1945 in the Nile Valley along with many other manuscripts of the Nag Hammadi Library. Most of the sayings are recognizable from the canonical Gospels. The value of the Gospel of Thomas in New Testament studies cannot be overstated. It is an example of the sort of document that scholars hypothesize Q to be, i.e., composed exclusively of sayings. Most scholars date the gospel of Thomas to the middle part of the 2nd century, but a minority dates it to the middle of the 1st century. If this were the case, it would be the oldest Christian document known and would make it a possible source for the composition of the Gospels.

Hadrian: emperor of Rome from 117 to 138 AD. He is responsible for the construction of many monuments, including Hadrian's wall in Britain. Between 133-135 AD he suppressed the second Jewish Revolt (The Bar Kochba Revolt), destroyed the city of Jerusalem, expelled Judeans from Judea and rebuilt Jerusalem, naming it Aelia Capitolina.

Hasmoneans: an Israelite family that ruled Judea from about 160 to 63 BC. They came to power in the revolt of the Maccabees that broke out when the Seleucid King, Antiochus IV attempted to pilfer money from the Temple treasury to support his war efforts. He also tried to impose foreign cult practices on the Temple authorities. After a successful campaign against the Seleucids, they struck a deal with the Seleucids in which they were given the office of the High Priest and ruling authority. Sometimes cast as the leaders of an anti-Greek revolt, the Hasmoneans were anything but anti-Greek. Indeed, they furthered the process of Hellenization among the Judeans. Their most successful rulers were John Hyrcanus and Alexander Jannaeus who enjoyed long reigns. When Pompey invaded Syria and Palestine in 64-63 BC, Hasmonean power was disrupted. A civil war ensued between them and the rising Herodian house. After a fifteen-year contest, power transferred to Herod the Great.

Hebrew Scriptures: consisting of thirty-eight books of legal codes, hymns and narratives, it has three sections: The first five books are called Torah or sometimes the Pentateuch. The Prophets (Neviim) include Joshua, Judges, 1 & 2 Samuel, 1 & 2 Kings and 1 & 2 Chronicles. The Writings (Ketuvim) include Job, Psalms, Proverbs, Song of Solomon and Ecclesiastes. The Hebrew letters for the names of these sections forms an acronym, *TaNaKh*. The

Hebrew Scriptures are often known by this name. The Hebrew Scriptures are distinguishable from the Old Testament, because the order of the books is different, reflecting a different interpretation of history.

Hebron: at about 3,000 feet the high point in the mountainous ridge, Hebron is also known as Mamre in the Old Testament. At one time Hebron was the capital of Judah (II Samuel 2: 1-11), but the city is best known as the traditional burial place of the patriarchs, Abraham, Isaac and Jacob and their wives, Sarah, Rebecca and Leah. Many biblical passages are situated there, e.g., Gen. 23 and Josephus refers to the construction of the wall around the Tomb of the Patriarchs (and Matriarchs). The Herodian structure is said to be a model for the Temple Mount.

Hellenistic Period: an archaeological and historical era beginning with the conquest of Alexander the Great of the territories of the Persian empire in 332 BC. In Greek history, the Hellenistic Period comes to a close in 146 BC when Rome conquered Greece. In Israelite/Palestinian history, the Hellenistic period ends with the conquest of the Levant by the Roman General Pompey in 64 BC.

Hellenization: the process of spreading Greek culture throughout the territories of the former Persian Empire.

Herod Antipas: upon the death of his father, Herod the Great, Antipas was given jurisdiction over Galilee and Perea. He rebuilt Sepphoris and adorned it to be the 'ornament of all Galilee.' He also founded a City, Tiberius, which he named in honour of the Emperor, Caesar Tiberius. According to Luke (Lk 13: 32), Jesus referred to him as 'that Fox.' This is the Herod who had John the Baptist beheaded, but ancient sources disagree as to why. Josephus says it was his fear of rebellion. The Gospels say it was because of John's denunciation of Antipas' incestuous marriage. Antipas is the Herod who interrogated Jesus after his arrest. In a typical story of royal intrigue, Antipas went to Rome in order to upgrade his title from tetrarch to king so that he could be like his family rival Agrippa. Agrippa, however, had prepared damaging accusations against him. He was exiled to Lyons in France where he died—some say of a broken heart.

Herod Archelaus: upon the death of his father, Herod the Great, Archelaus inherited rule over Judea and received the title ethnarch. Judea was half of Herod the Great's kingdom. He ruled from 4 BC until AD 6. He was not well liked. Matthew refers to him (Mt.2: 33) as ruler in Judea. When the Holy family returned from Egypt, they bypassed his administrative area out of fear and settled in Nazareth instead in order to evade him. Josephus tells us that Rome deposed him when a delegation of Judeans went to Rome to complain about him. From that time onward, Judea was ruled directly by Rome as a Roman province.

Herod the Great: one of five Herods mentioned in the New Testament and one of over forty mentioned by Josephus, he was the son of Herod Antipater, who was the governor of Idumea, a region to the south of Judea. Subsequent to Pompey's conquest of the Levant, Herod waged a twenty-year civil war with the Hasmoneans. He prevailed in this struggle after procuring the support of the Roman senate that proclaimed him king of the Judeans. Thus, he became the founder of a dynasty that became renowned for its splendid building achievements, ruthlessness and palace intrigue. He reigned until about 4 BC and was king of the Judeans at the time of Jesus' birth. In the birth narratives of Luke and Matthew, he is referenced as king. His reputation for brutality is preserved in Matthew's story of the massacre of the Holy Innocents as well as in Josephus who reports that Herod brutally suppressed opposition to his rule and even had a number of family members assassinated when he suspected them of sedition. Consequently, the Roman governor in Syria is said to have remarked, 'I would rather be Herod's pig than his son.' Notwithstanding his notorious ruthlessness, however, Herod left a sparkling legacy of building accomplishment. His architectural masterpieces were the artificial port at Caeserea Maritima on the Plain of Sharon and the city of Jerusalem itself. Upon his death, Judea was divided into three administrative areas. Subsequent generations referred to Herod as 'Herod the Great' to differentiate him from his sons.

Herod Philip: the third son of Herod the Great to receive a portion of the elder Herod's kingdom, Philip ruled over the Gaulinitis, Batanea and Trachonitis. He rebuilt and enlarged Caeserea Philippi, which he renamed after himself and his patron Caesar. Josephus reports that his reign was stable and prosperous. He is implicated in the story of the death of John the Baptist, but ancient sources are confused as to exactly what role he played.

Herodian: a fortress/palace in the Judean desert about three miles southeast of Bethlehem. Herod the Great built it by levelling a mountain and piling the rubble on top of the adjacent mountain, thus producing an artificial mountain stronghold. Archaeological remains include the royal residence and fortifications, a system of tunnels and cisterns, an administrative complex, a racetrack and a monumental pool. According to Josephus, Herod the Great is buried there, but his tomb has not been found. Rebels during the second

Jewish revolt used it.

Hippodamian plan: an urban plan, named after the 5th century BC Greek city planner, Hippodamus. Streets were arranged in a grid pattern in north-south and east-west directions. The main street was called the *cardo maximus*. It was intersected at a ninety-degree angle by the *decumanus maximus*. Streets ran parallel to these two main thoroughfares, thus creating 'blocks.'

The historical-critical method: the name given to the dominant scholarly approach to the Bible since the Enlightenment and especially in the 20th century. This method includes form, source, redaction, text, literary, sociological and rhetorical criticism. Each of these is a distinct form of analysis. The historical-critical method has produced monumental insights and discoveries. Predictably, seminarians loathe its rigorous demands, but no responsible student of the Bible can avoid the necessity of learning to use it. Neither can any serious student of the Bible escape its crushing burden of tedium and seeming irrelevance. For all its enormous influence and shining accomplishments, the historical-critical method is based on assumptions about knowledge that are accepted uncritically. For instance, the historical-critical method is based on the notion that truth is discovered by breaking down an object into its component parts. This, however, is a culturally conditioned idea. It is not at all clear that the Bible is best understood when it is approached as if it were an object. The effort to analyze the Bible into smaller and smaller molecular and atomic parts, e.g., forms, sources, pericopes, etc. has lead to an increase in specialization to the point where much scholarship is neither accessible nor relevant.

The Holy Land: a sub region of the Levant, representing about one half the total area of the Levant or about 7,200 square miles. It displays all of the major geographical subdivisions that characterize the Levant— a coastal plain, a mountainous hill country, the rift valley, the eastern mountains and the desert beyond them.

Iron Age: an archaeological period generally considered to begin around 1200 BC. Its ending depends on personal preference and the region one is considering, but in the Levant, it is usually considered to end with the beginning of the Persian Period ca. 536 BC. It is sometimes referred to as the Israelite Period. The events narrated in the Old Testament from the Exodus to the Babylonian Conquest occur against the backdrop of the Iron Age.

Israel: today, Israel is a nation-state situated on the eastern shore of the Mediterranean Sea. The region is historically referred to as Palestine. In biblical history, *Israel* is the name of a people who trace their ancestry to Abraham. The story of their history and relationship to the God Yahweh is the heart of the Hebrew Scriptures or Old Testament. In Western scholarship, the writing of the history of the people of Israel—modern and ancient—is characterized by the perpetuation of unquestioned and uncritically accepted presuppositions. Concerning ancient Israel, these presuppositions pertain to a past for which there is very little archaeological evidence and only Israelite literary evidence. Thus, ancient Israel is frequently conceived as a modern European styled nation-state. Most recently, Israeli, European and American historians are re-evaluating historical data and challenging some of the cherished assumptions about ancient Israel. It is generally agreed that Israel was one of many Canaanite peoples. Israel was a loose confederation of smaller clans or tribes that emerged mostly on the mountains of the Central Highlands in the southwestern part of the Levant. Historiography dates the emergence of the people Israel to the Late Bronze or Early Iron Age, but archaeological evidence is scanty and literary support dates to a period much later than that. The people of Israel produced distinctive writings that bear the characteristic traces of Near Eastern literature. These writings represent an enormous theological and historical legacy.

Jerash: a city in modern Jordan, about thirty miles northwest of Amman, in the mountains of Gilead, it is the site of ancient Gerasa, a city of the Decapolis. Jesus ministered through the region of the Decapolis and Mark mentions his activity in the region of the Gerasenes (Mark 5: 1-20). The excavations at Jerash reveal the best preserved Hellenistic city in the region of the Eastern Mediterranean Sea. The extensive site includes a massive monumental arch (built by Hadrian in AD 135), an enormous and well preserved stadium, most of the walls and another massive gate, several massive temple complexes, an unusual oval shaped agora, a Cardo that is 1,000 yards long, two decamani, a well preserved theatre and an odion, dozens of churches, shops, bath complexes and an ornate nymphaeum, among other things. The cardo is backed by stoa with both Corinthian and Ionian capitals and the water system for the city is well preserved. Although Jerash was founded about 198 BC and the Decapolis was established by Pompey the Great in 63 BC, most of the ruins date from the 2nd of 3rd centuries.

Jericho: situated on the floor of the Jordan River valley, several miles north of the Dead Sea, 15 miles east of Jerusalem and 1,250 feet below sea level, it is one of two Near Eastern cities which claim to be the oldest in the world (Damascus is the other one). It has 10,000 years of continuous human history associated with it. Settlement was sustained by a powerful spring that pumps

1,000 gallons of water per minute. Tel es Sultan is the oldest settlement and the first object of archaeological interest. Charles Warren first excavated the site in 1868. John Garstang announced that he had discovered the walls that came tumbling down at the time of Joshua's conquest, but Kathleen Kenyon rejected his theory in the 1950s with the aid of more sophisticated dating techniques. Today, most scholars agree that the city was unfortified at the time the Bible narrates Joshua's conquest. The city was greatly enlarged by Herod the Great who improved the irrigation system, built a stunning royal residence and added all the features of a city. The best known Old Testament story associated with Jericho is the conquest narrative (Joshua 5-7). Gospel references include the story of blind Bartimaeus (Mark 10: 46-52, the parable of the Good Samaritan (Luke 10: 29-37) and the story of Zacchaeus (Luke 19: 1-10).

Jerusalem: testifying to its theological and historical significance, it is mentioned in the Bible more often than any other city. Indeed, no other city in the world can claim such religious associations. No other city possesses the spiritual attraction of Jerusalem, holy to Jews, Christians and Muslims. It has over six thousand years of continuous human history associated with it. Its name derives from Canaanite usage and means 'foundation of Shalem.' Shalem was a local deity from pre-Israelite times whose worship was centred at Jerusalem. The popular belief that its name derives from Hebrew usage and means 'city of peace' is wrong. In Arabic, its name, 'Al-Quds,' means 'the Holy.' Originally, during the Islamic period, it was called 'the Holy House.'

Jerusalem was an unimportant village in pre-Israelite times. Prior to the arrival of Israelites, Jebusites, who continued to occupy the city even after the Israelite conquest, occupied it. At that time, occupation was restricted to Jerusalem's only water source, the Gihon Spring. The narratives in Joshua betray no early Israelite interest in Jerusalem. Nor is there any indication that Saul considered Jerusalem strategically or politically important. David made Jerusalem his capital, taking advantage of its location on the border of two Israelite tribes and the consequent fact that it did not belong to either the northern or southern tribes. Establishing his capital there thus enabled him to maintain the unity of the kingdoms. Solomon built the first temple on the top of Mount Moriah, north and uphill from the Jebusite and Davidic settlement.

The biblical narrative suggests that Jerusalem flourished as a centre of Israelite political and religious activity during the late Iron Age. In 586 BC, the city was sacked by the Babylonian King Nebuchadnezzar and its inhabitants were deported. The so-called *Babylonian Exile* lasted fifty years until the Persian King Cyrus defeated Babylon and the Judeans were allowed to return. Many stayed in Babylon, but those who returned reconstituted the Temple and its cult, marking the beginning of the so-called *Second Temple Period.*

By the time Jesus was born, Jerusalem had been rebuilt by Herod the Great as a Greek city and it had become world renowned as the cult centre of the people of Israel. The Temple of Yahweh, situated on the world's largest artificial platform, was a destination spot for Israelites and pagans alike.

Jerusalem was under construction during Jesus' entire life. Josephus provides copious information about the processes employed in the reconstruction and says that it took eighty years. Archaeological data in conjunction with Josephus' information suggest that Herod rebuilt the city along standard Hellenistic lines. No sooner had the Temple been completed, however, then the revolt against Rome broke out in Caesarea Maritima in the year AD 66. At the end of the revolt, the city of Jerusalem with its remarkable Temple was demolished. The finished product lasted only ten years.

Upon suppression of the second Jewish Revolt or Bar Kochba Revolt, the Roman Emperor Hadrian completely destroyed the city, rebuilt it on a much smaller scale and renamed it Aelia Capitolina. *Aelia* was the emperor's given name. *Capitolina* honoured the Capitolina gods of Rome. Hadrian also issued an edict expelling Judaeans from Jerusalem and the vicinity.

During the Byzantine period (AD 325-638), Christianity flourished in Jerusalem. The Emperor Constantine ordered the construction of a basilica to mark the place of Jesus' crucifixion and resurrection. Although Julian the Apostate, Constantine's nephew issued an edict allowing the reconstruction of the Jewish Temple, that order was never carried out. The site of the Temple was left derelict, used only as a garbage dump. Under Justinian, the city was remodelled once more. This city is depicted in the famous *Madaba Map.*

Islam arrived in Jerusalem in AD 638. The Islamic expansion in the Levant can hardly be called a conquest. Indeed, it was almost peaceful. By AD 638, the Byzantine Empire had lost much of its lustre in the Levant. It had become corrupt and wasted valuable energy and resources protecting itself from the Persian Empire in the east. When the Arab forces led by the Caliph 'Umar arrived in Jerusalem, they were welcomed as liberators. 'Umar ordered the restoration of the Temple Mount and renamed it the Harem esh Sharif or *Noble Sanctuary*. He issued an edict in which the religious privileges of Jews and Christians were to be protected and their property left intact. Since that time, Jerusalem, known as *Al Quds* or The Holy in Arabic, has experienced over 1,400 years of Islamic influence.

Jordan River Valley: the section of the Afro-Syrian Rift Valley between the Sea of Galilee and the Dead Sea.

Josephus: a 1st century Israelite who wrote a number of texts that together represent some of our best literary sources, among a small pool of such resources, for reconstructing the history of 1st century Palestine. He identifies himself as a member of the priestly caste and a Jerusalemite. He is evidently an aristocrat. He claims that he was general of the rebel forces in the revolt that broke out in AD 66. He defected to the Roman side midway through the revolt, became a confident of the emperor Vespasian and lived out the rest of his life in Rome under the emperor's patronage. His writings are his efforts to acquit himself and his people in the eyes of the Roman public.

Judea: this region constitutes the southern region of the mountain of the Central Highlands. Its terrain is similar to that of Samaria. It is suitable for farming and, like Samaria, most of its hills are terraced to support olive and almond orchards and vineyards. Indeed, the grapes that are produced there are legendary for their flavour and size (Numbers 13: 17-24). It is associated with Israelite society and derives its name from the name, Judah, one of the twelve Israelite tribes. In the Second Temple Period, *Judea* generally refers to the southern part of the mountains of the Central Highlands. In the Early Roman Period and later, *Judea* refers to a much larger territory including all of what is today Israel and the Occupied Palestinian Territories and parts of modern day Jordan, Syria and Lebanon.

Judean: a label attached to the people of Israel and their culture by non-Israelites. The name derives from the presumed geographical origin of Israelites, i.e., Judah or Judea. Even though there were large and flourishing populations of urban and rural Israelites throughout the Mediterranean basin by the late Second Temple period who had never stepped foot in Judea, the notion that the people of Israel maintained geographical roots in Judea was widespread. It was well known that the Israelite cultic centre was in Jerusalem in Judea.

Judean wilderness: a semi arid environment east of the mountain ridge defined by the Way of the Patriarchs. The Judean wilderness is a region of very little rainfall and stark landscapes. It is mountainous with deep v-shaped ravines formed by seasonal rivers. These are called *wadis* in Arabic. It served as a buffer zone between the population centres of Judah and the Jordan valley. Due to its terrain and isolation, it developed a reputation as a place of refuge for fugitives and robbers. It served this purpose for David when he sought refuge from Saul (I Samuel 23: 24; 24: 1). It also became known as a place of retreat for spiritual purposes. It is dotted with monasteries which were established in the Byzantine period, some of which remain active to this day, e.g. Mar Saba and St George's. Qumran, where the Dead Sea Scrolls were found is located there. No doubt, those who lived there sought its serenity for spiritual purposes and enjoyed the isolation and freedom from contemporary life that it afforded. John the Baptist is known to have been active in this region and tradition locates Jesus' temptation in the Wadi Qelt, a deep valley with precipitous cliffs on each side. The wilderness of Judea was also known as a place of treachery. The story of the Good Samaritan (Luke 10: 29-37) is located on the road to Jericho which traverses the Judean wilderness. First century listeners of Jesus' parable would have identified immediately with the report of a man who was ambushed along that road.

There is an abundance of imagery in the Bible that seems to be inspired by the terrain of the Judean wilderness. The Psalmist refers to the 'valley of the shadow of death' (Psalm 23: 4), an apparent allusion to the deep wadis formed by erosion over millennia of soft chalky limestone. The reference in Job to 'Terrors' which 'overtake them like a flood' (Job 27: 20), may be inspired by the prevalence of flash floods which result when rain falls heavily on the mountains and is channelled into wadis on the bedrock of hard dolomite.

Judea and Samaria: the hill country is divided into two subregions referred to in the Bible generally as Judea and Samaria. Modern day Israelis frequently point out that most of their biblical heritage is concentrated in these regions as opposed to the coastal plain or the rift valley. Indeed, the names of the cities that are found there, including Bethlehem, Jerusalem, Hebron, Bethel, Shiloh and Shechem (Nablus), are familiar to anyone with even a rudimentary acquaintance with biblical history. Today, this region is usually referred to as The West Bank and increasingly as Palestine.

The King's Highway: one of two ancient superhighways in the ancient Levant. It runs in a generally north-south direction along the ridge of the mountains of Transjordan.

The Levant: derived from a French word meaning 'the rising,' this term refers to the region of land on the shore of the eastern Mediterranean Sea, which includes modern day Lebanon, Syria, Jordan, Israel and Palestine. Rugged mountains, rich agricultural areas, semi-arid and desert environments characterize it. Its major geographical features are oriented in north-south directions. These include the Coastal Plain, the Central Highlands, the Rift Valley, the Eastern Heights or mountains of Transjordan.

Madaba map: a partially preserved mosaic on the floor of St George's Orthodox Church in Madaba, Jordan, it is an extremely important artifact that provides information about holy sites as they were known to have existed in the 6th century. Originally containing about two million tesserae, it was damaged during the construction of the modern church. The mosaic is a map of Palestine and lower Egypt. Jerusalem is clearly depicted, including the cardo, the Church of the Resurrection, the New Church, the northern (Damascus) gate and the forum of Hadrian. Also clearly shown are the Dead Sea, the Jordan River, including the place where Jesus was baptized north of the Dead Sea, Jericho, Nablus, Sinai, the Nile River and Alexandria.

Marcionism: an ancient belief declared heretical by the early Church. It is named after its first formulator, Marcion, who came from Asia Minor and lived in the 2nd century AD. Marcion was the first scholar to produce a Christian canon, i.e., a normative compilation of scriptural books that replaced the Old Testament for him and his followers. His list included no books of the Hebrew scriptures, a modified version of the Gospel of Luke—devoid of any hint of Jewish influence, and ten Pauline letters. Marcion's canon eliminated anything he believed to be Jewish adaptations of Christian writings and anything that was Jewish in origin.

Marl: an almost sterile form of soil that is peculiar to the Dead Sea Valley, in the vicinity of Jericho and to the south.

Masada: a remote desert fortress located on a mountain overlooking the western shore of the Dead Sea . It was first fortified by Alexander Jannaeus (104-76 BC). Its name means 'mountain stronghold.' During the civil war between the Hasmoneans and the Herodians, Herod the Great used the fortress to keep his family safe while he went to Rome to gain Roman patronage. When he prevailed over the Hasmoneans, Herod refortified the stronghold and built himself opulent living quarters.

   While Herod the Great never used Masada again, it was occupied by the Sicari, a group of Judeans rebels, during the 1st War of the Judeans. From there, the Sicari initiated raids against fellow Judeans, but took no further part in the Judean revolt. In AD 73, the Romans besieged the Sicari, setting the stage for Masada's most notorious episode. According to Josephus, our only written source for the events that allegedly transpired, the Sicari refused to surrender, preferring collective sacrifice instead. In all, Josephus says that 960 Sicari men, women and children took their own lives.

   The Masada story is one of the most widely misunderstood episodes in Judean history. While they are usually identified as 'Zealots,' it is clear from Josephus that the defenders on Masada were Sicari. Although they are frequently cast as nationalist heroes, Josephus' account clearly depicts the Sicari as Judean traitors, scoundrels and murderers. Rather than leave the reader with a positive impression of the Sicari, Josephus' narrative is meant to present his Roman audience with an explanation of how otherwise loyal Judeans were misled into rebellion. His story is meant to exonerate both the Romans and the Judean people from culpability in the Judean revolt. The entire uprising is blamed on the Sicari who accept their fate in the end as God's judgement on the folly of their cause.

The spectacular physical surroundings and extraordinary archaeological excavations, in combination with the infamous story told about the Sicari, make Masada a striking and popular site to visit. The Roman fortifications and siege ramp are well preserved, as are the defenders' fortifications on the summit. The sophisticated water collection systems testify to Herod's engineering skill. One cistern alone can hold three-million gallons of water. There are two palace complexes, storehouses, a bath complex and numerous other buildings.

Megiddo: one of the most important archeological sites in the Holy Land, it has over twenty-one layers of habitation reaching back over four thousand years in time, is situated on a branch of the Via Maris at one of the strategic crossroads leading to the Jezreel Valley. Megiddo protects the branch of the Via Maris which crosses the valley and leads up to the eastern heights, Damascus and the important markets and trade routes of the east.

Mesopotamia: literally 'between the rivers,' the region of the Tigris and Euphrates Rivers. Today this region consists of Iraq and Northern Syria. In ancient times it was the locus of the Babylonian and Assyrian Empires. The biblical narrative (Gen. 11: 30-31) tells us that Abraham was born there and began his sojourn to Canaan from there.

Mount Hermon: the tallest peak in the Levant it is situated in occupied Syria on the border with Lebanon. It is about 10,000 feet in elevation.

Mount of Olives: at about 2,500 feet, it is Jerusalem's highest point. Rich in ancient religious significance, it is believed, in Jewish tradition, to be the place from which Messiah would enter Jerusalem. It has many associations with Jesus in the Gospels. Jesus entered the city of Jerusalem from the Mount of Olives on Palm Sunday. He was arrested at the foot of the Mount of Olives in the Garden of Gethsemane. According to Acts, Jesus ascended into heaven from there (Acts 1: 9-12). Its association with Jesus' teaching here led to the building of several churches, including one built by Helena, Constantine's mother.

Myth: from the Greek word *mythos*, the history of this word oscillates between high esteem and extreme devaluation. While a myth is often understood to be a completely fictitious story, in its original Greek (Platonic) sense, it was understood as a story that expresses truths so deep and profound that they cannot be understood propositionally. Myth, in this sense, is an account of supreme reality.

Nablus: although its archaeological sites are largely neglected, Nablus is one of the most important sites in Palestine. Human occupation is attested here as early as the Chalcolithic Age (4500-3100 BC). Tel Balata is an enormous, well preserved Bronze and Iron Age site and there are important Hellenistic and Roman Age ruins, including a theatre, water systems, burial sites and temple complexes.

Known as Shechem in the Bible, according to the biblical narrative, Abraham received a promise of land from God there (Gen. 12: 6-7). Jacob purchased land to settle there (Gen. 33: 18-20). This site, where Jesus encountered the Samaritan women, is known in John and today as Jacob's Well. During the Babylonian Exile, those Judeans who stayed behind are said to have intermarried with the outsiders. Their offspring developed into the Samaritans who established their temple on Mt Gerazim, one of two mountains guarding the east-west pass through the city. The memory of this temple is still alive in New Testament times and is alluded to in John 4: 20.

The modern name is derived from the Latin name, Flavia Neapolis (new city of the Flavians), which was a Roman colony established by Flavius Titus in AD 72. Some scholars situate 'aenon near Salim,' where John the Baptist is depicted as operating (John 3: 23), about three miles east of Nablus. Jesus, Philip, Peter and John (Acts 8: 4-25) visited Nablus and Christianity flourished there during the Byzantine Period (AD 325-638). The Christian apologist, Justin Martyr, was born there (ca. AD 100).

The Nag Hammadi Library: one of two treasuries of New Testament era writings, these manuscripts were discovered in Nag Hammadi, one hundred fifty miles south of Cairo in the Nile River Valley. The discovery occurred two years prior to the discovery of the Dead Sea Scrolls in 1945. The manuscripts date from the 4th century and are written in Coptic. They are generally considered to be copies of Greek texts that were written in the second and third centuries, but some scholars date some of the documents to the middle of the 1st century. The collection includes twelve codices (papyrus pages bound together in book form) and one tractate which itself is a collection of other tractates. Forty of these works represent previously unknown material One work, *The Gospel of Thomas* is a collection of sayings attributed to Jesus. Many of these sayings are familiar to us from the canonical Gospels

Nazareth: situated in the central plain of the lower Galilee near the Via Maris and Sepphoris, it was Jesus' boyhood town. Nazareth is not mentioned at all in the Hebrew scriptures. It is not mentioned in a list of villages and towns in Josephus. It is not mentioned in a list of villages and towns in the Talmud. Its earliest reference is in the Gospels. The next earliest reference is from the early 3rd century AD. The scarcity of literary mention suggests that it was an unimportant town. At the time of Jesus, it was a small town, probably dependent upon nearby Sepphoris. Its points of archaeological interest include the spring, called the Well of the Virgin, ancient caves attesting Iron Age settlement, a complex of caves attesting early Christian veneration, and remains of ancient churches.

The Old Testament: the Christian designation for the books that make up three fourths of the Christian Canon. It includes the entire Tanak, but the books are arranged in different order, reflecting Christian understanding of the function of the books in pointing toward Jesus the Christ. Protestants recognize thirty-eight books of the Old Testament. Catholics include the seventeen books of the Apocrypha.

Ostracon: a pottery sherd inscribed in ink or etching (plural: ostraca). Ostraca were used to write messages, notes, receipts and letters, among other purposes. In ancient Greece, temporary banishment of a citizen was voted upon by using ostraca inscribed with the name of the person to be banished The person was thus 'ostracized.'

Palestine: derived from the name of the ancient civilization that flourished in the southern coastal region of the Levant, the Greek historian Herodotus first applied the name *Philisita* to the entire region which is today called Israel and the West Bank. In the year AD 135, after the suppression of the 2nd Judean Revolt, the Roman Emperor Hadrian incorporated the region into the Roman Empire, naming it *Provincia Palestina* after the Philistines, Israel's traditional enemy. From that time until 1948, it was known universally as Palestine. Since the establishment of the State of Israel in 1948, it has also been called Israel. In scholarship, the region is usually referred to as Palestine denoting a geographical area. However, this is an anachronism when it is applied to the region prior to the time of Herodotus. Today, in anticipation of the birth of a new nation-state, the term 'Palestine' increasingly carries political connotations. In this context, it refers to The Occupied Palestinian Territories of the West Bank and Gaza that will eventually become the State of Palestine.

Persian Period: an archaeological and historical era dated from the conquest of Cyrus the Great in 536 BC of the Babylonian Empire. It comes to a close with Alexander's conquest of the Persians in 332 BC. It corresponds to the period of the reconstruction of the Temple and the Books of Ezra and Nehemiah in Israelite history.

Philistines: known from the narratives of the Hebrew Scriptures where they appear frequently, the Philistines are popularly and simplistically considered the traditional enemies of Israel. Modern Western biblical scholarship and historiography have obscured and distorted the history of the Philistines by relying almost exclusively on the texts of the Old Testament to inform their search for a people called Israel. Indeed, in contemporary American English, to refer to someone as a 'Philistine' is to suggest that he or she is uncultured or barbarian. In fact, the Philistines were a sophisticated culture that flourished on the Coastal Plain of Palestine. Revisionist historians, with the aid of archaeological discoveries, are currently reconsidering Philistine culture.

Philo of Alexandria: a Judean who lived in Alexandria, Egypt between 20 BC and AD 40. He is the author of a vast collection of writings and one of the most important sources for information about Israelites outside of Palestine.

Phoenicians: a seafaring people, perhaps the 'sea people' of the Old Testament. They occupied the strip of land, about 130 miles long, along the seacoast in the Levant and cultivated an extensive trade network on the Mediterranean, with sea route to Egypt, Crete, Sicily, North Africa (Carthage) and Spain. Their cities included Byblos, Tyre, Sidon, and Carthage.

The Philistine Plain: one of several subdivisions of the Coastal Plain, it is located south of the Plain of Sharon and is named after the Philistines who settled the region. The Greek historian Herodotus applied the name of the Philistines to the entire southern region of the Levant, calling it Philistia.

The Plain of Acco: one of several subdivisions of the Coastal Plain. It takes its name from the ancient port city, Acco, which is easily accessible from the Via Maris and the Plain of Esdraelon. The Plain of Acco is separated from the

Phoenician Plain in the North by Ras ha Niqra and from The Plain of Sharon in the south by the Mt Carmel range.

The Plain of Esdraelon (Jezreel Valley): an east west running plain located in the lower Galilee connecting the Mediterranean coast to the Jordan River Valley. The shallow grade of the plain means that rainwater percolates into the ground rather than running off. Consequently, in the winter, the ground is often saturated and muddy. Two perennial streams, the Harrod and the Qishon are located here. It is a region of enormous agricultural productivity in Northern Israel. It is well watered, receiving about 1,000mm of rainfall each winter and has a mild climate. These factors made it a strategic location and one that has been hotly contested and coveted by empire builders. The combination of abundant water supply, fertile soil and gentle terrain guaranteed that the Jezreel Valley would be populated and cultivated throughout history.

The Jezreel Valley is not only a rich agricultural area, it is a biblically rich environment as well. Nazareth is located in its middle. Megiddo is located there as well. Known in the days of Jesus by its Greek name 'Esdraelon,' it was the scene of the some of the most dramatic stories in scripture. Saul sought out the seer at Endor near Esdraelon when he desperately needed the counsel of Samuel whom he previously had humiliated (1 Samuel 28). The Philistines defeated Saul's army in the battle in which Saul's sons were slain and Saul himself took his own life (1 Samuel 31). King Josiah of Judah was killed at Megiddo in a battle against an Egyptian army (2 Kings 23: 29-30; 2 Chronicles 35: 20-24). Barak defeated a Canaanite army under Sisera who was then delivered into the hands of Jael, the wife of Heber the Kenite (Judges 4). Jesus healed the widow of Nain's son (Luke 7: 11-17).

The Plain of Sharon: one of several subdivisions of the Coastal Plain, it is separated from the Plain of Acco in the north by the Mt Carmel mountains. It was generally unusable swampland until it was drained by Herod the Great's engineers and turned into productive farmland. In later years it reverted to unusable swampland.

Pseudonymous authorship: from Greek words meaning 'false name,' it is the custom, common in the ancient world, of naming a written work after another. There are several letters in the New Testament attributed to Paul that were not written by him. The Gospels and the Book of Revelation may be written pseudonymously. There are various reasons for writing pseudonymously. Naming a book after another is a way of honouring one's teacher or mentor There were times when it was dangerous to publish a book under one's true identity. When the canon of scripture was closed, naming a book after a recognized author was a way to gain readership.

Q: from the German word *Quelle* meaning 'source,' Q is the name given by scholars to a hypothetical document which was used as a source by both Matthew and Luke in the composition of their gospels. Q is considered to have been a collection of saying of Jesus. Although Q does not exist, i.e., no one has possession of it, scholars almost universally admit that it did exist and that it was a source in the writing of the Gospels of Matthew and Luke. To derive the composition of Q scholars remove from the Gospels of Matthew and Luke the parts they share with the Gospel of Mark. This is to say that the Gospel of Mark is largely included in both Matthew and Luke. When this is done, the remaining material is either unique to Matthew and Luke respectively or common to them. The common material consists of sayings. This 'sayings' material that is common to both Matthew and Luke is known as Q.

Qumran: the location of the discovery of the Dead Sea Scrolls on the northwest shore of the Dead Sea. The site is identified as Khirbet Qumran and is about five miles south of Jericho. The Ecole Biblique in Jerusalem and the Jordanian Department of Antiquities excavated the site during the 1950s. Eleven caves produced scrolls and dozens showed evidence of human habitation. Most scholars agree that the occupants of the site at the time of its destruction were Essenes, but the inhabitants referred to themselves a *covenanteers*. The site sprawls over a marl plateau that overlooks the Dead Sea and beyond to the mountains of Jordan. It is adjacent to Wadi Qumran from which it derives its name and from which it drew its water supply. Beyond the cliffs that overlook the site, the community maintained an agricultural centre where they raised livestock and grew grain. The site also included a manufacturing plant at Ein Feschka, about three miles to the south. There, they manufactured cosmetics and pharmaceuticals. Thus, it is evident that the Qumran community enjoyed a diverse economic base.

The main activity for which the Qumran community is known is the manufacture of biblical texts. These were produced on papyrus in the scriptorium that was discovered during the excavations. In AD 68, with a contingent of the Tenth Roman Legion under Vespasian approaching, the inhabitants of Qumran wrapped their most prized possessions in clay jars and hid them in caves, evidently hoping to recover them after the impending destruction by the Romans. However, they never returned. The Romans destroyed the site and after occupying it for several years, they evacuated it, its location was forgotten and the secrets of the covenanteers of Qumran were swallowed by the desert sands.

Rainfall: contrary to popular misconceptions, the Middle East is not a desert, although desert occurs. West of the mountains of the Central Highlands, rainfall is abundant in the winter months, falling most heavily on the mountains, but also on the coastal plain. The ridge of the Central Highlands receives about 1,000 mm of rainfall each year and enough rain falls during the winter to enable farming to occur. Elaborate water collection systems were developed over the ages, along with farming techniques suited to dry climates.

Redaction criticism: an ingredient of the historical-critical method. It is the process whereby the scholar discerns the hand of an editor, i.e., someone other than the author in the manuscript. Even after a text is completed and distributed, it is susceptible to modification by editors and scribes. These are called redactors. Sometimes, the redactor's interest is to clarify a portion of the text for a foreign audience. Sometimes he acts in order to place the text in a new situation. John 21: 24-25 bears the unmistakable marks of a redactor.

Rhetoric: the art of persuasion. Rhetoric was a highly cultivated discipline in the ancient world. It developed in the context of classical Greece, where political, philosophical and social debates and legal proceedings gave rise to the refinement of techniques of argumentation. Rhetoric was the most important subject taught in schools.

Rhetorical criticism: an approach to biblical study in which biblical texts are examined to discover the rhetorical devices used by their authors. Because a large volume of ancient treatises and handbooks on rhetoric survive, scholars can discern which authors use which rhetorical techniques. This reveals the author's purpose. Rhetorical analysis also helps scholars determine the social situation of a text and its author.

Roman Period: an archaeological and historical era. In Greece, it begins with Roman conquest in 146 BC. In the Levant it begins with the conquest of Pompey the Great in 64 BC. The Roman Period lasts until Constantine establishes his capital in Byzantium in AD 325. It is divided into two sub-periods. The Early Roman Period ends with the ascension of the Emperor Hadrian in AD 117. The birth and ministry of Jesus and the life of Paul occur within this period. The Late Roman Period extends from Hadrian to Constantine and coincides with the formative stages of Christianity.

Samaria: constitutes the northern region of the Central Highlands and was also called Mt Ephraim. The Israelite tribes of Ephraim and Mannassah originally populated the region. Subsequent to the time of the United

Monarchy, it was renamed Samaria after the capital city of the Northern Kingdom Israel (I Kings 16: 24). It received its name from King Omri who might have named it after the person (Shemer) from whom he purchased the property on which he built his new capital. The history of the city of Samaria illustrates the importance of its dubious location at the crossroads of civilizations in determining its historical development and role relative to other empires. The period of its greatest wealth and prosperity under Jeroboam II (786-746 BC) coincides with the high point of Phoenician power and commercial expansion in the Mediterranean. No doubt Samaria benefited from friendly relations with Phoenicia. Conversely, during periods of political instability in the outside world, Samaria's fortunes suffered. For instance, during the wars to determine the succession of Alexander the Great, Samaria came under the rule of Macedonians, the Ptolemies, the Seleucids and finally the Hasmoneans. Herod the Great rebuilt the city of Samaria, renaming it Sebaste, honouring Augustus Caesar, his benefactor. Sebaste is derived from *Sebastos* the Greek word for Augustus. Today it is the northern part of the West Bank and is often referred to as Palestine, along with the southern part of the West Bank.

Samaritans: in Jesus' day, Samaria was infamous among the Judeans as the home of the Samaritans, a religious sect which traces its ancestry to the tribes of Mannaseh and Ephraim, i.e. the original tribes of the northern kingdom of Israel. The Samaritans broke away from the Judeans when, under the reforms of Ezra, they located their temple in Jerusalem, the Judean capital instead of Mt Gerizim. The Samaritans claim that Mt Gerizim rather than Mt Zion is the true chosen place of God and so the temple should be situated there rather than in Jerusalem. Further, the Samaritans accept only the first five books of the Bible. For their part, the Judeans of Judea considered the Samaritans impure, because they alleged that the Samaritans had intermarried with pagans during the Assyrian and Babylonian occupations. By the time of Jesus, the schism had grown so great that the Samaritans were considered apostates and unclean. Consequently, Judeans avoided Samaria and contact with Samaritans (John 4: 9) Generally, according to the Gospel narratives, Jesus and his disciples seem to have minimized their contact with Samaritans by travelling around Samaria rather than through it (Matt. 19: 1; Luke 17: 11), but on at least one occasion, Jesus travelled through Samaria (John 4: 4-9). If Jesus himself had any ambivalence about Samaritans, he seems to have overcome it. Three of the best known stories of the gospels feature Samaritans in prominent and complimentary roles. In the story of the Good Samaritan (Luke 10: 30-36), two representatives of the Judean establishment are unfavourably compared with the Samaritan who comes to the aid of an unidentified man who was victimized by robbers. In the story of the ten lepers (Luke 17: 11-19), Jesus heals ten people who were afflicted with leprosy, but the only one who returns to thank Jesus is identified as a Samaritan. Jesus praised his faith. Finally, in the story of the woman at the well (John 4: 4-9), a Samaritan woman becomes the vehicle through which many in the Samaritan community come to believe in Jesus. In each of these stories, the traditional hostility between Judeans and Samaritans is the backdrop against which the events of the stories unfold.

The Sea of Galilee: situated in the Afro-Syrian rift valley, 650 feet below sea level, it was known by different names in different periods. In the Gospel of John, it is known as *The Lake of Tiberius.* The Synoptic Gospels refer to it as both *lake* and *sea.* In the Old Testament it is called *Kinneret.* Pliny the Elder refers to it as *The Lake of Tarichaea.* It is the largest body of fresh water in the Levant and has been an important source of life and livelihood throughout history. It is about thirty miles in circumference, about twelve miles long from north to south and about seven miles wide at its widest point. It reaches a depth of 150 feet. It is fed primarily by the Jordan River from the north, by smaller tributaries and by springs on the northwestern shore. It is most well known for the biblical stories that are located on it and around its shores.

Sepphoris: the provincial capital of Galilee at the time of Jesus' upbringing, it is located in the central part of the lower Galilee, about twenty miles from the Mediterranean coast, fourteen miles from the Sea of Galilee and three miles from Nazareth. Its impressive archaeological excavations, including some of the best mosaics in Palestine, date mainly to the second and third centuries AD, but the theatre and water systems date to the 1st century AD. Some scholars (e.g., Strange) date the theatre as early as the first half of the 1st century AD. It was rebuilt by Herod Antipas and surely controlled the surrounding farm area.

The Septuagint: the Greek version of the Hebrew Scriptures that was translated from Hebrew in Alexandria and includes additional seventeen books. By the time of Jesus and Paul, the Septuagint was the normative version of the Hebrew Scriptures.

The Shephelah: meaning 'lowlands' in Hebrew, this region was a buffer zone between the territory of Judah and the territory of the Philistines. Several important cities were situated here, including Lachish and Gezer and major Old Testament stories were staged here including the story of David and Goliath.

Soil and fertility: the composition of the mountains of the Central Highlands is an important factor in agriculture productivity, because they are composed primarily of porous limestone. This deteriorates into a very rich soil with a distinctive red colore from which it derives its name, 'terra rosa.' This soil is able to sustain farming and pasturing of livestock. Olive orchards and grape vineyards abound. Agricultural productivity was sufficient in ancient times to sustain large cities, such as Jerusalem, Hebron and Shechem.

The limestone of which the mountains are composed is important in another respect. Rainfall percolates through this porous material until it reaches a deeper layer of hard dolomite. It then travels horizontally for great distances, sometimes twenty miles or more, until it emerges in springs on the coastal plain or as oases in the desert valley to the east. The city of Jericho, 15 miles east of Jerusalem is one such oasis as is Ein Gedi ten miles to the south.

In the Jezreel Valley, the combination of fertile soil and abundant rainfall (ca. 1,000 mm per year) sustains agriculture three seasons per year without artificial irrigation. A wide variety of crops were grown throughout history. Josephus indicates that the entire region was under cultivation in his day (1st century). Over the past 50 years, Israel has introduced irrigation technology that enables growing to occur throughout the year. Today, the Jezreel Valley supports various grains, cotton, fruits, including Olives, melons and citrus, and sunflowers.

Source criticism: one of the fundamental ingredients of contemporary biblical analysis, source criticism is the process of examining the books of the Bible to discern sources used in their composition. No serious scholar questions the notion that the books of the Bible were composed using earlier written and oral sources. Source criticism examines these component sources. An almost universal consensus among scholars, e.g., is that the Gospel of Mark is the earliest of the four canonical Gospels and that Matthew and Luke rely on Mark. Mark is included in the Matthew and Luke almost in its entirety. Matthew and Luke follow Mark's chronology. Further, the consensus is overwhelming that both Matthew and Luke used a second written source. This was a collection of sayings of Jesus called 'Q.' Source theory is applied to every book of the Bible. In Pauline studies, the letters of Paul are scrutinized for sources and scholars now believe that 2 Corinthians, e.g., is made up of portions of at least two letters of Paul.

Stoa: a standard feature in Hellenistic architecture, it was a colonnaded hallway. The philosophical school called Stoicism derives it names from these, because its members met in these public hallways.

Synagogue: from a Greek word meaning 'assembly' or 'gathering together.' There is much scholarly debate on the history and purpose of the synagogue. In particular, the long and popularly held belief that the synagogue was a *building* has come into question over the past fifteen years. The consensus is emerging that in the 1st century in Palestine, at least, synagogues were not *buildings*. First it is impossible to tell from a foundation what the purpose of a particular building was, unless there is more explicit means of identification (like an inscription). The three structures commonly held to be synagogues (Masada, Herodian, Gamla) cannot be positively identified. The fourth structure often claimed to be a 1st century synagogue is the foundation under the 4th century limestone synagogue at Capernaum, but Victor Corbo, who excavated the site did not call it a synagogue, but rather identified it as a public building. Nothing positive identifies the 1st century foundation as that of a synagogue. Second, the two literary references to the 'building' of a synagogue are ambiguous. In the case of the Lucan reference (Luke 7: 5), it might reflect the situation in Asia Minor where Luke is writing. In the case of the so-called Theodotus inscription, its date cannot be established and it might come from a later time period. In both cases, the Greek word 'build' *(oikodomeo)* is ambiguous and does not necessarily mean 'build' as in construction of a physical structure. The Greek word could mean 'build' as in strengthen, build up morally, etc. Based on this, it is likely that in the time of Jesus, the synagogue was the assembly itself and not the place where the assembly met.

Syncretism: a technical term used by historians to describe the process whereby cultures blend with one another. During the period of Hellenization, Greek culture was superimposed upon the cultures of the Near East. At the same time, Greek culture was influenced by those cultures. Greek architecture, political values, language and educational systems were inculcated into the eastern cultures. Eastern religious forms, especially mystery religions, were transmitted to Greece.

Synkrisis: a standard technique in ancient rhetoric. It can be fairly translated as 'comparison' and is the practice of contrasting values, people, ideas, positions for the purpose of persuading people to adopt a new position.

Synoptic Gospels: from Greek, meaning 'one view,' the synoptic Gospels are Matthew, Mark and Luke. They are so named because they seem to be harmonious with one another in their accounts of the life and ministry of Jesus. For the purpose of comparison and study, they can be put into columns alongside one another. Such an arrangement is called a *synopsis*. By contrast,

John's Gospel was recognized from very early in the history of biblical scholarship to be very different from the synoptics. However, it was only in the mid-18th century that the similarity between the first three Gospels and their strong dissimilarities with John came to be called the *synoptic problem*. Since that time, it has been studied carefully. Over the past 100 years an overwhelming consensus has emerged to explain the synoptic problem. Today, it is taken almost without dissent that Mark is the oldest and first Gospel to have been written. Matthew and Luke used Mark as one of their sources and closely followed Mark's chronology, but each writer worked independently. Each writer also used another common source called *Q* from the German word *quelle*, which means *source*. Finally, Matthew and Luke also used individual sources as well as their own. These are called *special sources*.

Tanak: the Jewish name for the Hebrew Scriptures, it is an acronym from the Hebrew words Torah (the first five books of the Bible), Neviim (the Prophets) and Ketuvim (Writings).

Tel: an Arabic word meaning 'mound,' it refers specifically to an artificial, archaeological hill consisting of layers (strata) of civilizations built one on top of the other. In Hebrew, the word is sometimes synonymous with 'ruin.' Tels have a characteristically cone-shaped appearance.

Tesserae: the cubes from which mosaics are made (singular, *tessera*).

Text criticism: an ingredient of the historical-critical method. It is the examination of biblical manuscripts to determine the best reading of a particular passage. There are about 5,000 ancient Greek manuscripts that contain all or part of the New Testament. The most complete, most widely circulated and oldest are the collection called the *Chester Beatty Papyri* and the codices called *Sinaiticus, Alexandrinus, Vaticanus, Ephraeimi, Western* and *Bezae*. These preserve widely circulated copies of large parts of the New Testament that date to as early as the middle of the 2nd century AD. Scholars recognize that ancient manuscripts vary due to the ancient processes used to reproduce and translate texts. These processes were error prone and so, for example, a manuscript produced in Alexandria might contain variant readings compared to one produced in Antioch. One good example of textual variations is Mark 5: 1. The best manuscripts variously state that Jesus went to the country of the *Gerasenes, Gadarenes* or *Gergushines*. One problem is that the preferred reading, that Jesus went to the country of the *Gerasenes* does not fit with the geographical setting of the story, since the story requires the Sea of Galilee, but Gerasa is thirty miles away from there.

Tiberias: located on the western shore of the Sea of Galilee, between the shore and the mountains behind it, Tiberias had replaced Sepphoris as the provincial capital of Galilee by the time of Jesus' adult ministry. It was founded by Herod Antipas, who was tetrarch (ruler of a third of his father's kingdom). It was built over an ancient Israelite burial ground and thus, was considered unclean by some Judeans. He named it in honour of his patron, Tiberius Caesar (ruled AD 14-37), settled it with former soldiers, non-Judeans and freed slaves and erected a number of buildings, including a palace, a stadium, a gymnasium and a fortress. Tiberius became a centre for Jewish learning after the destruction of the Temple in AD 70.

Tiberius Caesar: successor to August Caesar, he reigned from AD 17-37. In the Gospel of Luke, association with the reign of Tiberius (the 15th year) gives the dates of Jesus' ministry. He is named in Luke 3: 1 and all references to Caesar in the Gospels refer to him.

United Monarchy: the period of time (roughly 100 hundred years beginning around 1022 BC) in the history of biblical Israel when the tribes of Israel were ruled by a monarch. Late in the period of the Judges, the elders of the Israelite tribes realized that only a centralized administration would enable the Israelite tribes to survive Canaanite and Philistine domination. Saul was the first king in Israel's United Monarchic Period, evidently appointed as a result of his successes in battle against Israel's enemies. The biblical narrative indicates that David succeeded Saul when Saul's effectiveness waned. Solomon succeeded David and was the third king in Israel's United Monarchy Period. Following Solomon's reign, which is known in Israelite legend as one of exceptional grandeur and majesty, the united monarchy collapsed and split into two separate kingdoms. The northern kingdom was called Israel. The southern kingdom was called Judah.

Vespasian: emperor of Rome from AD 69-79. He was commander of the three Roman Legions that suppressed the first Judean Revolt (AD 66-70). During that operation, upon the death of the emperor, his troops declared him to be the emperor. Referring to the practice of the deification of emperors upon their deaths, a custom he disdained, he remarked on his deathbed, 'Alas, I think I am becoming a god.'

The Via Maris: or the 'way of the sea,' (Isaiah 9: 1) was one of two major super highways in the Levant. It ran along the coast of the Mediterranean from Egypt to the Galilee and from there toward the east and north to Asia Minor. The Via Maris ran through the Jezreel Valley which is a natural east-west passageway through the north-south running mountains of the Central Highlands. It was well travelled with peoples from far-flung empires. Consequently, it was ethnically diverse and culturally pluralistic through the ages. Anyone growing up in the proximity of the Via Maris (Nazareth) would have been exposed to a wide variety of peoples and cultures.

Wadi: an Arabic word meaning gully or gorge or ravine. It refers to the intermittent riverbeds or ravines formed by runoff from rainfall

The Way of the Patriarchs: an ancient road that ran from Beer Sheva in the south to Shechem (Nablus) in the north and further to the Jezreel Valley in Galilee. It passed through Hebron, Bethlehem, Jerusalem and Ramah (modern day A Ram). The road marks the major divide in the Palestinian watershed. A sort of Palestinian 'Continental Divide,' water that falls to the east of the ridge makes its way to the Jordan river and the Dead Sea. Water that falls to the west eventually reaches the Mediterranean.

The West Bank: when the armistice of 1949 went into effect, ending the 1948 war between the newly formed State of Israel and its neighbouurs, the Arab Legion had control of a region on the West Bank of the Jordan River which included the cities of Jericho, Hebron, Bethlehem, the Old City of Jerusalem, Ramallah, Nablus, Latrun, Tulkarm, Qalqilya and Jenin. The Arab Legion became the army of the Hashemite Kingdom of Jordan. Jordan annexed the West Bank and maintained sovereignty over it until 1967, when Israel in the 1967 (Six Day) War conquered the region. Consequently, it is also referred to as The Occupied Territory of the West Bank or The Occupied Palestinian Territory of the West Bank. In 1988, Jordan relinquished its claim to sovereignty over the West Bank. Today, its status is disputed. Israel continues to maintain military control over about 90 percent of the West Bank. Israel and the Palestinian National Authority are in a process of negotiating the ultimate status of the territory. The Palestinians claim all of the territory that was under Jordanian control until the 1967 War. This includes occupied East Jerusalem, which they claim as the future capital of a Palestinian State. Israel claims security interests, as well as interest in water resources and control of commercial markets.

Wilderness or desert: in general, the term 'wilderness' in the Bible refers to desert terrain, defined by the amount of annual rainfall, while the word 'desert' refers to any isolated place devoid of human habitation (cf.: Acts 8: 26 with Matt. 3:1, 4:1, 11:7).

BIBLIOGRAPHY

Aharoni, Yohanan. *The Land of the Bible: a Historical Geography*. Philadelphia: Westminster Press, 1979.

Alter, Robert. *The Art of Biblical Narrative*. New York: Basic Books, 1981.

Angus, S. *The Mystery Religions: a Study of the Religious Background of Early Christianity*. New York: Dover Publications, Inc.

Baeck, Leo. *The Pharisees and Other Essays*. New York: Schocken, 1960.

Bailey, Kenneth. *Poet and Peasant*. Grand Rapids: William B Eerdmans, 1976.

_____. *Through Peasant Eyes: More Lucan Parables, Their Culture and Style*. Grand Rapids, MI: Wm B Eerdmans Publishing, 1980.

Baron, Salo Wittmeyer. *A Social and Religious History of the Jews*. New York: Columbia University Press, 1952.

Barrett, C K. *Jesus and the Gospel Tradition*. London: SPCK, 1967.

_____, ed. *The New Testament Background: Writings from Ancient Greece and the Roman Empire that Illuminate Christian Origins*. San Francisco: HarperSanFrancisco, 1987.

Bauer, Walter. *A Greek-English Lexicon of the New Testament and Other Early Christian Literature*, 2nd edition. Revised by F Wilbur Gingrich and Frederick W Danker. From Walter Bauer's 5th Edition. Chicago: University of Chicago Press, 1979.

Borg, Marcus. *Meeting Jesus Again for the First Time: the Historical Jesus & the Heart of Contemporary Faith*. San Francisco: HarperSanFrancisco, 1994.

Bowker, J. *Jesus and the Pharisees*. Cambridge: Harvard University Press, 1973.

Bright, John. *A History of Israel*. Philadelphia: Westminster, 1981.

Brown, Raymond E. *An Introduction to the New Testament*. New York: Doubleday, 1997.

_____. *The Birth of the Messiah: a Commentary on the Infancy Narratives in Mathew and Luke*. Garden City, NY: Image Books, 1977.

_____. *The Death of the Messiah: From Gethsemane to the Grave: a Commentary on the Passion Narratives in the Four Gospels*, vols. 1 and 2. New York: Doubleday, 1994.

_____. *The Gospel According to John*, vols. 1 and 2. Garden City, NY: Doubleday and Company, Inc. 1970.

Brown, Raymond E, Fitzmeyer, Joseph A and Murphy, Roland E, eds. *The New Jerome Biblical Commentary*. London: Geoffrey Chapman, 1990.

Brueggemann, Walter. *The Land: Place as Gift, Promise, and Challenge in Biblical*

Faith. Philadelphia, PA: Fortress Press.

Bultmann, Rudolph. *History of the Synoptic Tradition*. Peabody, MA: Hendrickson Publishers, Inc., 1963.

Chadwick, Henry. *The Early Church: the Story of Emergent Christianity from the Apostolic Age to the Dividing of the ways Between the Greek East and the Latin West*. London: Penguin Books, 1993.

Charlesworth, James H, ed. *Jesus and the Dead Sea Scrolls*. New York: Doubleday, 1992.

Cross, Frank Moore. *The Ancient Library of Qumran*, 3rd ed. Minneapolis, MN: Fortress Press, 1995.

Crossan, John Dominic. *The Historical Jesus: The Life of a Mediterranean Jewish Peasant*. San Francisco: HarperSanFrancisco, 1991.

Davies, Philip R. *Qumran*. Guildford, Surrey: Lutterworth Press, 1982.

Davies, W D. *The Gospel and the Land: Early Christianity and Jewish Territorial Doctrine*. Berkeley: The University of California Press,1974.

_____. *The Territorial Dimension of Judaism*. Berkeley: The University of California Press, 1982.

_____. *The Territorial Dimension of Judaism: With a Symposium and Further Reflections*. Minneapolis: Fortress Press, 1991.

Derwachter, F M. *Preparing the Way for Paul: The Proselyte Movement in Later Judaism*. 1930.

Durkheim, Emile. *The Rules of Sociological Method*. New York: Free Press, 1966.

Edwards, O C. 'Sociology as a Tool for Studying the New Testament', *Anglican Theological Review* 65 (1983): 431-438.

Elliot, John. *What Is Social Scientific Criticism?*, Minneapolis: Fortress Press, 1993.

Elliot, John. 'Social Scientific Criticism of the New Testament and Its Social World', *Semeia* 35. 1986.

Ellison, John W, ed. *Nelson's Complete Concordance of the Revised Standard Version Bible*, 2nd ed. New York, NY: Thomas Nelson Inc., 1957.

Esler, Philip F. *The First Christians in their Social Worlds*. London: Routledge, 1994.

_____, ed. *Modelling Early Christianity: Social-scientific Studies of the New Testament in its Context*. London: Routledge, 1995.

Ferguson, Everett. *Backgrounds of Early Christianity*. Grand Rapids, MI: W. B. Eerdmans Publishing Co., 1993.

Finegan, Jack. *The Archaeology of the New Testament: the Life of Jesus and the Beginning of the Early Church*. Princeton, NJ: Princeton University Press, 1969.

Finkelstein, Louis. *The Pharisees: The Sociological Background of their Faith*. Philadelphia: Jewish Publication Society of America, 1962.

Finley, M I. *Slavery in Classical Antiquity*. New York: Barnes and Noble, 1968.

Finn, Thomas M. 'Social Mobility, Imperial Civil Service and the Spread of Early Christianity', *Studia Patristica*. Edited by Livingstone. New York: Pergamon Press, 1982.

Fitzgerald, John T, ed. *Friendship, Flattery, and Frankness of Speech: Studies on Friendship in the New Testament World*. New York, NY: E.J. Brill, 1996.

Fitzmyer, Joseph A. *The Dead Sea Scrolls and Christian Origins*. Grand Rapids, MI: W B Eerdmans Publishing Co., 2000.

_____. *The Gospel According to Luke*. Vol. 1. Garden City, NY: Doubleday, 1981.

_____. *The Gospel According to Luke*. Vol. 2. Garden City, NY: Doubleday, 1985.

Flavius, Josephus. *The Jewish Wars*, trans. H. St J Thackeray. Cambridge: Harvard

University Press, 1997.

_____. *Antiquities*, vols. XII-XIX . trans. Ralph Marcus and Louis H. Feldman. Cambridge: Harvard University Press, 1943, 1963, 1965.

_____. *The Life of Flavius Josephus*. trans. H StJ Thackeray. Cambridge: Harvard University Press, 1997.

Fox, Robin Lane. *Pagans and Christians*. San Francisco: HarperSanFrancisco,1986.

Fredriksen, Paula. *From Jesus to Christ: The Origins of the New Testament Images of Jesus*. New Haven: Yale University Press, 1988.

Freyne, Sean. *Galilee from Alexander the Great to Hadrian, 323 BCE-135 CE: A Study of Second Temple Judaism*. Wilmington, Del: Michael Glazier, 1980.

_____. *Galilee, Jesus and the Gospels: Literary Approaches and Historical Investigations*. Philadelphia: Fortress Press, 1988.

Gager, John. *Kingdom and Community: The Social World of Early Christianity*. Englewood Cliffs, NJ: Prentice-Hall, 1975.

Georgi, Dieter. *The Opponents of Paul in 2 Corinthians: A Study of Religious Propaganda in Late Antiquity*. Philadelphia, PA: Fortress Press, 1985.

Gingras, George E, trans. *Egeria: Diary of a Pilgrimage*. New York: Newman Press, 1970.

Haenchen, Ernst. *The Acts of the Apostles*. Philadelphia: Westminster Press, 1971.

Hamel, G. *Poverty and Charity in Roman Palestine, First Three Centuries C.E.* Berkeley, CA: University of California Publication: Near Eastern Studies 23, 1990.

Hengel, Martin. *The Hellenization of Judea in the First Century After Christ*. Philadelphia: Trinity Press International, 1989.

Hengel, Martin. *Property and Riches in the Early Church: Aspects of a Social History of Early Christianity*. Philadelphia: Fortress Press, 1974.

Hengel, Martin. *Judaism and Hellenism*. Philadelphia: Fortress press, 1974.

Herford, R Travers. *The Pharisees*. Boston: Beacon, 1962.

Horsley, Richard A. 'Bandits, Messiahs and Longshoreman: Popular Unrest in Galilee Around the Time of Jesus', *Society of Biblical Literature Seminar Papers* (1988).

_____. *Jesus and the Spiral of Violence*. San Francisco: Harper and Row, 1987.

_____. *Sociology and the Jesus Movement*. New York: Continuum, 1994.

_____. *Galilee: History, Politics, People*. Valley Forge, PA: Trinity Press International, 1995.

_____ and Gottwald, Norman K. *The Bible and Liberation: Political and Social Hermeneutics*. Maryknoll, NY: Orbis, 1993.

_____ and Hanson, John S. *Bandits, Prophets and Messiahs: Popular Movements in the Time of Jesus*. New York: Seabury, 1985.

_____ and Silberman, Neil Asher. *The Message and the Kingdom: How Jesus and Paul Ignited a Revolution and Transformed the Ancient World*. New York: Grosset/ Putnam, 1987.

Jaffee, Martin. *Early Judaism*. Upper Saddle River, NJ: Prentice Hall, 1997.

Jeremias, Joachim. *Jerusalem in the Time of Jesus*. Translated by F H and C H Cave. Philadelphia: Fortress Press, 1969.

_____. *The Parables of Jesus*. Translated by S H Hooke. New York: Charles Scribner's Sons, 1963.

Johnson, Luke Timothy. 'The New Testament's Anti-Jewish Slander and the Conventions of Ancient Polemic.' *Journal of Biblical Literature* 108.3 (1989): 419-441.

_____. *The Real Jesus: The Misguided Quest for the Historical Jesus and the*

Truth of the Traditional Gospels. San Francisco: HarperSanFrancisco, 1996.

Keck, Leander E and Martyn, J Louis, eds. *Studies in Luke-Acts*, Philadelphia: Fortress Press, 1980.

Kee, Howard Clark. *Christian Origins in Sociological Perspective: Methods and Resources*. Philadelphia: Westminster Press, 1980.

_____, and Lynn H Cohick, eds. *Evolution of the Synagogue: Problems and Progress*. Harrisburg, PA: Trinity Press International, 1999.

_____. *Medicine, Miracle and Magic in New Testament Times*. Cambridge: Cambridge University Press, 1986.

_____. *Miracle in the Early Christian World: a Study in Socio-historical Method*. New Haven, CT: Yale University Press, 1983.

Kennedy, George A. *A New History of Classical Rhetoric*. Princeton, NJ: Princeton University Press, 1994.

Kittel, Gerhard, ed. *Theological Dictionary of the New Testament*, vol. 1-10. Translated and edited by Geoffrey W Bromley. Grand Rapids, MI: Wm. B. Eerdmans Publishing Co., 1964.

Koester, Helmut. *Introduction to the New Testament: History, Culture and Religion of the Hellenistic Age*. Philadelphia: Fortress Press, 1982.

_____. *Ancient Christian Gospels: Their History and Development*. Philadelphia: Trinity Press International, 1990.

Mack, Burton L. *The Lost Gospel: The Book of Q and Christian Origins*. San Francisco: HarperSanFrancisco, 1993.

_____. *Rhetoric and the New Testament*. Minneapolis, MN: Fortress Press, 1990.

Malina, Bruce J. *Christian Origins and Cultural Anthropology: Practical Models for Biblical Interpretation*. Atlanta: John Knox Press, 1986.

Malina, Bruce J. *The New Testament World: Insights from Cultural Anthropology*, Atlanta: John Knox Press, 1981.

Marhsall, I. Howard. *Commentary on Luke*. Grand Rapids, MI: Wm B Eerdmans, 1978.

Marshall, Peter. *Enmity in Corinth: Social Conventions in Paul's Relations with the Corinthians*. Tubingen: J C B Mohr, 1987.

Matthews, Victor H. *Manners and customs in the Bible: an Illustrated Guide to Daily Life in Bible Times*. Peabody, MA: Hendrickson Publishers, Inc., 1991.

Meeks, Wayne. *The Moral World of the First Christians*, Philadelphia: Fortress Press, 1986.

Meier, John P. *A Marginal Jew: Rethinking the Historical Jesus*, vols. 1 and 2. New York: Doubleday, 1991.

Metzger, Bruce Manning. *The Text of the New Testament: Its Transmission, Corruption, and Restoration*. New York: Oxford University Press. 1968.

Meyers, Eric M and James F Strange. *Archaeology and the Early Rabbis*. Nashville, TN: Abingdon, 1981.

Mitchell, Margaret M. *Paul and the Rhetoric of Reconciliation: An Exegetical Investigation of the Language and Composition of 1 Corinthians*. Tubingen: J C B Mohr, 1991.

Negev, Avraham, ed. *Archaeological Encyclopedia of the Holy Land. Jerusalem*: The Jerusalem Publishing House, 1980.

Neusner, Jacob. *The Idea of Purity in Ancient Judaism*. Leiden: E.J. Brill, 1973.

_____. *From Politics to Piety: The Emergence of Pharisaic Judaism*. Englewood Cliffs, NJ: Prentice Hall, 1973.

_____. *The Rabbinic Tradition About the Pharisees Before 70*. Leiden: Brill, 1973.

Neyrey, Jerome H. *The Social World of Luke-Acts: Models for Interpretation*. Peabody, MA: Hendrikson Publishers, 1991.

Osiek, Carolyn. *What Are They Saying About the Social Setting of the New Testament*. New York: Paulist Press, 1992.

Prior, Michael. *The Bible and Colonialism: A Moral Critique*. Sheffield: Sheffield Academic Press, 1997.

_____. *Christians in the Holy Land*. London: World of Islam Festival Trust, 1994.

_____, ed. *They Came and They Saw: Western Christian Experiences of the Holy Land*. London: Melisende, 2000.

_____. *Zionism and the State of Israel: A Moral Inquiry*. London: Routledge, 1999.

Pagels, Elaine. *The Gnostic Gospels*. New York: Vintage Books, 1979.

Philodemus. *De Libertate Dicendi*. Translated by David Konstan et al., Atlanta, GA: Scholars Press, 1998.

Pliny the Elder. *Natural History*, vols. V and XIII. Translated by H. Rackham. Cambridge: Harvard University Press, 1944.

Reynolds, J and Tannenbaum, R. *Jews and God-fearers at Aphrodisias: Greek Inscriptions with Commentary*. Cambridge: 1987.

Ringgren, Helmer. *Israelite Religion*. Philadelphia: Fortress Press, 1966.

Rousseau, John J and Rami Arav, eds. *Jesus and His World: An Archaeological and Cultural Dictionary*. Minneapolis, MN: Fortress Press, 1995.

Saldarini, Anthony J. *Matthew's Christian-Jewish Community*. Chicago, IL and London: The University of Chicago Press, 1994.

_____. *Pharisees, Scribes, and Sadducees in Palestinian Society: A Sociological Approach*. Wilmington, Del: Michael Glazier, 1989.

Sanders, E P. *Jesus and Judaism*. Philadelphia: Fortress Press, 1985.

_____. *Judaism: Practice and Belief (63 BCE-66 CE)*. Philadelphia: Fortress Press: 1992.

Schneemelcher, Wilhelm, ed. *New Testament Apocrypha*, vol. 1: *Gospels and Related Writings*. Translated by R McL Wilson. Louisville, KY: Westminster/John Knox Press, 1991.

Silberman, Neil Asher. *Between Past and Present: Archaeology, Ideology and Nationalism in the Modern Middle East*. New York: Anchor, 1989.

Simon, Marcel. *Jewish Sects at the Time of Jesus*. Philadelphia: Fortress Press, 1967.

Smith, Robert H. 'Were the Early Christians Middle Class? A Sociological Analyses of the New Testament', *Currents in Theology and Mission* 7 (1980): 260-276.

Stambaugh, John E and Balch, David L. *The New Testament in Its Social Environment*. Ed. Wayne A. Meeks. Philadelphia: The Westminster Press, 1986.

Sternberg, Meir. *The Poetics of Biblical Narrative: Ideological Literature and the Drama of Reading*. Bloomington, IN: Indiana University Press, 1985.

Tarn, W W. *Hellenistic Civilization*. New York: Meridien Books, 1975.

Theissen, Gerd. *The First Followers of Jesus: A Sociological Analysis of the Earliest Christians*. London: SCM Press, 1978.

_____. *The Gospel in Context: Social and Political History in the Synoptic Tradition*. Minneapolis, Fortress Press, 1991.

_____. *The Miracle Stories of the Early Christian Tradition*. Philadelphia: Fortress press, 1983.

_____. *Social Reality and the Early Christians: Theology, Ethics, and the World of the New Testament*. Minneapolis: Fortress Press, 1992.

_____. *Sociology and Early Palestinian Christianity*. Philadelphia: Fortress Press, 1978.

Troeltsch, Ernst. *The Social Teaching of the Christian Churches*. New York: Harper and Brothers, 1960.

Twelftree, Graham H. *Jesus the Exorcist: A Contribution to the Study of the Historical Jesus*. Peabody, MA: Hendrickson Publishers, Inc. 1993.

Vermes, Geza. *The Dead Sea Scrolls in English*, 4th ed. London: Penguin Books, 1995.

_____. *The Dead Sea Scrolls: Qumran in Perspective*. Philadelphia: Fortress Press.1981.

_____. *Jesus the Jew: a Historian's Reading of the Gospels*. Minneapolis: Fortress, 1973.

_____. *Jesus and the World of Judaism*. Philadelphia: Fortress Press, 1981.

_____. *The Religion of Jesus the Jew*, Minneapolis: Fortress, 1993.

Vogt, Joseph. *Ancient Slavery and the Ideal of Man*. Cambridge: Harvard University, 1975.

Wallace-Hadrill, Andrew, ed. *Patronage in Ancient Society*. New York, NY: Routledge Press, 1989.

Westermann, William L. *The Slave Systems of Greek and Roman Antiquity*. Philadelphia: The American Philosophical Society, 1955.

Whitelam, Keith W. *The Invention of Ancient Israel: the Silencing of Palestinian History*. London: Routledge, 1996.

Wiedemann, Thomas. *Greek and Roman Slavery*. Baltimore: Johns Hopkins, 1981.

INDEX

[Page references in **bold** refer to Glossary entries]

Lebanon 45
leitourgia 59
Lessing, Gottwald 105
Levant 43, 44, **170**
lingua franca 54

M

Madaba map **171**
magi 36
Magic 74
Marc Antony 66
Marcion 102
Marcionism 102, **171**
Marl **171**
Masada 98, 99, **171**
Megiddo **172**
Mesopotamia 42, **172**
Mithras 72, 80
Mount Hermon **172**
Mount Moriah 16
Mount of Olives **172**
Mt Gerazim 92
Mt. Gerazim 91
Mt. Nebo 46
Mt. of Olives 37
Myth **173**

N

Nablus **173**
Nag Hammadi Library 107, **173**
Nazareth 38, 112, **174**
Nebuchadnezzar 43
Northern Kingdom of Israel 43

O

Old Testament **174**
Old Testament Apocrypha 22
Ostracon 22, **174**
Oxyrhyncus 27

P

Palestine 36, 48, **174**
papyrus 22
Paul 17
Peloponnesian Peninsula 17

Persia 50, 51, 53
Persian Period **175**
Pharisees 23, 37, 40, 94
Philip II 50
Philippi 60
Philistine Plain 45, **175**
Philistines 175
Philo of Alexandria 22, **175**
Phoenicia 45
Phoenicians **175**
Plain of Acco **175**
Plain of Esdraelon (Jezreel Valley) **176**
Plain of Sharon **176**
Plato 57, 68
Pliny the Elder 22, 77
Pontius Pilate 113
Provincia Palestina 87
Pseudonymous authorship **176**

Q

'Q' 32, 116, **177**
Queen of Sheba 43
Quirinius 97
Qumran 91, 92, 93, **177**
Qumran texts 26

R

Rabbi Hillel 13
Rainfall **178**
Redaction criticism 32, **178**
redaction criticism 32
Reimarus, Hermann 104
Renan, Ernst 105
Rhetoric **178**
Rhetorical criticism **178**
Robinson, Edward 106
Robinson, James 102
Roman Period **178**
Roux, Georges 34

S

Sadducees 23, 40, 94
Samaria 87, **178**
Samaritans 89, 91, **179**
Saronic Gulf 17